Wet-Fly Tying
and Fishing

Wet-Fly Tying and Fishing

ROGER FOGG

THE CROWOOD PRESS

First published in 2009 by
The Crowood Press Ltd
Ramsbury, Marlborough
Wiltshire SN8 2HR

www.crowood.com

© Roger Fogg 2009

British Library Cataloguing-in-Publication Data
A catalogue record for this book is available from the British Library.

ISBN 978 1 84797 127 2

Frontispiece: Tying the Red Palmer.

Designed and typeset by Focus Publishing, Sevenoaks, Kent

Printed and bound in Malaysia by Times Offset (M) Sdn Bhd

CONTENTS

FOREWORD

Communication between the many generations of anglers who have contributed to our modern knowledge of the history of fly fishing only works in one direction and, sadly, not all anglers are interested in, or even aware of, the history of our sport. Anglers who are inclined to take the time to read books, and are of a certain vintage themselves, may well recall the printing of Roger Fogg's *The Art of the Wet Fly* in 1979. Time has moved on since those days and there have been vast improvements in fishing tackle, clothing, techniques and in communication. The speed of communication alone has changed angling forever.

But are we better anglers or merely more efficient catchers of fish? When we use Kevlar braided leaders and tungsten beaded flies, fluorocarbon line and plastic indicators, do we run the risk of losing some of the skills and folk knowledge of our ancestors who, for the most part, used wisps of silk, fur and feather? However, when we try to answer these questions is it too easy to fall into misty-eyed nostalgia?

Nostalgia can sometimes play us false. When chaps, and happily and increasingly chapettes, spend time in the tackle shop when the river is out of sorts, the conversation often takes a nostalgic turn and a kind of fuzzy collective memory emerges – waxed jackets, early carbon rods and some of the old glass rods are marvelled over. It is easy to forget the kind of fug we used to get with non-breathable waders!

The book you are holding goes some way to answering such questions. This overview of wet-fly history, tactics and fly patterns emerges in the same year that at least two major rod makers are returning to the action of fibreglass rods for small river fishing. Today's interested and thinking angler, and those of generations to come, owe a debt of gratitude to Roger Fogg and The Crowood Press for this timely issue of an important book.

Peter Arfield (AAPGAI)
The Bakewell Fly Fishing Shop
November 2008

DEDICATION AND ACKNOWLEDGEMENTS

This book is dedicated to my grandchildren – Isabel Mia, Samuel William and Jessica Lauren.

Acknowledgements

First of all, I owe a debt of gratitude to all at The Crowood Press for their belief in the project and support during the production of my book.

I am extremely grateful to my son, Chris Fogg, for taking all the photographs and for accompanying me on some very enjoyable fishing trips. Equally, I am indebted to my daughter, Catherine Gregory, for devoting time to proof reading, and to my wife, Christine, for putting up with me during the production of this book.

I must also thank my fishing buddies, Peter Harrison and David Gregory, for companionship and useful exchanges of ideas, and the same goes for all the members of Buxton Fly Fishers. Thanks to Peter Arfield for his perceptive Foreword and for his ability to seduce me into buying expensive reels and lines (the odd whisky helps). Many thanks to Stuart Richards for the loan of valuable photographic equipment, without which the photographs for this book would not have been possible. Finally, thanks also to Stephen Cuthbert for providing help and advice during the photography sessions on his delightful Arnfield Reservoir.

PREFACE

In the intervening years since my book, *The Art of the Wet Fly*, was published in 1979 my ideas on fly fishing have changed a little. Entomology seems less important now, as most wet-flies serve to provide impressions of several naturals; there is no need for an individual artificial to imitate each and every insect. The trout certainly don't seem to mind. I am now a little less worried about having to convince myself that a trout has taken my fly because it really looks like the large dark olives that it is currently feeding on; it has taken my fly and that is sufficient. Approximation is enough and if a wet-fly is consistently effective under given circumstances, and at certain times of the season, then that will do for me. Don't get me wrong, entomology is very interesting, but it was a great deal more interesting thirty years ago when there seemed to be a greater variety of aquatic flies in evidence. The upwinged flies, mayflies, or ephemeridae, call them what you will, seem to have suffered most and on some pools where I might have seen up to ten different species, I now see a dominance of chironomid midges and a few olives. I do not propose, therefore, to list every natural insect and to provide detailed descriptions of appearance, habitat, life cycles and seasons of emergence. John Goddard's books will tell you everything you need to know about natural insects and you will find his valuable reference guides listed in the Bibliography.

While my ideas on wet-fly fishing have been modified a little during the last thirty years, one thing that hasn't changed is my belief that it is a fascinating way to fish and far from the 'chuck-and-chance-it' approach that some would make it out to be. It makes no pretence at 'exact imitation', but that does not exclude it from being considered a broadly imitative approach. A range of wet-flies (listed in Chapters 7 to 10) will imitate all the insects, and other creatures, that trout feed on, but these flies must be fished in precise ways and that is something I will outline in the forthcoming chapters. Furthermore, to fish wet-flies with the correct techniques, then the right tackle must be employed. A short, fast and tip-actioned rod, perhaps one of the most commonly encountered rods today, will not allow the angler to fish wet-flies effectively, so we will consider the importance of tackle in Chapter 4.

These days I mix-and-match, fishing the wet-fly much of the time, but also the nymph or dry-fly as occasion dictates, or even as fancy takes me. It's nice to have a change sometimes and, as they say, variety is the spice of life. I think that I became quite typecast after writing *The Art of the Wet Fly* and I still get surprised looks even today when others see me casting a dry-fly or nymph. Undoubtedly, there are times when the wet-fly ought to be used because it will provide the best chance of a fish or two, but I am certainly not suggesting that it is the only way to fish for trout. There are times when only a weighted nymph will get down to trout lying in a deep pool and times when the dry-fly will be the order of the day. Of course, things are never clear cut and there are typical dry-fly days that produce nothing but frustration. I have known many a good evening rise when the dry-fly has proved utterly useless and only a wet-fly, fished close to the surface, has tempted a trout. In summary, this is a book about tying and fishing wet-flies, but it is not a book that promotes the wet-fly as a kind of angler's panacea rendering nymphs and dry-flies redundant.

During the last few years I have been asked quite a few times if I was intending to produce a revised version of *The Art of the Wet Fly*. I certainly considered doing so, but, on reflection, decided that a new start was required – a completely new book, in fact. Not only would a fresh start enable me to update ideas on tackle and techniques, it would also allow me to rethink some of the basic concepts involved in tying and fishing wet-flies. I hope the reader will find something of interest over the course of the following pages.

Roger Fogg
December 2008

1 INTRODUCTORY MATTERS

That great angler of the past, Francis Francis, once said that 'the judicious and perfect application of dry, wet and mid-water fly-fishing stamps the finished fly-fisher with the hall-mark of efficiency'. He was a wise man, an all-round angler and an entertaining writer; *A Book on Angling* (published 1867) is still a very good read. I would not describe myself as anything like 'a finished fly-fisher', but I do enjoy catching trout by different methods, so that in writing about the wet-fly I do not wish to imply that it is the only method to use. The traditional art of the wet-fly is, however, a somewhat neglected art and I hope that I will be able to convince the reader that it is a very worthwhile technique and complementary to the use of the dry-fly or nymph.

What Is a Wet-Fly?

A full understanding of what I mean by the 'wet-fly' will hopefully emerge during the present chapter, but, for the moment, let me simply say that the 'wet-fly' is clearly different from a 'dry-fly' and is also neither 'nymph' nor 'lure'. For F.M. Halford, writing in 1889 (*Dry-Fly Fishing in Theory and Practice*), everything seemed clear-cut, so that he could say: 'The simplest definition of the term "floating-fly" is – an artificial fly fished *on* the surface; and that of the term "sunk-fly" – one fished *below* the surface of the water.' For Halford , there were simply 'dry-flies' (flies that float) and 'wet-flies' (flies that sink), but it is now more complicated and particularly with respect to flies 'fished below the surface of the water'. The single category 'wet-fly' hardly seems adequate as a description of trout flies as disparate as Zonkers, Pheasant Tail Nymphs,

Snipe and Purples, Dog Nobblers, Hot Spot Shrimps, Blobs, Mallard and Clarets, Czech Nymphs, Butchers, Montanas, Gold Ribbed Hare's Ears and a whole host of other patterns. They are all fished under the surface of the water, but they differ in terms of the locations they are suited to, the tackle required to fish them and the methods by which they are fished. For example, fishing a Czech Nymph, with a 6ft (1.8m) wand of a rod and AFTM (Association of Fishing Tackle Manufacturers) no.2 line on the Cherry Brook or Hampshire Bourne, would not be appropriate. Ethics apart, trying to fish heavily weighted lures or nymphs on a tiny, shallow stream, and with light tackle at that, would simply not be practical. However, on appropriate tackle, most of the patterns referred to above might be fished in different ways on a large reservoir so that the angler may choose his or her preferred method and style of fly.

There are thus matters of appropriateness and effectiveness, as well as matters of choice, when it comes to 'sunk' flies. In spite of Francis Francis's definition of 'the finished fly-fisher', we all have a tendency to prefer a particular technique when in fact a variety of methods may achieve the same end. Wherever we fish, lake or river, it is rare for my angling companion, Peter, to fish anything but the dry-fly and there is nothing snobbish about this, he simply prefers that method. On the other hand, I might fish the wet-fly, nymph or dry-fly as fancy takes me. Sometimes Peter catches more trout than me, sometimes I catch more than him; it evens out in the end. As far as we are concerned, it's just a matter of preference and no value judgements are attached to the choice of flies or methods. That said, prejudice certainly plays a part in fly fishing and we are all perhaps guilty of it. Trout flies tend to be divided into a kind of social stratification, with the imitative dry-fly at the top of the pile and the lure or wet-fly at the bottom. In this kind of hierarchy, the split-winged dry-fly becomes the aristocrat, the nymph probably a bit of a reformed rebel but now respectably middle class, the lure represents flash new money (with more than a touch of bling), while the wet-fly is viewed as old working class: 'ee bah gum', cloth caps, brass bands and all that.

This inherent hierarchy of methods and styles of fly is quite misguided. In many ways, fishing dry-flies is quite a straightforward matter and there is no reason to think it superior to the wet-fly. The belief that the dry-fly is superior is generally attributed to Halford. While F.M. Halford is viewed as the high priest of dry-fly fishing, and is thought to have sneered at wet-flies, this impression might have been partly created by a few mischievous comments made by G.E.M. Skues (*see* Chapter 2). Halford certainly believed that the dry-fly was more effective on the chalk streams than the wet-fly, but its denigration, or at least its neglect, is probably of more recent origin. In *Dry-Fly Fishing in Theory and Practice*, Halford writes:

> There is far too much presumption of superior scientific knowledge and skill on the part of the modern school of dry-fly fishermen, and I should be the last to wish to write a line tending to encourage this erroneous assumption of superiority, or to depreciate in any way the patience and perseverance, coupled with intuitive perception of the habits of the fish, requisite for a really first-rate performer with the wet fly.

Many anglers undoubtedly claim superiority for the dry-fly, and for the nymph too, so that any newcomer to the sport will be forgiven for thinking that spider patterns, winged wet-flies and loch flies are things of the past. They are missing out therefore on a whole host of effective flies and pleasurable ways of fishing them. Lure fishermen too may be missing out by neglecting old patterns such as the Alexandra, Butcher or Peter Ross, which are as good as any creations invented to imitate fry and it is unfortunate that

there seems to be an obsession with this season's new lure, which often turns out to be a 'here today, gone tomorrow' affair. Traditional wet-flies, though they may be fished exclusively and effectively throughout the season, offer a perfect complement to dry-flies, nymphs and lures and any fly-box is incomplete without them.

From time to time, some of the old wet-flies make an appearance in the pages of fly-fishing magazines, but not that often, because what sells magazines are those new wonder flies guaranteeing huge catches of enormous trout. I will try to redress the balance by offering the best of the old wet-flies but I make no claims that they will help the reader to break records. The old wet-flies will certainly catch big fish, and plenty of fish, they have always done that, but I would argue that their true value lies in the fact that they are particularly enjoyable to fish. Angling is a pastime and I do not therefore subscribe to the idea that the ends justify the means, for if the means are not pleasurable then the ends are irrelevant. If your sole purpose in going fly fishing is to catch a 'double', or a 'twenty', or a limit bag for every visit to a fishery, then perhaps this book is not for you.

I hope that I have established a number of important points, but I am fully aware that further explanations are required if I am to make clear what I mean by the 'wet-fly'. It's not an easy thing to explain. Defining a dry-fly is easy enough: whether it has double-split wings, single wings or no wings at all, whether it has a hackle or no hackle, whether it is made of foam or dressed with a cul-de-canard feather, if it floats on the surface it is a 'dry-fly'. It might then be assumed that all flies fished subsurface would be termed 'wet-flies' and this was basically Halford's approach, so that whether a sunk-fly imitated a shrimp, nymph, emerging fly or drowned fly he classed them as 'wet-flies'. That will no longer do. I could say that a wet-fly is a fly which is fished subsurface and is neither nymph nor lure, but that would not be very precise. Even defining a modern nymph is as difficult as defining a wet-fly. Talking to a river keeper on the Test recently it became clear that his antipathy towards nymph fishing was really a product of the fact that many of his clients plied large weighted abortions that bore no

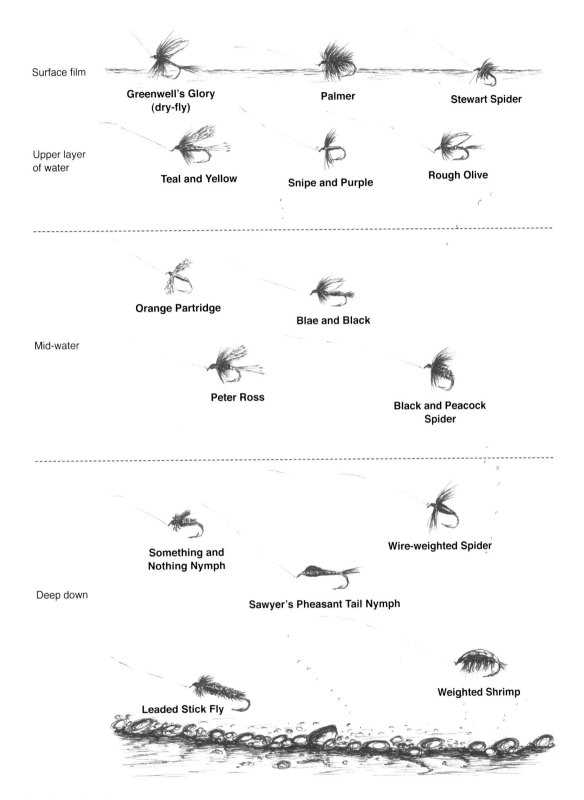

Surface film

**Greenwell's Glory
(dry-fly)**

Palmer

Stewart Spider

Upper layer
of water

Teal and Yellow

Snipe and Purple

Rough Olive

Mid-water

Orange Partridge

Blae and Black

Peter Ross

**Black and Peacock
Spider**

**Something and
Nothing Nymph**

Wire-weighted Spider

Deep down

Sawyer's Pheasant Tail Nymph

Leaded Stick Fly

Weighted Shrimp

Wet-flies and depth.

resemblance to any natural nymph. The term 'nymph' might embrace the little unweighted hackled patterns used by Skues (in reality little different from soft-hackled wet-flies), the weighted Pheasant Tail nymph developed by Frank Sawyer, leaded shrimp, bloodworm or caddis larva imitations, heavy Czech Nymphs and weighted fancy patterns bearing no resemblance to any living creature. None of the above are strictly 'wet-flies', although the Skues nymphs were close enough because they were fished just under the surface rather than deep down. The 'weighted fancy patterns bearing no resemblance to any living creature' should, in reality, be termed 'lures', while the rest may legitimately be termed 'nymphs', because they are imitative and are fished nymph-style regardless of the fact that Skues thought that 'only the larval stages of the Ephemeridae are represented in nymph fishing'. What Pheasant Tails (and similar nymphal-shaped patterns), shrimps, bloodworms, caddis larvae and Czech Nymphs have in common is that they are weighted patterns intended to sink to the depth at which a trout is feeding.

In my own mind, I draw a distinction between nymphs, which are weighted (whether it is with fine wire, lead wire or a tungsten bead), and wet-flies, which are unweighted so that they will sink slowly yet remain close to the surface. Nymphs and wet-flies do lie on the same continuum, but there is a wide gap between a heavily weighted Czech Nymph bumping the bottom of a stream and a tiny soft-hackled spider pattern drifting just under the surface. However, it would be very difficult to separate an unweighted Skues nymph, fished close to the surface, and a soft-hackled pattern such as the Poult Bloa, and it is likely that a trout takes both patterns for the same stage in an insect's life cycle.

So far then, we have dry-flies that float *on* the surface and nymphs which are capable of sinking to mid-water, or to the bottom of a stream or lake. The simple view of the wet-fly is that its province is the levels not completely covered by dry-flies and nymphs and that is *in*, or just under, the surface film and in the upper layers of water. With reference to natural insects, this may translate as follows: dry-flies imitate adult aquatic flies, either newly hatched or returning to lay their eggs, and terrestrial flies blown by accident onto the water; artificial nymphs imitate active nymphs, mature nymphs ascending to hatch into adult flies and creatures that inhabit the bottom of a stream or lake; wet-flies imitate adult flies in the very process of emerging at the surface, duns which fail to hatch and are drowned, flies which descend in the water to lay their eggs and drowning terrestrial insects. In broad terms, I am assuming that dry-flies, nymphs and wet-flies are primarily imitative of natural creatures, not necessarily 'exact' imitations but impressions nevertheless, and that the stimulus for a trout to take them is the feeding instinct. In contrast, the flash, colour or movement of a lure is intended to stimulate a trout to strike through an instinct of aggression or self-preservation. While this definition provides a perspective on the differences among dry-flies, nymphs, wet-flies and lures, as the following chapters will show, it is still a little simplistic. For example, even when trout are visibly feeding on floating natural flies there are times when a wet-fly will actually work better than a dry-fly, but more of that at a later stage.

Then again, there will be some fine distinctions. Is, for example, a loch fly such as the Peter Ross a wet-fly or a lure? I have implied that wet-flies stimulate the feeding instincts of trout, but it is not always clear whether a pattern may be classed as a stimulator to feeding or to aggression. A wet-fly/lure continuum will reveal sharp contrasts at the extremes, for example between a Mallard and Claret dressed on a size 14 hook and a Minky Booby tied on a size 6 long shank hook, but other cases pose more of a problem. It may be argued that there is little difference between a loch fly such as a Connemara Black, tied on a size 12 hook, and a lure such as a mini-Viva dressed on an identical hook. There may, of course, be a difference in the way that they are fished – the Connemara Black cast short on a floating line and retrieved slowly, the Viva cast long on a sinking line and retrieved quickly – but that is a different point. Nevertheless, the way we fish a fly, plus the tackle we use to fish it, does have a bearing on whether we are likely to call a fly a 'wet-fly' or a 'lure'.

The Traditional Wet Fly

It is high time that we looked more specifically and precisely at traditional wet-flies. On rivers in the north of England, it is not uncommon to find an angler still casting flies such as the Orange Partridge, Snipe and Purple, Poult Bloa or Dark Watchet, with these tiny, soft-hackled patterns enjoying something of a renaissance in recent years. There are a few anglers who use them on rivers elsewhere and they have developed quite a following in North America. If you visit the River Clyde you will find fishermen still casting the most delicate of wet-flies, mere wisps of things with small bodies and narrow upright wings; they are as fragile-looking as any real ephemeridae. Those flies have been fished there for centuries and trout are still duped by them. On Irish loughs, Welsh and English lakes and Scottish lochs, there are fly fishermen who still prefer to use a three-fly cast of traditional wet-flies (although flies designed for use on English reservoirs are gaining ground on those waters too). They fish their traditional flies with long rods from bank or boat, forever moving and casting short lines in a relaxed manner; not for them the double-hauling of heavy sinking lines hurled into the distance. Traditional loch flies have not completely vanished from English reservoirs, although they are perhaps only in favour among the older generation.

Traditional flies rarely appear these days in fishery logs, not because they are ineffective, but because few anglers use them. I visited a fishery recently and was informed by a fellow angler that what I needed to use was an Orange Sparkle Blob because 'that's what everybody was catching them on'. I didn't have an Orange Blob, or any other colour of Blob for that matter, but I still caught fish and by all accounts the trout soon went off Orange Blobs. They presumably became 'educated', turned on to the next wonder fly, perhaps a Lime Green Sparkle Blob, became 'educated' again, turned on to the next popular pattern and so on. 'Wonder flies' are often short-lived. Traditional wet-flies are more consistently effective and that is why they have lasted for so many years. I think it has something to do with the imitative qualities they possess and the fact that they suggest 'food' as opposed to an invader that stimulates either a trout's curiosity or its aggressive and territorial instincts. Tiny soft-hackled spider patterns are clearly imitative, but even an ostensibly flashy fly such as the Peter Ross (*see* Chapter 10) seems to be a more consistent performer than most lures. For one thing, it is a much smaller fly than the average lure and it doesn't depend on speed to irritate a trout into striking; I have caught plenty of fish on it when I have not been retrieving the flies so it must bear some close scrutiny. While I would gladly fish a Peter Ross at fry-bashing time, I have also done well with a small Peter Ross when trout have been feeding on emerging chironomid midges and it may just be that the Peter Ross exaggerates trigger features of the naturals. The Peter Ross is supposed to be primarily a loch fly, but a small version of the pattern is often surprisingly effective on rivers with a little colour in them. I caught one of my largest river trout on a tiny size 16 Peter Ross, a rock-hard, silver and fin-perfect rainbow, a fraction over 5lb.

However, this raises an important point. Classifying wet-flies into separate categories such as 'river flies' (mainly soft-hackled spiders and small winged wet-flies) and 'loch or lake flies' is a dangerous business, for the boundaries are blurred. While a Peter Ross, and many other 'loch flies' for that matter, will catch river trout, I have also caught plenty of reservoir trout on 'river flies' such as the Snipe and Purple, Greenwell Spider and Orange Partridge. The Snipe and Purple has proved a particularly good early season reservoir fly, while the Greenwell and Orange Partridge have saved a number of potential blank days in summer. Classifying trout flies into categories may be a useful kind of shorthand, but it acts as a rough guide only. It occurs to me that the boundaries are also blurred between 'exact imitations' (if such flies exist), 'impressionistic imitations', 'general flies' and 'attractors' because although the angler may distinguish between them, we really cannot be sure how a trout perceives a fly. To human eyes, a dressing may appear extremely realistic, but its inert behaviour and appearance in the water may suggest otherwise to a trout. In contrast, an artificial may only loosely resemble a real insect to human eyes, or seemingly resemble nothing at all, but to a trout it may trigger a programmed feeding response. The late Richard Walker was a great believer in exaggerating the key feature, or features, of an insect because he believed this would act as a stimulus to a trout, but it is not an exact science and we will never really unravel the mystery of the way of a trout with a fly.

Traditional wet-flies are far from uniform in appearance. Some are drab, while others are bright and colourful. Some are tiny wisps of things with nothing but plain tying silk bodies and a single turn of hackle, while others have dubbed bodies, wings, tails, ribbing and other embellishments. But, apart from being 'traditional', all these wet-flies are unweighted patterns designed to be fished close to the surface of the water and the techniques used to fish them are pretty standard, as we shall see in subsequent chapters. For the moment, however, it may be useful to summarize the kind of variety of functions that we have within the group of patterns that I term 'wet-flies':

- flies that provide reasonable imitations of the appearance of specific insects, whether as mature nymphs, emerging adult flies, or drowning aquatic and terrestrial flies
- flies that provide a general impression of the appearance of a variety of insects at various stages in their life cycles
- flies that attract principally because they emulate the movement of insects (for example, insects struggling to emerge from nymph or pupal case, or struggling to escape drowning)
- flies that imitate the appearance and/or movement of food items other than insects (for example, fish fry)
- flies that exaggerate trigger features of food items in order to simulate the feeding instincts of trout
- flies that induce a take principally through flash, colour and the movement given to them; such flies are usually labelled 'attractors' and are akin to lures.

None of these categories of wet-fly is exclusive and it is quite possible for a pattern to fulfil more than one of the functions listed above. Equally, it may be difficult to decide which category a fly should be fitted into; this is particularly the case with many commercial tyings of standard patterns. For example, the Blae and Black is an excellent little winged wet-fly imitation of black chironomid midges, or 'duck flies', yet I have seen commercial dressings on hooks as large as size 8, which would make the fly more suited to the role of attractor. Wet-flies, if they are to fish properly, should be lightly or even sparsely dressed, not only to emulate the delicate appearance of a natural insect, but also so that they will be mobile and lively in the water. Heavily dressed flies are inert and lifeless and depend on a fast retrieve. Invariably, most commercially dressed wet-flies are overdressed and on hooks that are too large for the specified pattern. I often see dressings of the Snipe and Purple with chubby floss silk bodies and masses of hackle and wonder how many anglers really know what the fly should look like.

In conclusion, to be effective traditional wet-flies must be dressed correctly and must be fished in the correct manner. In order to ensure that the dressings are correct, there is really no substitute for tying your own flies. In the following chapters I will explain how to dress wet-flies and exactly how they should be fished.

Why Fish with Traditional Wet-Flies?

I suppose that what I have said so far has only partially addressed the not unreasonable question, 'Why should we fish with traditional wet-flies as opposed to more modern patterns?' For a complete answer to this question the reader must bear with me throughout the rest of the book, but for the moment I will simply assert that wet-flies are very effective and the techniques by which they are fished are so pleasurable that it makes wet-fly fishing a wonderful branch of the sport. Of course, this assertion is subjective and I do not suggest that there is no pleasure in fishing either the nymph or dry-fly. On the other hand, those who fish the nymph and dry-fly often regard wet-fly fishing as merely a game of 'chuck-and-chance-it', but I believe they are missing the point. Wet-fly fishing is an art to rival any branch of fly fishing, requiring as much knowledge of lake and river craft as the most 'socially acceptable' of techniques.

I cannot deny that for me the wet-fly is partly a nostalgic emblem of a past age. A world inhabited by small boys who got dirty, were free from the shackles of health and safety and went fishing because they hadn't discovered the 'delights' of mobile phones, fake designer gear, iPods, computer games and under-age sex. We didn't have much pocket money, but we spent hours in tackle shops before buying a single float or a packet of hooks. Local shops specialized mainly in coarse fishing tackle and that is why we didn't mind a shopping trip to Manchester with our parents because there was a different kind of shop there. It sold game fishing tackle and although most of it was well beyond the reach of our meagre budgets, it was the gateway to the mysterious world of fly fishing that we had read about in Bernard Venables' classic, *Mr Crabtree Goes Fishing*. In my imagination, the shop was owned by a famous tackle manufacturer, but it was actually called 'Hardy Bott' and had been there a long time; Arthur Ransome bought tackle there when he worked for the *Manchester Guardian*. It closed down many years ago and now an Arndale Shopping Centre hides its exact location.

That tackle shop was an old-world emporium of wooden cabinets, classy reels and expensively built cane rods. It didn't smell of rank maggot bran like our local tackle shops, but was exotically perfumed with the intoxicating smell of linseed oil from landing nets and oil-dressed silk lines. I bought my first flies there even before I possessed the tackle to fish them with. By the time I got my first fly rod, reel and silk line, which would have been in 1959 or 1960, I had built up a nice little collection of flies, mainly wet-flies because the dry-flies were much dearer. The flies were initially kept in an Elastoplast tin, but I graduated to a Loch Leven Fly Box with rows of metal clips. There were soft-hackled spiders such as the Snipe and Purple, Snipe and Yellow and Orange Partridge – they were the cheapest flies – and there were loch flies, mostly dressed with teal wings, but I also had Invictas, Alexandras and Butchers. I liked the look of them.

There was a small Pennine reservoir within walking distance of home and trout fishing season tickets were pretty cheap. It was an ideal place to fish, particularly because the stream which entered at the top end provided the bonus of twenty or thirty yards of 'river' fishing. It did, however, also provide the menace of steep bracken-covered banks which claimed plenty of flies before I mastered the art of casting. I lost many flies during that first season, but I also caught trout and although they were only small brownies the sense of satisfaction was great. The lost flies were a problem, however, and no amount of searching in the bracken retrieved more than a small percentage of them. I decided to tie my own flies because I couldn't afford to replace those I had lost. My first attempts at fly-tying produced rough copies of spider patterns because they were seemingly the simplest flies to dress. I tied without a vice and on coarse fishing hooks, beginning with feathers from a dead starling that had flown into our lounge window. They worked, so I gained the confidence to tie further flies and extended my materials kit by adding various colours of wool, feathers from next door's budgies and fur from our spaniel.

My first fly rod was a short split-cane affair more suited to fishing dry-flies than wet-flies, but I caught trout on both. The first magical rises I experienced to a dry Greenwell's Glory will be forever imprinted on my memory, but I remember too the evening rises when the performance of the dry-fly was disappointing, so I turned to wet-flies in order to catch a couple of fish. That was a lesson I learned early on. I learned too the benefits of moving around, exploring all the reservoir's banks instead of staying in favoured spots. When you don't have much tackle, you are much more mobile and mobility is important for fishing the wet-fly, both on reservoirs and on rivers.

I cannot understand why some modern fly fishers carry so much gear. A large plastic tackle box may not be a problem on a boat, since the boat itself provides the wherewithal to cover an expanse of water, but it is not uncommon to see reservoir bank fishers sitting on such boxes so that they remain rooted to a single spot. There is a key principle here. To fish traditional wet-flies from the bank, whether on river, loch or reservoir, it is essential that the angler travels light, for it is necessary to move around in search of fish. The adjective 'light' is also something to apply to the tackle itself. Whether fishing a river, or from bank or boat on a stillwater, only light tackle will fish the traditional wet-fly effectively. That said, it is not as easy to acquire a long and light pliant rod suited to fishing wet-flies on lakes, lochs and reservoirs as it is to buy shorter and more powerful tip-actioned rods designed for hurling heavy lures long distances. Rods suited to wet-fly fishing on small and medium rivers are less of a problem and light line nymph rods will usually suffice. On lakes and reservoirs, either from boat or bank, a long and light rod is necessary to make repeated short casts, to control the flies and to 'dabble' or 'dibble' the top dropper fly at the surface at the end of the retrieve. This technique also calls for the use of a light line, so that we are looking for a stillwater rod of between 10ft (3m) and 11ft (3.4m) that will take lines of AFTM no.4 or no.5 and certainly no heavier than no.6. Naturally, such a long rod would be nothing but an encumbrance on a small overgrown stream where, even for wet-fly fishing, a rod of only 7ft (2.1m) or 8ft (2.4m) might be practical, while a nine-footer (2.7m) is satisfactory for most other rivers. In essence, the rule of thumb is to use as long a river rod as the environment of the stream will allow, for a long rod will allow the angler to keep as much of the light line off the stream as possible while maximizing line control. On rivers, line control means minimizing the effects of drag caused by the currents of the stream, either by holding the line above them, or by 'mending' the line frequently (*see* Chapter 5). River rods also require a through action, or middle to tip action, rather than a tip action, for they must be able to throw an open loop on the back-cast in order to avoid tangling a team of wet-flies. Distance-casting is not a consideration, nor the quick false casting of dry-flies, and the rod will be required to handle lines in the AFTM no.3 to no.5 range. Unfortunately, the majority of river rods seem to be designed with a quick tip action which is not suited to the leisurely short casting of wet-flies.

I have emphasized the fact that wet-fly fishing on rivers, as well as on lakes and reservoirs, involves fishing with light lines and although this may mean making sacrifices in terms of the distance cast, there are undoubted benefits in terms of the delicacy with which the flies can be presented. Distance is rarely a factor on rivers anyway (although chest waders may be needed to reach the fish with short casts on larger rivers), but it is surprising how effective short casting may be even from the bank of a reservoir, providing that the shallows have not been ploughed barren by wading anglers. The light line, generally a floating line, also guarantees that the wet-flies will fish close to the surface – traditional wet-fly fishing is aptly described as a 'top-of-the-water' technique and is far removed from the use of high-density sinking lines, which is a different style of fishing altogether. In due course, I will say more about flies, tackle and techniques, for the function of this introductory chapter is essentially to provide just an overview of wet-flies and wet-fly fishing.

Some anglers are turned on by innovation in the form of new flies, new techniques and the latest tackle, but I freely admit that one of the things that interests me is the historical heritage of wet-fly fishing. To fish one of Charles Cotton's flies on the River Dove would rival playing a piano that Mozart, Beethoven or Schubert once played. I cannot play the piano – but I can follow in the footsteps of anglers such as Cotton, Stewart, Theakston, Jackson, Pritt, Walbran, Tod, Edmonds and Lee, and I can fish with the same wet-flies that they once used. Of course, light modern tackle improves efficiency and it would be foolish to return to the heavy rods and horse-hair lines of past centuries, but for me fishing the same flies as used by anglers of the past, and in a similar style too, creates an added dimension to the pleasure of fly fishing.

In days gone by, when travel was difficult and hazardous, and communication systems were relatively primitive, many fly patterns and styles of dressing them were unique to a particular locality. Even the universal patterns were given parochial names and were subjected to various modifications. Generally, however, it was a matter of local solutions to the challenge of catching trout and this involved making the best use of materials provided by local fauna in dressing flies to represent dominant local insects. Styles of fly were also often quite different from region to region and this is illustrated by the contrast between the slim winged wet-flies of the Tummel, Tweed and Clyde as opposed to the hackled 'spiders' favoured in Yorkshire. However, even some areas of Scotland preferred hackled flies to winged flies, as we can see with W.C. Stewart's 'trio' of spiders. All this helps to explain the rich diversity of wet-flies, particularly spider patterns and loch flies, that have lasted the course of time, although there must have been many more creations of silk, fur and feather that were lost along the way. Those patterns were circulated either by word of mouth, or occasionally by handwritten manuscripts, and at some stage they disappeared; an old man died without an heir to pass his manuscript to; the inhabitants of a rural hamlet left to find employment in the cities, or emigrated and so on.

We can thank a few individuals, however, for rescuing some effective wet-flies that might otherwise have disappeared, men such as Theakston (*British Angling Flies*, 1853), Jackson (*The Practical Fly-Fisher*, 1854) and Pritt (*Yorkshire Trout Flies*, 1885, republished as *North-Country Flies* in 1886). Unfortunately, there seems to have been no parallel collation of the old Scottish loch flies – patterns such as the Teal and Black, Mallard and Claret, Woodcock and Yellow, or Grouse and Green – so that both their inventors and the original dressings remain obscure. Many patterns have probably been lost, but enough have lasted the course. They were discovered by English Victorian gentlemen who visited Scotland in order catch fish and kill the odd stag, and the Scottish flies travelled back to England with them. It was during this period that enhanced geographical mobility among the middle classes ensured that once parochial wet-flies spread beyond their original localities.

For some reason, most of the wet-flies that have lasted the course tend to be of northern origin, with Derbyshire and Staffordshire being the southern limit. Of course, there are exceptions and someone may remark, for example, that the Butcher came from Kent and the Invicta from Gloucestershire. However, I might add that even James Ogden of Cheltenham, who invented the Invicta, lived originally in Derbyshire. There was something different about wet-flies of the south. For one thing, they tended to be more heavily dressed and even in 1676 we find Charles Cotton hanging a portly dressed London fly in his window to laugh at each morning. Southern wet-flies began to disappear primarily because of the emergence of chalk stream dry-fly fishing in the 1880s, which made wet-fly fishing appear anachronistic. The slowly rolling chalk streams were ideal for floating-flies. In contrast, the rain-fed rivers of the north were generally more suited to the wet-fly. There were similar rough streams in Devon and Cornwall, but these produced a rather different kind of wet-fly. In *Trout Fishing on Rapid Streams* (1863), H.C. Cutcliffe describes a unique breed of wingless wet-flies quite unlike those of Lancashire and Yorkshire. Instead of soft hackles from starlings, snipe or waterhen, Cutcliffe's wet-flies were hackled with sparkling and steely feathers from old English gamecocks. Those hackles were designed to 'kick' in the roughest of rapid currents and by all accounts they made very effective flies, but such feathers are pretty rare today and Cutcliffe's patterns have all but disappeared.

There is a fair amount of diversity among the order of patterns that we might term 'traditional wet-flies'. In subsequent chapters I will give the dressings of a selection of wet-flies, dressed in different styles, and I will provide some idea of how and when they may be fished.

2 THE HISTORICAL PERSPECTIVE

It is often assumed that fly fishing developed in a linear and rather uncomplicated way. In the beginning, anglers fished with sunken flies, because they didn't know any better, then Halford announced the birth of the dry-fly towards the end of the nineteenth century. The wet-fly was now as dead as a dodo. G.E.M. Skues discovered nymphs, debated his right to fish them with Halford, and thus prepared the ground for Frank Sawyer and Oliver Kite to develop weighted nymphs and the 'induced take' method. And so we arrived at modern times, with the wet-fly condemned to the dim and murky past. Well, the history of fly fishing isn't as straightforward as that.

Did Halford, Marryat and company actually invent the dry-fly in the 1880s? In one of his occasional pieces, G.E.M. Skues informed his readers that James Ogden was fishing a dry-fly on Derbyshire streams as early as the 1860s and I am sure he wasn't the first to use it. So the dry-fly has a long history and we cannot presume that the wet-fly preceded it as a more primitive method. It is probably more accurate to suggest that the dry-fly, or to put it more precisely, the 'floating-fly', preceded the wet-fly. Just think about it for a moment. A man looks at a river and sees trout rising to take floating natural flies; wouldn't he then try to copy nature by floating his artificial fly on the stream? He would, and he might well conclude that that is how trout feed, for their subsurface feeding habits are far less obvious to him. Thus, he casts an artificial fly to float on the surface of the river, but his fly sinks after a time as it drifts downstream and yet he still catches fish. He soon realizes that both the floating-fly and sinking-fly catch fish and he feels no need to make a distinction between the two methods. They are one and the same, for when his fly first lands on the stream it floats for a while before it begins to sink. That is the way it is. Eventually, he learns that there

Our fly-fishing heritage.

are times when the floating-fly works better and times when it is the sinking-fly's turn to produce food for the table. It is my belief that both the dry- and wet-fly originated from the same roots.

In providing this perspective on the wet-fly, I am not intending to offer a detailed history of fly fishing; there are good books by a number of authors on that subject and *A History of Fly-Fishing for Trout* (1921) by John Waller Hills has rarely been bettered. My intent is solely to provide a better understanding of what traditional wet-fly fishing is really about. There is, however, a very evident problem in trying to examine the history of the wet-fly, which is that we are restricted to the evidence provided by the printed word. There was undoubtedly an oral tradition whereby patterns and techniques were passed from generation to generation. In most cases, though thankfully not all, there is little recorded evidence of the substance of this tradition and there is something of a regional slant to this. For example, while printed texts on wet-fly fishing commonly emanated from the north of England, little was written before the twentieth century about the flies used on Scottish lochs. Accordingly, while there is a wealth of information relating to soft-hackled north-country 'spiders', the origins of many Scottish loch flies remain obscure and some patterns have undoubtedly been lost. I suspect that many Scottish loch flies, tied with feathers from indigenous birds such as the grouse, have been in existence for centuries, but as part of an oral rather than a written tradition. Unfortunately, our view of history is always controlled by written documents and without them there are gaps in our knowledge and understanding. For example, we know that the Peter Ross was developed by a fisherman of that name who came from Killin in Perthshire and lived from 1873 to 1923. He suggested a small modification to the standard Teal and Red, created a much better fly and earned himself everlasting fame, but that does not help us to understand the origins of the Teal and Red. When was that loch fly developed, and by whom? It is impossible to say. Ironically, we know more about flies cast in obscure places centuries before fly fishing came to Britain.

Early Words

The first known reference to fly fishing dates back to the second century AD and provides an account of fishing in Macedonian rivers. Claudius Aelianus, in *De Animalium Natura*, describes the catching of fish with speckled skins, presumably trout, and I am grateful for a translation provided by William Radcliffe in *Fishing from Earliest Times* (1921). What is being described seems to be the casting of a floating artificial to fish observed feeding on natural flies at the surface: 'When a fish observes a fly on the surface, it swims quietly up, afraid to stir the water above, lest it should scare away its prey; then coming up by its shadow, it opens its mouth gently and gulps down the fly ...' So fish are observed feeding at the surface, more obvious you will agree than the observation of subsurface feeding, and the angler casts his artificial in imitation of the floating natural fly:

> They fasten red wool round a hook, and fix onto the wool two feathers which grow under a cock's wattles, and which in colour are like wax. Their rod is six feet long, and their line is the same length ... the fish comes straight at it, thinking from the pretty sight to get a dainty mouthful; when, however, it opens its jaws, it is caught by the hook and enjoys a bitter repast, a captive.

I imagine that the fly used was hackle-less, the feathers being tied on to represent wings, yet it would still float well enough. It might not have been dry-fly fishing as Halford knew it, but I am sure that fly fishing did begin with attempts to float an artificial fly, rather than with the wet-fly. No, wet-fly fishing is not the primitive and ancient method that it is often thought to be; it is not with this method that fly fishing began.

Who knows when fly fishing actually did first begin? We know that it was practised in the second century AD in Macedonia but there are no earlier records. After that, there is a great gap in time before the next significant reference to fly fishing in the second edition of the hunting bible, *The Book of St Albans*, published in 1496. The book, or 'Boke', as it was originally called, was printed at Westminster by Caxton's curiously named successor, Wynkyn de Worde, and the second edition had an added fourth part entitled 'The Treatyse of Fysshynge with an Angle', generally attributed to Dame Juliana Berners (or Barnes), though of this there is some doubt. Dame Juliana was seemingly an abbess, though we know nothing else about her, and there are those who have challenged a woman's authorship. Dame Juliana, for we will assume her authorship of the 'Treatyse', provided a list of twelve apostolic trout flies to be used from March to August, a similar season to our own. What the flies actually imitate is of historical interest only, although G.E.M. Skues had a good shot at identifying all the naturals imitated. It is self-evident in several cases, such as the 'stone flye' for 'Apryll' fishing. What intrigues me about Dame Juliana's flies is whether they were dressed to float or sink. Of the twelve flies offered by the Dame, nine are definitely dressed with bodies, wings and no hackle; three are possibly hackled patterns. As with the Macedonian flies, this does not mean that they wouldn't float, nor does it mean that they were not intended to float. So did she fish a floating- or sinking-fly? I think that with a longish rod and buoyant horse-hair line, the Dame's flies would have floated for at least a time. Thomas Barker, who published *The Art of Angling* in 1651, was not much of an original thinker, but that is useful in itself for it informs us how flies had been fished for many years before him. The way he fished a fly was probably little different from the way Dame Juliana fished it, so that when he advises us that 'no part of your line touch the water but your fly only' it seems as if flies were fished in a dapping style which would ensure that they fished on, or at, the surface. I believe that the genuine wet-fly has yet to make an appearance.

If nine of the flies in the 'Treatyse' of 1496 were hackle-less, but probably fished at the surface, then the other three patterns, quoted below, were undoubtedly floating-flies, although we cannot be sure that they were hackled entirely in the modern manner. All three flies were to be fished in May:

- 'In the begynnynge of May a good flye. The body of roddyd wull and the lappid abowte with blacke sylke: the wynges of the drake & of the redde capons hackyll.'

- 'The yellow flye. The body of yellow wull: the wynges of the redde cocke hackyll & of the drake lyttyd yellow.'
- 'The blacke louper. The body of blacke wull & lappyd abowte with the herle of the pecok tayle: & wynges of the redde capon wt a blewe heed.'

May is certainly a good month for rising trout and I am sure that the above patterns were early 'dry-flies'. I am equally sure that the other nine flies in the 'Treatyse' were principally intended to float. Early illustrations of trout flies generally show wings much broader than we dress them today and therefore much more likely to provide the fly with buoyancy. Dame Juliana's flies might have sunk and still caught fish, but then the 'wet-fly' would simply have been a kind of happy accident.

Observations from the Seventeenth Century

Little of note, and certainly nothing of originality, was written after the 'Treatyse' until 1676, a date that proves a milestone in the history of the wet-fly. It was in 1676 that Charles Cotton, at Izaak (or Isaak) Walton's request, added a Part II to *The Compleat Angler* and entitled it 'Being Instructions How to Angle for a Trout or Grayling in a Clear Stream'. Written, if we take Cotton at his word, in only ten days, his excellent little treatise introduces observations on subsurface feeding and makes specific reference to the wet-fly on his beloved Derbyshire Dove. In spite of the fact that Cotton adopted the rather stodgy pastoral dialogue form of Walton, whereby 'Piscator' advises a compliant and two-dimensional 'Viator' on the pleasures of angling, Cotton's understanding of natural insects, fly-dressing and fishing techniques comes as a breath of fresh air after the fanciful stories, florid prose and dubiously sylvan milkmaids of Walton's famous original. Still, the popularity of Walton's book guaranteed a considerable readership for Cotton, who was no borrower but a first-hand observer of the natural world; he did not simply pass on received wisdom as others had done before him.

I like Cotton, not only because he was clearly

a fine angler but a character too. He lived in Beresford Dale, on the River Dove. The basic facts of his life can be told quickly: he was born into the landed gentry in 1630; married twice and fathered many children; fished and wrote poetry; and died in 1687. He seems to have let most of the turmoil of the Civil War pass him by, though he had royalist sympathies and certainly adopted a 'cavalier' approach to Oliver Cromwell's Protectorate:

'Let me have sack, tobacco store,
A drunken friend, a little whore,
Protector, I will ask no more.'

Of course, he also wanted to be left alone to fish the Dove and Manifold and it is with Charles Cotton that we first see an emerging distinction between floating- and sinking-flies. Cotton undoubtedly fished artificial flies at the surface as occasion dictated and live flies too, for he informs us that he gathered live 'green-drakes' (mayflies) which 'we commonly dape, or dibble with'. While many of Cotton's flies would have been intended to float, he also reveals a remarkable knowledge of what happens under the surface and, as far as I know, he is the first writer to do so. Observation of the trout's sub-aqueous food items is the very foundation of fishing the wet-fly.

Cotton began his season as early as January and although he used flies when he could, he was not averse to using the minnow or the worm. As soon as he caught a fish, he wanted to know what it had been feeding on so that he could adopt an imitative approach. Admittedly, his approach to an autopsy lacked delicacy: 'Then thrusting your finger through his Guills, to pull out his Gorge, which being opened with your knife, you will then discover what flie is taken, and may fit yourself accordingly.'

Cotton thought it equally important to study the insects of the stream in their natural habitat. Thus he studied the aquatic forms of mayflies, caddis, or sedge flies, and stoneflies. I particularly like his description of the nymph of the large stonefly:

'This same Stone-fly has not the patience to continue in his crust or husk, till his wings be full grown; but so soon as ever they begin to put out, that he feels himself strong, at which time we call him a Jack, squeezes himself out of his prison, and crawls to the top of some stone, where if he can find a chink that will receive him, or can creep betwixt two stones, the one lying hollow upon the other, which, by the way, we also lay so purposely to find them, he there lurks till his wings be full grown ... His body is long, and pretty thick, and as broad at the tail, almost, as in the middle: his colour a very fine brown ribbed with yellow, and much yellower on the belly than the back: he has two or three whisks also at the tag of his tail, and two little horns upon his Head: his wings, when full grown, are double, and flat down his back, of the same colour, but rather darker than his body, and larger than it ...'

This is a detailed, unique and ground-breaking observation. Cotton fished both with live stonefly nymphs and with artificials. While he fished his mayflies at the surface, knowing that stoneflies occupied more rapid water, he adopted a different approach and particularly on windy days: 'we seldom dape with this [i.e., the artificial stonefly] but in the streams, for in a whistling wind a made Flie in the deep is better, and rarely, but early and late, it not being so proper for the mid-time of the day.'

Although Cotton's prose is a little tortuous in this passage it is plain enough that he was intentionally fishing his artificial fly under the surface ('in the deep') and was indeed practising the wet-fly. It is therefore a passage of great significance. Charles Cotton's importance then, is that he is the first really to observe insects in detail, and particularly their aquatic stages, and subsequently to realize that there are times when the artificial fly must be fished intentionally, rather than accidentally, beneath the surface. In that sense, he is the father of the wet-fly – at least in print.

If Cotton's detailed observations of underwater insect life, and his adoption of the wet-fly as occasion demanded, laid the foundations for wet-fly fishing, then James Chetham is perhaps no less important. Seemingly from Smedley, in Lancashire, though my *AA Road Atlas* lists no such place, James Chetham published *The Angler's Vade Mecum* in 1681. It is easy enough to dismiss the importance of Chetham. He plagiarized all of Cotton's patterns and had a penchant for the macabre, believing that it was efficacious to anoint his baits and flies with 'man's fat or the powdered Bones or Scull of a dead man'; now those are materials no longer available by mail order! On the other hand, Chetham's inclusion of additional flies ('Another Catalogue of Flies, practised by a very good Angler, and useful to be known by the young Anglers in clear, Strong Rivers') is of great interest. These flies are much slimmer in construction than flies used elsewhere in the country and they employ many of the same materials that we find in the traditional north-country spider patterns of T.E. Pritt. Given Chetham's reference to 'a very good Angler', we may assume that he did not create these flies himself and is simply recording in print the products of an oral tradition. The slim construction of these flies, when fished on rapid streams, makes it very unlikely that they were intended to float. They are genuine wet-flies and it leads us to wonder just how old the north-country wet-fly tradition really is. It probably predates Cotton, though it only eventually first appears in print via Chetham in 1681.

James Chetham used an extensive and impressive palette of fly-dressing materials and dubbed slim fly bodies from a wide range of hair: bear, camel, badger, spaniel, hog, sheep, colt, calf, squirrel, black cat, hare, weasel, mole, fox, otter and ferret. He also used herls from the peacock, ostrich and heron for bodies; silks of various colours for tying and the construction of bodies; and gold and silver twists for ribbing his flies. His list of materials is more extensive than Cotton's, although his book was published only five years later. Chetham is also the first in print to make reference to the use of soft hackles from birds such as partridges, starlings, fieldfares, lapwings (sometimes also called plovers or 'peewits'), golden plovers, blackbirds and coots. These are the stock-in-trade hackles of north-country spider patterns; the very same feathers used in the flies of Pritt, or Edmonds and Lee, two centuries later. Thus, although the most famous books on fishing the wet-fly generally began to appear in the nineteenth century, it is clearly a much older art. Chetham's take on the

age-old Blue Dun ('Made of the Down of a Water-Mouse [water shrew], and the Blewish Dun of an Old Fox mixt together, Dub'd with Sad Ash-colour'd Feather of a Throstle.') is very similar to Pritt's Waterhen Bloa (*see* Chapter 7). It was probably also a hackled fly, with the thrush feather being wound around the hook, and therefore represents the first reference to a genuine north-country soft-hackled fly. In print at least, Chetham introduced the use of soft hackles and spun bodies of blended furs, lightly dubbed on other colours of silk so that the tying silk shines through.

Expansion of Angling Literature in the Nineteenth Century

Although a number of good angling books were written between 1681 and 1800, they generally reveal little about the development of the wet-fly. For example, the father and son team of Richard and Charles Bowlker, who fished around Ludlow on the Teme and Onny, resulted in the publication of *The Art of Angling* (1747) which was widely read and went through many reprints. Nevertheless, the flies they tied were rather heavily dressed and little different from the London fly that Charles Cotton hung in his window to laugh at. Ultimately, *The Art of Angling*, whatever its past fame, makes little contribution to the development of trout flies, either wet or dry. However, in the north of England, the wet-fly continued to evolve. In 1806, an expatriot Scot, Alexander MacKintosh, published *The Driffield Angler* and, while he probably often fished floating-flies, he also includes a number of soft-hackled wet-flies. For example, he dressed one fly with a body of dark olive mohair, mixed with fine gold-coloured hog's wool and hackled with a soft reddish-brown feather from a cock grouse. Was this a local Yorkshire pattern, or did he bring his grouse-hackled flies with him from Scotland? Was the traditional hackled wet-fly already in use in Scotland fifty years before W.C. Stewart? It is impossible to answer this question as angling books of note have yet to appear from over the border. In Scotland around 1800, the tying of trout flies remained essentially an oral rather than a written tradition. Even in England at the beginning of the nineteenth century, and with few notable exceptions, many of the publications on angling were locally based rather than aimed at a national audience. MacKintosh may have limited the circulation of his book by entitling it *The Driffield Angler* and this was certainly the fate too of John Swarbrick, who published *Wharfedale Flies* in 1807. Swarbrick's little work is of interest because some of the typical Yorkshire Bloa patterns make their first appearance in its pages. There were probably other little books like Swarbrick's and I am sure that parochialism has resulted in the loss of much interesting angling literature.

Parochialism was not the mistake made by George C. Bainbridge, who published his list of trout flies in Liverpool under the title of *The Fly-Fisher's Guide* in 1816, although, having said that, it is not a book that has had the fame it deserves. Bainbridge's book offers forty-two flies; some of them are typical hackled wet-flies, many are winged wet-flies, while others are winged but hackle-less. It is not always clear whether his patterns are to be fished wet or dry and the consistent use of the soft-hackled wet-fly has not yet fully established itself. Among the hackled patterns, there is the usual take on the Blue Dun theme (body of water rat fur mixed with lemon-coloured mohair; pale blue poultry hackle) and an interesting Black Midge (brownish-black silk body and blue dun cock hackle). After Bainbridge, William Blacker's *The Art of Fly Making*, or *The Art of Angling and Complete System of Fly-Making and Dyeing of Colours*, was published in London in 1843. What is interesting about Blacker's book is that it contains hackled wet-flies from the south of England. There are, for example, 'Five Flies for the Axe, Devon' and 'Four Celebrated Evening Flies for Thames at Weybridge'.

Blacker was a great believer in palmer dressings (*see* Chapter 9) and among several included in his book, the Red Palmer makes its appearance, but there are also interesting soft-hackled wet-flies such as the Grouse Hackle dressed with a gold or orange silk body and reddish-brown grouse hackle. The Grouse Hackle was recommended for fishing in May and June, although it is not clear what it was

intended to imitate. Soft-hackled wet-flies had seemingly moved to the south by 1843, although they remained few in number. However, we must not neglect the possibility that separate southern and west-country wet-fly traditions also existed and that Blacker's Grouse Hackle may have originated from one of those localities rather than from the north.

Before Blacker published his book, a very notable publication on natural insects and artificial flies had made its appearance – *The Fly-Fisher's Entomology* by Alfred Ronalds, published in 1836. Ronalds in many ways represented the new Victorian 'scientific' approach to work and leisure. It was an excellent and influential book and in many ways surpassed Halford's work on fly-fishing entomology of some fifty years later. *The Fly-Fisher's Entomology* contains colour plates illustrating natural flies and their respective artificials and there are excellent and familiar dressings in the book. Many of the flies actually look like wet-flies, with wings and hackles sloping backwards, and they would undoubtedly make good wet-flies, although most likely they were principally intended to be fished as 'floaters', as seems clear from Ronalds' account of how he fished them:

> When a fish has just risen at a natural object, it is well for the fisherman to try to throw into the curl occasioned by the rise, and left as a mark for him; but should the undulations have nearly died away before he can throw to the spot, then he should throw (as nearly as he can judge) a yard or two above it, and allow the flies to float down to the supposed place of the fish ...

Ronalds wrote a good book, teaching anglers much about the insects of the stream, but he was principally a floating-fly man and therefore only of marginal interest in terms of the development of the wet-fly.

Meanwhile, further north from Ronalds' native Staffordshire, the wet-fly was gaining ascendency. There is a preponderance of winged and hackled wet-flies among the ninety or so patterns offered by Michael Theakston in his *British Angling Flies*, published in Ripon in 1853, and further soft-hackled wet-flies listed by another Yorkshireman, John Jackson, in *The*

Practical Fly-Fisher of 1854, the year war broke out in the Crimea. Jackson, in particular, made good use of feathers from the waterhen, snipe, dotterel, woodcock, coot, grouse and starling. At the time, both Theakston and Jackson tended to favour winged wet-flies above hackled patterns, although this had changed radically by the time Pritt went to print in 1885. As with Bainbridge and Blacker before them, Theakston and Jackson were more interested in providing lists of patterns rather than focusing on the methods by which their flies should be fished. The opposite is true of a very influential wet-fly book that appeared from over the border in 1857; the year of the Indian Mutiny.

Published in Edinburgh, W.C. Stewart's *The Practical Angler* is almost a wet-fly fisherman's bible. Stewart only fished a limited number of flies and believed correct presentation to be the key factor. Indeed, he is remembered principally for his famed semi-palmered 'trio of spiders' (the Black Spider, Red Spider and Dun Spider). Palmered flies, with hackles wound the length of the hook, had been around for centuries, but Stewart's flies were palmered only halfway down the shank. They were wet-flies designed to suggest the 'buzz' of movement created by emerging or drowning flies and the dressings of the three spiders are given in Chapter 9. Stewart fished an exacting wet-fly method. The wet-fly was fished upsteam, generally to individual fish, and in this sense it has an affinity with the later art of nymphing on chalk streams. Stewart also placed great emphasis on the importance of the semi-palmered hackle to suggest a 'buzz' of movement and this design of fly is beginning to gain popularity once more as anglers recognize the importance of fishing specific emerger patterns. Apart from his 'trio of spiders', Stewart is also remembered for his insistence on fishing flies upstream and with short casts. He maintained that this would scare fewer fish, resulting in more hooked fish, than by fishing downstream and this too became the hallmark of the wet-fly technique as practised in the north of England. Stewart writes that, 'The greatest error of fly fishing as usually practised … is that the angler fishes downstream whereas he should fish up.'

While Stewart was very much a wet-fly man, it would be wrong to imagine that his flies were fished deeply sunk. Indeed, the very essence of traditional wet-fly fishing is that the flies are fished in the upper layers of water and even at the surface. When a three-fly leader is cast only a short distance upstream, or upstream and across, not only will the dropper flies remain close to the surface, but the point-fly will also. Initially, the flies will be *on* the surface before sinking as they drift downstream. Stewart describes this process: 'The moment the flies alight – being the only one in which the trout take the artificial fly for a live one – is the most deadly in the whole cast. There is no reason for keeping them on the surface, they will be quite as attractive a few inches under water.' It may therefore be said that this method combines both the floating- and sinking-fly. Stewart is important in terms of teaching us how to fish the wet-fly on rivers and we will have more to say about him and his technique in Chapter 5.

I have already suggested that a west-country wet-fly tradition may have been in existence for some time; it appeared first in print, however, only in 1863 when H.C. Cutcliffe (F.R.C.S.) published *Trout Fishing on Rapid Streams*. The little book was actually written while Cutcliffe was practising medicine in India and perhaps feeling a touch of nostalgia for the rivers of north Devon. He writes that, 'The inquiries which were constantly made of me, when I was in England, led me to think that an exposition of my views of the art of trout fishing would prove acceptable and useful to my old friends at home.' My copy is a treasured possession, though I have to agree that the fear Cutcliffe expresses in the preface – 'some will think me tediously prolix' – is generally borne out by the text. Even the preface requires us to wade with caution through the pages of *Trout Fishing on Rapid Streams*:

> For my incompetency for the execution of my desires, for the many errors in expression, and haste with which the type has been allowed to appear, I claim leniency of my readers in their criticism, and trust that as I have set about my task with the utmost desire to exercise my feeble powers, to the furtherance of the sport of North Devonians, so they in kindly feeling, acknowledging the intention of the author, will

less consider the rhetorical construction of sentences, than the practical matter contained within the work.

Cutcliffe is the very Polonius of fly-fishing literature, but while we would require of him more matter and less art, there are certainly good things in his book. Cutcliffe's wet-flies were often hackled patterns but quite different to north-country flies. They were rather heavily hackled and, to provide 'kick' in the rough water of rapid streams, he dressed his flies with stiff-fibred and sparkling feathers from old English gamecocks. Bodies were of various dubbed and mixed furs such as fox, squirrel, cow's hair, water rat and rabbit and he had a penchant for ribbing his flies with bright gold tinsel to attract trout in the turbulent rivers. Above all, Cutcliffe prized his cock hackle feathers and favoured a range of uniquely coloured hackles described as 'rusty brownish blue', 'black red', 'smoky blue' and so on. He kept his feathers stored in a hackle book and cared for them in a way that verges on eccentricity: '... but now comes the most valuable, the highest treasured of all – the book with the hackles, oh these precious beauties! Does one project beyond its especial case? Take it gently, handle it respectfully, and place it tenderly where no harm can reach it; where it may rest undisturbed.'

Fishing alongside Cutcliffe, or observing him tying his flies, might have taught us a great deal, but I am not sure that I would have been quite so happy with him as my family GP! Cutcliffe fished a three-fly cast, more flies if it was not too windy and, on the point, which he calls the *'stretcher'*, he favoured a 'red fly with gold twist'. This he described as a conspicuous fly to be 'thrown into any little hole, or under a stone, or by the side of the current', so that the trout would dash out for it. Not very specific about things entomological, Cutcliffe believed his 'red fly' to be taken for 'some worm or grub'. Both the middle fly and the top dropper were to be fished 'bobbing and dapping about on the surface', so that the wet-fly was once more combined with a kind of floating-fly. In keeping with most anglers of the period, Cutcliffe did not exclusively fish the artificial fly and would use natural flies, live beetles, maggots, worms and

minnows as he thought fit. Is it not strange that we now compartmentalize different techniques in fishing, as with everything else in life, and become specialists rather than all-round anglers?

Cutcliffe wrote *Trout Fishing on Rapid Streams* only a couple of decades before Pritt's classic wet-fly book came into print, but before we reach Pritt, there is a real curiosity to arouse our interest. In 1876, W.H. Aldam published *A Quaint Treatise on Flees and the Art of Artyfichall Flee Making*, a real anachronism in an age of scientific discovery; Bell invented the telephone in the same year. Aldam's book is a rare collector's item, which includes wet-flies beautifully tied in the north-country style by Mary Ogden-Smith and her father, James Ogden. (James Ogden of Cheltenham, though originally from Derbyshire, was generally acknowledged to be the greatest fly dresser of his age.) The book is something of a mystery and while Aldam informs us that the book is based on a manuscript from 'an old man well known on the Derbyshire streams as a first-class fly-fisher', we cannot be sure whether this was the truth or merely a fiction. There may well have been such an old man, and such a manuscript, but I have my doubts and wonder whether Aldam had simply come up with a novel idea. However, suspending my disbelief, it would certainly be very rewarding to think that we at last had evidence from what had largely been an oral tradition. G.E.M. Skues was also fascinated by the puzzle posed by Aldam's book and wrote:

> But I am sure that I have read somewhere that the manuscript was but one of many, which, before books on fly-dressing became generally accessible, were handed down from generation to generation in farmhouses and cottages in country districts where trout fishing was available. So it is far from improbable that the Treatise was not itself original, and it may have been a copy of a copy, and the use of the soft-hackled fly may go back much further than we know, though perhaps not to Cotton ...

Now I agree that the soft-hackled fly probably goes way back in time, but I am still not convinced that there were many such manu-scripts. How many were literate enough to read them in farmhouses and cottages? Surely, the odd original manuscript would have turned up sooner or later, wouldn't it? I may be wrong, but I still subscribe to the idea of a mainly oral tradition and think that Aldam had dressed up his book in pseudo-anachronistic and semi-literate language as part of an imaginative fiction. To my way of thinking, there is a lack of consistency in the incorrect spellings of words that smacks of artifice. Of course, this does not exclude the possibility that the patterns, materials and methods of dyeing them were passed orally to Aldam by an old and renowned Derbyshire fly fisherman. That remains a distinct possibility.

There are some fascinating things in the *Quaint Treatise*, such as the instructions given for dyeing 'Hare or Rabbitts belley' with 'aquafortis' to produce a dubbing called 'Yellow Caritted Stuff' and the warning that the reader should use 'a rag at the end of a short stick and fark to keep your fingers from being bruned'. Consider also the plea that we should keep our fly bodies as slim as those of natural insects and should dub them with soft rather than coarse furs:

> It makes your flee much nater and comes more to nature then than stiff brisley Dubbing – You find nothing coace in nature – When you have made a Artyfichall flee as nate as hand can make It is a thousand times behind a natural one when dresst with the natest meatearills – When wee come to Examin those small beautiful tender dellagate and nate water bred Duns that ought to be the Anglers coppiing – I can find no room for coace meatearills ...

The above passage provides a good flavour of the style of Aldam's book and, in my opinion, the artificial use of dialect and idiosyncratic spelling. Nevertheless, it is still an interesting book from a fly-fishing point of view and contains a good range of winged and hackled wet-flies, many of them the patterns we generally associate with T.E. Pritt and Edmonds and Lee. There are various March Brown patterns, a Dotterel Dun, a Watchet (or Iron Blue), a Black Gnat, Little Chap, Orange Brown (or Woodcock Fly) and so on, all patterns we encounter with later authors. The Little Chap is an interesting beetle pattern

dressed with a body of copper-coloured peacock herl and hackled with a dark dun hen feather. The Little Chap even turns up a few decades later as one of F.M. Halford's chalk stream dry-flies! It is very probable that the Little Chap had been around for some time as a beetle pattern before Aldam acquired the dressing and published it. It undoubtedly was a pattern passed around the country, and modified from area to area, if not from angler to angler. In some books, for example, it acquires a silver rib, becomes the 'Smoke Fly', and is a pattern recommended for grayling. Alternatively, dressed with a marginal covert feather from a snipe it becomes the Black Snipe.

Only ten years after Aldam's unique *Treatise* the book often considered the definitive work on North-Country wet-flies appeared. In 1885 Khartoum fell, Gilbert and Sullivan produced *The Mikado*, the internal combustion engine was invented and T.E. Pritt published *Yorkshire Trout Flies*. It is better known by its 1886 republished title of *North-Country Flies*. To wet-fly fishermen of the north of England, Pritt has become almost a deity and even in North America he enjoys a cult following among the growing numbers who fish soft-hackled wet-flies. *North-Country Flies* is undoubtedly an important book, though I feel we do need to put it into perspective. Pritt did us a great service by collating patterns and by codifying them, but he was not an innovator *per se*. Many of the dressings within the pages of *North-Country Flies* were passed to him by angling friends, or were the result of his library research, which included books by Bainbridge, Theakston, Jackson *et al*. Pritt's real value lies in the fact that he tied everything together in a volume that celebrated the north-country wet-fly tradition. As such, it is greatly valued today, although its original publication came at something of an unfortunate time, in that F.M. Halford published *Floating Flies and How to Dress Them* in 1886 and that book signalled the so-called 'dry-fly revolution'. Halford's work resulted in much subsequent literature being focused on the chalk streams of the south and it also led to a tendency to denounce the wet-fly, even if this had not been Halford's intention.

T.E. Pritt was born in 1848 near Preston, in Lancashire. For the working classes, 1848 was a momentous year; it was the year of *The Communist Manifesto*, the collapse of Chartism and the year of revolutions across Europe, but Pritt was born comfortably into an 'arty' middle-class family. He enjoyed a successful banking career in Manchester before furthering that career in Leeds. He became the angling editor of the *Yorkshire Weekly Post* in 1884 and enjoyed a wide circle of eminent fishing companions and exponents of the wet-fly such as Francis Walbran, four years Pritt's junior. (Walbran drowned in 1909 while fishing the River Ure.) Pritt's entertaining articles in the *Yorkshire Weekly Post* (a selection was published in 1896, the year after his death, as *An Angler's Basket*) guaranteed that his book would succeed in the north, but a competing period of dry-fly 'enlightenment' was emerging in the south. It is likely that the chalk stream fraternity would have regarded Pritt's book as quaintly old-fashioned. However, Pritt offers excellent and timeless hackled wet-fly patterns, matched to natural insects, and many of them will underpin Chapter 7 of this book. Although he attributed each fly to specific months of the fishing season, Pritt counselled wisely that, 'the seasons are given approximately, the actual appearance of each fly being dependent on the mildness of the previous winter and the prevailing spring weather'. Pritt also gave an excellent account of what the soft-hackled wet-fly represents:

> It is far more difficult to imitate a perfect insect and to afterwards impart to it a semblance of life in or on the water, than it is to produce something which is sufficiently near a resemblance of an imperfectly developed insect, struggling to attain the surface of the stream. Trout undoubtedly take a hackled fly for the insect just rising from the pupa in a half-drowned state; and the opening and closing of the fibres of the feathers give it an appearance of vitality, which even the most dexterous fly-fisher will fail to impart to the winged imitation.

Thus, while those in the south pursued the philosopher's stone of 'exact imitation', Pritt and his companions sought sufficient resemblance to emerging flies but a more important impression of movement and life. Unlike passively floating and fully emerged natural duns, emerging and drowning flies struggle and it is this buzz of movement that attracts trout. It is also this movement that the wet-fly emulates – a factor which is often neglected. Even that great thinker on fly fishing, J.C. Mottram, somewhat missed the point when he wrote, 'Because the majority of flies when on the water keep quite still, it is only in exceptional cases that this quality [i.e., movement] needs to be considered.' (*Fly Fishing: Some New Arts and Mysteries*, 1915). That statement may be true of dry-flies imitating static emerged duns, but it is not true of the wet-fly fished in imitation of emerging or drowning insects. There had developed a real north–south divide in terms of fly fishing, symbolized by the differing techniques of wet-fly and dry-fly, and there was a growing sense of division in many other aspects of life too.

Into the Twentieth Century

Pritt's *North-Country Flies* was followed in 1916 by the publication in Bradford of *Brook and River Trouting* by H.H. Edmonds and N.N. Lee. Like most other books of the period, it contains something on bait fishing but its principal interest lies with the wet-fly. On publication, 1,000 standard copies were printed plus fifty de luxe editions each containing thirty-six artificial flies dressed by Hardy Bros, along with a selection of materials. Now that would be a copy worth having! To a degree based on Pritt's book, Brook and River Trouting provides an excellent list of flies and good advice on tying and fishing them. Soft-hackled wet-flies dominate the book, but there are also a few winged wet-flies and a handful of dries. One of the most significant aspects of this book is that it provides precise instructions about the selection of correct hackle feathers from a bird's wing and provides colour plate illustrations of these feathers and other materials. When first published, the book's circulation was small and it was also published at a time when many young men, who would rather have been waving fly rods on the rivers of England, were carrying rifles and wading through the mud and barbed wire of the First World War battlefields. What is most striking about the book is that the colour plates not only provide a precise guide to correct materials, but also display flies dressed as slim and delicate as it is possible to achieve; even the 'old man' celebrated by Aldam's book would have been satisfied that they were suitably 'dellagate and nate'. When fishing these delicate creations, Edmonds and Lee were clearly of a mind with W.C. Stewart and Pritt and were firmly in the upstream camp. They were also very keen to stress the perils of drag impairing the effectiveness of artificial flies and advocated casting a wavy line 'as the current has to pick up the slack before the drag takes effect on the flies'. While they may well have cast on occasions to individual sighted fish, they outline a method for systematically searching the stream by short casting:

> To fish a stream or length of river systematically, crossing and re-crossing, each time a few yards higher up, until the whole has been thoroughly covered, takes time, but it is far better that the angler's flies should be on the water, searching every spot fit to hold a fish … we are to pay especial attention to every little run, eddy, channel and slack water behind boulders.

The Edmonds and Lee method of searching the stream is the antithesis of what had developed on the chalk streams whereby the angler would only make a cast once he had spotted a rising fish. Most of the time, therefore, the chalk stream angler's dry-fly would be off the water rather than on it. Edmonds and Lee, like Pritt before them, certainly did not neglect the rationale behind the use of the wet-fly and provide a very good outline of the theory:

> Why, it may be asked, should the fish be more partial to the wet fly than the dry fly on Northern streams. The reason is not far to seek; for, owing to the roughness and rapidity of such rivers, a large percentage of insects, as they rise from the bed of the river preparatory to hatching out, are carried many yards downstream before they reach the surface of the water. Others, getting into rough water, find themselves unequal to the effort of emerging from their nymphal case, or emerge with wetted and helpless wings, while

many flies, surviving these natural difficulties, are carried down some rapid almost immediately after they reach the perfect state, and get water-logged before ever they have the opportunity of using their wings. Hence, the trout become used to taking much of their insect food in a submerged or partially submerged state. Therefore so long as those streams remain as heretofore, the wet fly is likely to continue to hold premier position in the filling of a North Countryman's creel.

This is a fair argument, although the authors do not perhaps focus adequately on the full significance of the stage of emergence from nymph to adult fly. That came a little later and from the other side of 'the pond'. In 1941, the American, James Leisenring, published *The Art of Tying the Wet Fly*, which was republished in 1971 as *The Art of Tying the Wet Fly & Fishing the Flymph*. Leisenring's original book was concerned only with tying flies and contained little on fishing them, while the new edition, with additional material from Leisenring's disciple, Vernon S. Hidy (known whimsically as Pete Hidy), focused on fishing techniques and what Leisenring's wet-flies imitated. It still remained a small book, but a good one nevertheless. Hidy coined the term 'flymph' to describe that stage between mature nymph and adult fly, in other words the stage we would generally term an 'emerger'. The flymph then is a wet-fly cast upstream and across, and fished close to the surface, as Hidy puts it: 'for the trout to take just below or within a few inches of the surface film'. The soft-hackled wet-fly, with its semblance of movement, is appropriate for this method of fishing and the semi-palmered Stewart Spider may be considered ideal.

The Leisenring/Hidy book is really the last in a line of books on the development of the wet-fly on rivers; the literature of dry-fly and nymph somewhat took over after that. Ironically, while the history of the wet-fly was formerly dominated by river fishing, at the point at which the river literature begins to wane, the literature of fishing wet-flies on lochs and reservoirs comes a little more to the fore, but it is still relatively thin on the ground. Notable exceptions are books such as R.C. Bridgett's *Loch Fishing in*

Theory and Practice (1924) and T.C. Ivens' *Still Water Fly-Fishing* (1952). T.C. Ivens, though he occasionally used dry-flies, was very much of the opinion that the sunk-fly was much more effective on reservoirs and writes:

> Looking back over my 1947 to 1952 angling diary in which I recorded weather and light conditions, my takes and those of other anglers (and the blanks too!), I find that I took only six fish on the dry fly over the six-year period. On many occasions I devoted the whole of the rise to testing the worth of dry flies; on others I fished wet near to another successful angler fishing dry. The results of tests, fairly conducted by several of us, prove that the wet fly is far and away more deadly than the dry fly, even in a rise.

Ivens invented a number of good nymphs and lures, but it is interesting to note that he also put faith in traditional patterns such as the Butcher and Alexandra. His thoughts on wet- and dry-flies are included in a section headed, 'The Dry/Wet Controversy', yet this tends to further the idea that they are competing rather than complementary techniques. In this respect, I can think of no better way of rounding off this brief history than by quoting the wise words of Viscount Grey of Falloden. In *Fly Fishing*, first published in 1899, and a book which makes most anglers' 'top ten' fishing books, Viscount Grey wrote:

> The enthusiasm which was the result of dry fly fishing led at one time, among those who were fortunate enough to be able to enjoy it, to a tendency to disparage the older art of using the wet fly. A comparison of the two methods is always interesting, but it must never be forgotten that it is not necessary, nor even appropriate, to exalt the one at the expense of the other.

Grey was one of those fortunate enough to enjoy dry-fly fishing on the chalk streams of the south, but he had grown up fishing the wet-fly on the burns and rivers of the north and so understood the ways of the wet-fly. A little less fortunately, Viscount Grey happened to be Foreign Secretary when the First Word War started; the lamps went out all over Europe and Grey himself went blind. However, Edward Grey fished on and though he could no longer see to respond to the rise of a trout to a dry-fly, the wet-fly became his salvation. When *Fly Fishing* was republished in 1930, with an additional chapter entitled 'Retrospect', Grey wrote:

> There remains wet fly fishing for trout in still water and across or down stream. When there is no slack line, a certain proportion of trout – a good proportion when they are taking well – that come at an angler's fly will hook themselves. There is of course some bungling ... the mere touch of a trout, even if it does not hook itself, gives a little thrill; the feel of a small, single-handed rod, its quick and delicate motion, and its response to the hand, are delightful: it is very pleasant to spend a day by rippling streams with a background of trees and the air lively with the songs of birds in April and May.

I think that Grey captures the very essence of fly fishing for trout in his book, while the above passage alone should make us wish to revisit the old upstream versus downstream debate. We will do that in Chapter 5.

3 WHEN TO FISH THE WET-FLY

Introduction

Chapters 5 and 6 below are concerned with *how* and *where* to fish wet-flies, but there is also the matter of *when* to fish them. If I were asked the not unreasonable question, 'When should I fish the wet-fly?' then I might be tempted to answer glibly, 'Whenever you feel like it'. Strangely, there would be an element of sense in that reply. The answer may appear to be no answer at all and yet it remains true that whenever a wet-fly is fished, no matter what the circumstances, and if it is the right fly fished in the correct manner, there is a very high chance that the angler will be successful. It is possible to fish the wet-fly exclusively throughout the season and to maintain a high catch rate; I have done that. In the 1880s, when many chalk stream men would only cast dry-flies, their counterparts in the north fished the wet-fly exclusively and consistently took good catches of trout. It must be said, however, that it is equally possible to fish with either a nymph or dry-fly throughout the season without greatly reducing one's tally of trout caught.

I am not so sure about the exclusive use of lures. It all boils down to personal choice and on many occasions whether we choose to fish a nymph, dry-fly or wet-fly doesn't matter; each method will stand an equal chance of catching a fish or two. I have caught trout on wet-flies while others have used nymphs or dries and there has been little difference in the number of fish landed by each method. Thus, there is a considerable overlap in terms of the effectiveness of different methods and I would go as far as to argue that it is impossible to divide the season, month, or even a single fishing day,

neatly and predictably into 'wet-fly time', 'nymph time' or 'dry-fly time'. By means of illustration, even during the storied 'evening rise' I have known a wet-fly to do better than a dry, and I have also known many times when trout lying deep down in clear water will just as happily rise to take a dry-fly on the surface, or wet-fly just under it, as a leaded nymph sunk down to their depth. Nothing is ever straightforward in fly fishing.

In spite of what I have said, there are undeniably times when the dry-fly will be more effective than the wet, or times when the wet-fly is more effective than the dry, or times when the nymph will outfish anything else, yet it is unwise to generalize on the basis of any individual instances. When, for example, trout are swimming slowly close to the surface and are taking tiny flies, a dry-fly may prove the only way of catching them, as anything that sinks more deeply will not be seen. At other times, trout seem to be fixed on flies emerging just under the surface film and neither nymph nor dry-fly will take them; the only solution is a wet-fly fished very close to the surface. In slightly coloured water, trout may be cruising for food at mid-water and will only take wet-flies or weighted nymphs fished at that depth. Then there are fat trout that feed almost exclusively on a rich supply of shrimps in a deep river pool and no dry-fly or wet-fly will tempt them; a leaded imitation of a shrimp is the only method to use and when such trout are caught their bellies literally crunch with natural shrimps. In really turbulent water also a leaded fly may be the only pattern to get down to the fish and dry-flies or wet-flies would simply be swept away too quickly by the rapid current – but then I have caught trout from tumbling runs on both dries and wets. As I said, it is dangerous to generalize and there are exceptions that break the seeming rules of all the above examples.

In Chapter 1, Francis Francis was quoted as saying that the 'finished fly-fisher' was he who was capable of fishing effectively at all levels of the water and that would seem, at face value, a reasonable assumption. The 'finished fly-fisher' would be the man who is equally skilled at plying the dry-fly, nymph and wet-fly on rivers or lakes. I suppose, by modern standards, he would also be accomplished in all the latest techniques including Czech nymphing (or 'high sticking') on rivers and fishing a team of dry-flies with a 'slime line' (clear intermediate line) on reservoirs. Some of the latest techniques originate from the match circuit where rapid switches of method are necessary in order to catch the greatest number of trout within a finite amount of time. Extremely proficient anglers will make several switches of flies, techniques and tackle within a short space of time and by doing so will maximize their catch rate in order to beat other anglers in a competition. This has also tended to become the norm in non-competition fishing, and particularly on reservoirs, because anglers seem to think that they are losing out if they do not catch huge numbers of trout. With a few variations, it is possible to stick with a single method – as long as you find pleasure in using that particular method – and to reap adequate rewards for your efforts. You may not catch 'over sixty trout in a day', as someone I was in conversation with recently claimed to have done, but then what pleasure is there in that?

When wet-fly fishing I like to travel light so that I can move around and explore as much water as possible. With the exception of boat fishing (since a boat provides both mobility and storage space), that means carrying a single rod, whereas radical changes of technique require the use of several rods. Thus, while I may vary my approach to counter any given situation, as opposed to making a repetitively identical sequence of casts and retrieves, the broad technique will generally remain constant because the tackle will stay the same. I will use one rod, and more often than not the same floating line, and only the flies and the way I use them will be subject to change.

Fishing is a pastime and should therefore be relaxing, so that frequent changes of tackle seem to me to be quite pointless if I am not trying to fill my freezer or to catch more trout than everyone else. At a pinch, the wet-fly rod may be used to fish a dry-fly or nymph when it is really essential, for no angler truly enjoys a blank day, but it was my inherent laziness in not wanting to change tackle and techniques that led me to discover that the wet-fly will work more often than not – even when it may be least expected to. I discovered, for example, that rising trout will accept a wet-fly and that a deep-lying trout may be tempted to rise to a wet-fly fished just below the surface.

It is now time to consider the 'when' of wet-fly fishing in more detail and the best approach is to examine rise forms and signs of feeding fish. Some anglers will disagree with the conclusions I draw from my experiences, but I can only write as I find it. I may upset the dry-fly specialists by claiming that some classic 'dry-fly rises' are as effectively countered by the wet-fly, but I will try to balance this out by suggesting that there are also apparent sunk-fly situations when the dry-fly may actually work better.

Signs of Feeding Fish

No-Shows

When there are no signs at all of fish feeding at the surface, or close to it, then the wet-fly or nymph would seem to be the order of the day, although in clear water trout will sometimes rise to a dry-fly even when there are no natural flies hatching. No visible rises may either mean that trout are feeding deeper down or not feeding at all! In rivers it is usually possible to locate fish and to try them with a wet-fly, or to search the water as described in Chapter 5. Searching the water will also be necessary on lakes and reservoirs (*see* Chapter 6) and this may also require experimenting with different depths and possibly trying floating, intermediate and sinking lines. There *are* times when trout remain very deep down so that only a leaded nymph will reach them.

Bow waving trout at fry time.

Bow Waves

During high summer, or late in the season, trout, and big ones at that, often charge and crash around the reservoir as they feed on fry, sticklebacks or minnows, and a common sight is to see the 'bow wave' of a trout as it ploughs into a shoal. There will probably be several bow waves produced by a number of trout working in tandem and this often occurs in shallow water close to the bank. A degree of stealth is always advisable when approaching trout lying in shallow water, although fry-feeding frenzies do tend to make trout less cautious. (Although this kind of episode is normally associated with lochs and reservoirs, it is also far from an uncommon occurrence in some of the quieter pools of large rivers.) A lure will catch trout at such times and there are some very good lures which create impressions of sticklebacks, minnows or fry. In the past, I have caught fry-feeding trout on lures that resemble small roach and perch, on Muddler Minnows, on a fry pattern developed by Richard Walker and on very large versions of the Pheasant Tail Nymph. When these lures were employed it seemed necessary to strip them quite quickly through the water in order to provoke a response and I am not particularly fond of that method, nor do I particularly like employing the heavier tackle required for lure fishing.

There are times also when lures seem strangely unsuccessful in taking trout. A trout may either ignore the lure, or repeatedly nip at it without taking. In contrast, a smaller wet-fly is often taken quite confidently and it may be fished more slowly on a lighter rod and line. The leader must be strong, however, as takes are often violent. I have found that attractor loch flies are effective when retrieved erratically in little pulls, since this suggests an injured fish and an easy prey; the fly is frequently taken during the pauses between pulls. Wet-flies dressed on hooks in the size range 12 to 8 are about right, a size 10 hook is a good average, and a small fly bears closer inspection than a lure, which is why lures generally have to be fished rather more quickly. Among the wet-flies suited to this kind of fishing are the Butcher, Peter Ross, Teal Blue and Silver (a good roach fry imitation) and the Alexandra (a good perch fry imitation). As is the case with lures, there are times when the loch fly also gets nipped at rather than taken. This is where an unusual minor tactic comes into its own – the use of a dry-fly, and I did say that I would be honest enough to indicate when the dry-fly might be used in a typical wet-fly situation. Why it should be I really don't know and I am not even going to attempt to offer an explanation, but it is sometimes the case that a big dry-fly will work very well when cast into the general area of fry-feeding activity, taking the trout when other methods have failed. It is the perversity of trout, but I prefer things that way because the unpredictable nature of fishing prevents monotony.

The Big Rise

The 'big rise' is what might be thought of as the archetypal dry-fly rise and it is generally a rise form produced when a trout engulfs a floating natural insect. Every angler will recognize the rise form described by G.E.M. Skues as a 'kidney shaped double whorl'. It is depicted in illustrations as a series of concentric circles. The theory goes that if you hit the rise form with the right dry-fly then you will catch a fish. Of course, on a fast-flowing river the rise form will drift quickly downstream so that pin-pointing the exact location of the trout is not always that simple. On a reservoir, the rise form poses further problems in that trout often move quickly in search of their food, which can mean that, as the circles of the rise spread slowly outwards, the trout is already some distance away.

The classic rise may be produced by trout surface feeding on duns of the ephemeridae, chironomid midges, stoneflies, small sedges, terrestrial flies and a host of other creatures including caterpillars, beetles and ants. A bubble of air left after a fish has risen is a fair indication that a floating natural has been taken. However, the big rise occurs too when trout are feeding on insects emerging in, or just below, the surface film, so that a wet-fly fished close to the surface works better than a dry-fly fished on the surface. Even when trout are feeding on floating natural insects it does not mean that they will ignore a wet-fly and it all depends on the depth at which they are swimming. If a fish is swimming a couple of feet below the surface during a good hatch then it will take a wet-fly fished above it just as readily as a dry-fly. We must remember that during a hatch of duns, for example, while the adult flies will be obvious to the angler as they float on the surface, there will also be ascending nymphs below the surface and trout may be feeding on both. They may feed on both insect stages simultaneously, but they sometimes do become preoccupied with a single stage such as the ascending nymph, emerging fly or hatched dun. However, even when trout are seemingly locked onto feeding solely on the floating-fly, there are times when wet-flies score better than dry-flies, and particularly on reservoirs.

The speed of the rise *sometimes* acts as an indication of the size of a trout. In general, small fish rise quickly, while larger fish conserve energy and rise more slowly. There are times, however, when even a large fish rises quickly if it believes that a nice juicy item of food is about to escape from the water. The strength of a rise

The big rise.

form may be partially controlled by the size of fish involved, but a further conditioning factor is the depth from which a fish has risen; stronger rise forms are produced by trout lying deep down than by trout swimming close to the surface. It is also quite possible that a trout lying a few feet down feeds on plenty of nymphs below the surface, then occasionally makes a foray to the surface where it takes a floating-fly and creates a very distinct rise form. Such inter-mittent rise forms, particularly on rivers, indicate a fish which may be prepared to rise for a dry-fly but would be more consistently caught on wet-fly or nymph. In shallow rivers, a trout lying near to the bottom only has a short distance to rise to the surface in order to take either an artificial or natural fly, yet that still requires the expenditure of more energy than taking a nymph or wet-fly at its own depth.

Trout are often prepared to take either a wet-fly or a dry-fly, unless a hatch is so intense that they become preoccupied with floating-flies. During most hatches of aquatic flies there will not only be adults floating on the surface but also nymphs and emergers, as well as drowned adults that have failed to escape the surface film. Adult flies become swamped by the current of a river, or by the wave on a reservoir, and trout pick them off underwater where a good imitation wet-fly is likely to dupe them. The same is true of terrestrial insects, for some will struggle at the surface while others are swept under, and this therefore gives the angler the option of using wet-flies or dry-flies.

So far, we may conclude that big rise forms do not necessarily mean that we have to use dry-flies, but if the surface of the water is positively littered with floating naturals then the majority of trout are likely to stay close to the surface and only take floating artificials even though there will be plenty of ascending nymphs or pupae below them. It is pretty obvious on rivers when this is the case, for both trout and flies will be very visible. On lakes and reservoirs the same kind of situation might occur when the water is very calm and the meniscus makes it difficult for adult flies to escape the surface film. Once again, it should be obvious that this is the case from the number of flies visible on the surface and a dry-fly will seemingly make more sense than a wet-

fly. On the other hand, I have witnessed a good number of occasions on reservoirs when the dry-fly is refused simply because there are so many naturals around that the chances of a trout locking onto an artificial are minimal. Why should they choose our dry-fly sitting in the middle of thousands of natural insects? The solution here may be to offer something completely different and a wet-fly retrieved slowly close to the surface is worth a try. It will attract a trout's attention more readily than our static dry-fly and there is a good chance that it will be taken. This is a 'minor tactic' that succeeds pretty frequently.

While the large number of surface flies may indicate that the dry-fly is to be preferred to the wet-fly, the frequency of rises is not necessarily a good indicator. There may, for example, be plenty of trout creating rise forms, but they are not taking flies on or above the surface. Though there are lots of rising fish we see few adult flies actually *on* the surface and this suggests that a wet-fly (or 'damp-fly' may be a more accurate description) is the better option. Imagine that we are beside a good pool on the river, trout are rising everywhere and there are clouds of dark olive duns in the air. We watch a good brown trout rise three times close up against the far bank, but we didn't see a dun sailing down towards it and there was no bubble of air after each rise. In fact, there appear to be very few duns on the surface, even though the air is full of them and the trout are feeding avidly. A closer observation makes everything clear, for we notice duns popping out here and there and flying off almost immediately. The trout are obviously feeding on duns in the very act of emerging from their nymphal cases, for that is the time when they linger a little just below the film and become an easy target. A soft-hackled wet-fly fished close to the surface will take more fish than a bona fide dry-fly. Only occasionally does a fish take the odd dun that has failed to escape the water. Duns are emerging very quickly and it seems to be only smaller and more energetic fish that slash at the flies just before they take off. Trout taking emerging flies sometimes produce a different rise form from those taking floating duns, a kind of 'sipping rise', but more often than not the big rise is in evidence when trout take emergers, just as it is when they take floating-flies.

It is easy to misinterpret rise forms, but whenever a dry-fly fails it is always worth moistening it so that it fishes just below the surface. Like many anglers, including Skues, I discovered the importance of copying emerging flies by accident rather than by observation. I hadn't had a rise to my fly all morning. After lunch I stuck to the same dry-fly and saw a good fish rising close to some bushes against the far bank. My Grey Duster was refused many times and through sheer laziness I neither dried it nor changed it. Almost losing interest, I flipped the fly once more upstream of the fish and it sank. Instantly there was a rise and half-unconsciously I tightened into an angry brown trout which eventually came to the net. The same scenario was repeated several times during the afternoon and it gradually dawned on me that the preference for a wet-fly over a dry-fly was because the trout were feeding on emerging insects rather than hatched duns.

Both soft-hackled spider patterns, such as the Poult Bloa or Hare's Lug and Plover, and tiny winged wet-flies, such as the Gold Ribbed Hare's Ear or Greenwell's Glory, make excellent emerger patterns and it is important that they are fished very close to the surface. Received wisdom has it that our leader should always be degreased even when using dry-flies (which, however, considerably impairs a quick strike), but I have little time for received wisdom and don't believe that a greased leader scares fish other than in the calmest of flat calms. When fishing a wet-fly emerger pattern, both on rivers and lakes, lightly grease the leader to within a few inches of the fly, or flies, for they must fish as close to the surface as possible. If the right approach is taken, the trout should see the fly first anyway, so that a greased leader improves our chances of success by keeping the fly at the correct level in the water and it certainly doesn't scare the fish if we are careful.

Rises to Terrestrials

Wet- or dry-flies may be used when trout are taking terrestrial insects, though that was not my opinion and when I published *The Art of the Wet Fly* in 1979 and wrote:

The picture changes somewhat when considering a trout rising to floating insects which derive from terrestrial rather than aquatic pupae. In this case there is no consciousness of a sub-aquatic stage (saving the drowned adults which are usually present in broken water) and the trout becomes attuned only to the surface fly. Thus it seems a negative approach to cast a wet-fly to a trout feeding exclusively on terrestrial insects such as hawthorn flies because the dry-fly is certainly more killing. An obvious exception is the trout which takes up its feeding position where rough water is likely to draw the struggling insect under the water; usually a wet fly is the order of the day for him.

I have modified my views on wet-flies and terrestrials over time. Thirty years ago I undoubtedly underestimated the number of terrestrials that get swamped and end up being eaten under the surface. I am sure that I also overestimated the awareness that trout have of insect life cycles when I wrote, with reference to trout taking terrestrials, that they have 'no consciousness of a sub-aquatic stage' and thus become fixed on the surface fly. At the time this must have seemed logical, but it was nonsense and trout will take terrestrial imitations under the surface as readily as on it, regardless of how many natural flies do, or do not, drown. Since I wrote the above, I have probably caught as many trout at hawthorn time on a small Black Pennell wet-fly as I have on dry hawthorn imitations. If it looks like a hawthorn fly, either on the surface or under it, then a trout will have it and a slowly retrieved wet-fly stands more chance of attracting a trout's attention and inducing it to take than does a static dry-fly.

Sucking Rises

'Sucking rises' are really a version of the big rise, but are distinguished by the trout making a very audible sucking sound as it takes an insect in the surface film, or just beneath it. Sometimes it is produced when trout take spinners (female ephemeridae lying dead in the film after egg-laying), or terrestrials that have given up struggling, but more often than not trout will be taking medium-sized emergers (ephemeridae, chironomids or sedges) in a leisurely fashion, knowing full well that they have no means of escape. A dry-fly resting right in the surface film may succeed, but a better bet is a wet-fly fished very close to the surface. On rivers, sucking rises are more likely to be encountered in quieter pools rather than rapid runs.

Sipping Rises

'Sipping rises' are the cause of much frustration because they occur when trout are feeding on either the nymphs and pupae, or the adults, of tiny flies such as reed smuts, caenis (the smallest ephemeridae), tiny stoneflies, small midges or aphids. Even a large trout is capable of making only a tiny dimple at the surface at such times. It is likely that there are a vast number of these insects at the surface, which means that an artificial dry-fly imitation will be lost among them. Trout become preoccupied with small flies and can browse along just under the surface almost like a basking shark feeding on plankton. It is as if they are feeding 'blindly' and it is frustrating when a delicate dry-fly, tied on a size 22 hook, is completely ignored. There are two main options: either to cast a large dry-fly in the hope that contrast will be more effective than 'exact imitation'; or to retrieve a single wet-fly close to the surface. Sometimes, the movement of the wet-fly diverts the trout's attention from its preoccupation with tiny naturals.

Slashing Rises

The last surface rise I will discuss is the 'slashing rise'. On both rivers and reservoirs, slashing rises are produced by trout feeding on large insects, including mayflies, but particularly moving insects such as sedge flies skittering across the surface on a summer's evening. Slashing rises may also occur when trout are feeding on large struggling terrestrial insects such as hawthorn flies, crane flies (daddy long-legs) or drone flies. Static dry-flies sometimes work. A better bet might be a buoyant pattern like the Deer Hair Sedge nudged across the surface; it is effective at times, although often provokes follows and swirls without solid takes. Strangely, although slashing rises occur at the surface, a moving wet-fly skipped through the surface film, or retrieved erratically just under the surface, proves more consistently effective. When trout are taking sedge flies, palmer dressings are a good choice (*see* Chapter 9), as is the Invicta (*see* Chapter 10). On lakes and reservoirs, retrieving wet-flies through ripple or waves on a warm evening can produce exciting sport and a few smash takes, so a strong leader is required. On rivers, dealing with slashing rises as dusk approaches may mean breaking the accepted rules of wet-fly fishing, as the trout will be less cautious. Casting downstream and across, so that the fly swings towards the near bank, is more effective than casting

A large trout lying in shallow water prepares to sip in a fly.

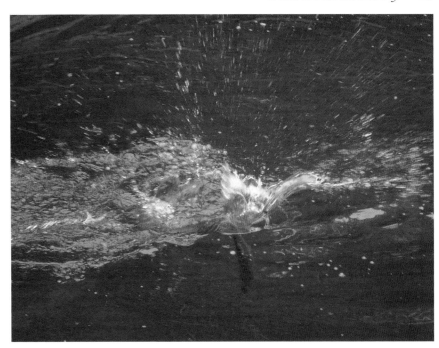

The slashing rise: this trout actually took a palmer fished on the top dropper.

upstream. We usually avoid 'drag' at all costs, but on this occasion it will make the fly skate and skitter at the surface and that is what the fish want.

The Porpoise Roll

The 'porpoise roll', also known as 'head-and-tailing', occurs when a trout's head breaks the surface, its back arches out of the water and then rolls downwards again; it looks for all the world like a porpoise or dolphin. The fish may be feeding on a number of different items – including mature nymphs, spinners, or even aquatic snails – but by far the commonest cause is feeding on chironomid midge pupae ('buzzers' or 'duck-flies'), or small sedge pupae. Porpoise rolls more frequently occur on lakes and reservoirs, but they are also fairly common on quiet river pools that have a silt or mud bottom. Nearing the emergence of the adult fly, pupae are very active and make little forays towards the surface; a wet-fly fished in a 'sink-and-draw' method may therefore be effective. However, porpoise rolls are usually in evidence when pupae are hanging in the surface film, just before eclosion occurs, so that the artificial fly needs also to be close to the surface. A lightly greased leader is helpful in all but the calmest of conditions. There are many effective and realistic pupal imitations, but the fault with some of them is that they sink too quickly. Lighter wet-flies are preferable and especially soft-hackled spider patterns such as the Black Spider and Snipe and Purple to imitate midge pupae and the Woodcock Spiders (dressed with different body colours) for small sedge pupae. On the rare occasions when trout are taking aquatic snails, the Black and Peacock Spider is deadly.

Boils, Bulges and Dinner Plates

'Boils', 'bulges' and 'dinner plates' all occur when trout are feeding on active nymphs or pupae, or other creatures such as the corixa, a little way under the surface but close enough to it for the displacement of water, caused by the trout turning quickly, to be evident at the surface. These are excellent signs for the angler because trout are obviously feeding in earnest and the choice of wet-fly or nymph is often immaterial; it is simply a matter of the individual's personal taste. The strength or definition of the bulge or boil gives some indication of the depth at which trout are intercepting nymphs, although this may be

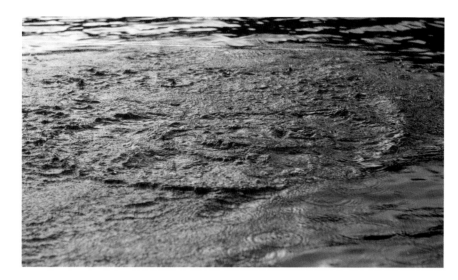

Boils and bulges are rarely this obvious: a trout feeding on nymphs very close to the surface.

difficult to detect on rivers where the water boils and bulges as it flows over rocks and boulders. Generally speaking, a distinct hump or bulge of water reveals a trout feeding close to the surface, while a little boil of water means that it is a somewhat deeper. On rivers, it is difficult to pinpoint the exact location of a fish, since the whirl of water will travel downstream before reaching the surface and it is necessary to take into account the speed of the stream. Boils and bulges are common too on lakes, lochs and reservoirs when it is calm or there is only a slight ripple. However, when there is a good wave, the displacement of water produced by a feeding fish is likely to form a little flat area in the wave and about the size of a dinner plate.

Boils, bulges and dinner plates provide classic situations for top-of-the-water wet-fly fishing and although a normal drift is effective on rivers, a dead-drift technique is less effective on lakes and reservoirs. The team of flies used on lakes and reservoirs should be retrieved in order to emulate the active nymphs or pupae and although a standard figure-of-eight retrieve will be effective on many occasions, it is often necessary to experiment. Little pulls, with pauses in-between, or an erratic retrieve, may provoke more responses than pulling the flies in at a steady or uniform pace.

Finally, the absence of boils, bulges or dinner plates at the surface does not mean that trout are not feeding actively on nymphs. They may be feeding on them deeper down, so it is always wise to search the water and to experiment with choice of fly, style of retrieve and the depths at which the flies are fished. This is something we will discuss further in Chapters 5 and 6.

4 TACKLE FOR WET-FLY FISHING

I am not a technical kind of angler so there won't be a great deal of complex physics in this chapter. What advice I am able to give on tackle comes from nearly half a century's experience. Theoretically, tackle for wet-fly fishing is little more than a means to an end and in that respect it must be practical and fit for purpose. However, there are other dimensions to consider. One rod may be more pleasurable to cast with than another, even though both rods will do the job. A reel may be perfectly serviceable but it may equally be cheap and nasty, not the kind of object we might treasure like a traditionally crafted model, and I know which reel I would rather fish with and lovingly clean and oil during those long winter evenings. So it is that objects of aesthetic value become part of the holistic experience of fishing the wet-fly. In this respect, a double-tapered floating line also enhances the experience. I have put my cards on the table.

Rods

In past ages, rods were invariably very long. The rod described in the *Treatyse of Fysshynge with an Angle* of 1496 must have been between 12ft (3.7m) and 18ft (5.5m) in length. Secured to the tip of the rod would be a horse-hair line, several hairs twisted together and joined in sections and then tapered down to between one and three hairs at the point. Rods with the line tied directly to the rod's tip became known as 'loop rods'.

Wet-fly fishing from a boat necessitates a very long rod.

The long wet-fly rod enables line to be kept off the water when short casting.

Cotton too, writing in 1676, was using rods from 15ft (4.6m) to 18ft (5.5m) in length and with the horse-hair line tied directly to the tip of the rod. By the time W.C. Stewart was publishing *The Practical Angler* (1857) and reels were commonly in use, much shorter rods were employed for fishing the wet-fly, although David Webster was still advocating the use of a 'loop rod' in 1885 (*The Angler and the Loop Rod*) and around the same time Francis Francis used rods up to 12ft 8in (3.9m) in length.

The long rod, with its flexible tip and middle section, would have been pliable enough to have cushioned the pull of even a large trout on a light horse-hair line. Long rods enabled their users to keep most of the line off the water and thus to both avoid scaring fish and to combat drag caused by varying river currents. No distinction was made between wet-fly and dry-fly fishing, as short casts made with a long rod resulted in the fly initially floating and then sinking slowly as it drifted downstream. This is how they fished – and it clearly worked. Of course, I have no desire to return to the 'loop rod', which must have been a bit of a wrist-breaker and I certainly wouldn't want to go to the trouble of making a horse-hair line either. On the other hand, there are things

to be learned from the tackle of the past and things that we may wish to replicate with our modern gear.

By the late nineteenth century the great push was for lighter, shorter and stiffer hexagonal cane rods that would punch a dry-fly into the wind, cast long distances and dry the fly with crisp false casts. Rods designed for fishing the wet-fly were rarely fashioned entirely of split cane, which was considered too stiff, and were less easy to obtain commercially. At the time of the First World War, Edmonds and Lee advocated incorporating woods that had largely fallen out of use on the chalk streams in order to achieve the correct action for a wet-fly rod:

The length of the rod the writers find most useful is 10ft. 6ins., and, if it is to be used for wet-fly fishing exclusively, they would unhesitatingly recommend a two-piece rod made of greenheart, or of hickory for the butt, with greenheart top, not too whippy and not too stiff. Such a rod is softer in the action and less tiring to the wrist than one made of split cane. That is a matter well worth consideration when one is whipping the stream for long periods at a stretch.

Subsequent innovations in rod-building materials did not tend to further the development of a wet-fly rod that Edmonds and Lee would have considered suitable – that is, 'not too whippy and not too stiff'. Initially, rods built out of hollow fibreglass seemed to be a gift from the gods. They were much lighter than split cane or greenheart, and tougher too. Up to a length of around 9ft (2.7m), there were rods perfect for fishing wet-flies, for they had a lovely mellow action, but longer rods made of fibreglass were simply too sloppy. In the 1970s, and concurrent with the production of some of the later fibreglass rods, carbon fibre came onto the scene and effectively revolutionized rod production, yet longer wet-fly rods remained relatively rare. There was an excellent long rod manufactured by Bruce and Walker – The Century – and this really was a wet-fly weapon. The Century was 11ft 3in (3.43m) and was rated for no.4 to no.6 lines; it was the ultimate rod for fishing wet-flies on stillwaters and on larger rivers too. It was surprisingly light for such a long rod, wasn't tiring to cast with and enjoyed quite a reputation for a while before unfortunately disappearing from production.

I have beside me an array of catalogues from all the major rod producers and mail order companies and while there are plenty of relatively short light-line rods suitable for wet-fly work on rivers, longer rods for larger rivers and stillwaters are rare. However, I have just purchased a 10ft (3m) Orvis rated for no.4 lines and there are similar rods from other manufacturers. It is generally the case that longer rods are rated for lines of no.6 and above, often no.7 or no.8, and are more suited to heavy reservoir work, although some of the no.6 rated rods may be suitable for wet-fly fishing. Glancing at the current catalogue of one of the largest British mail order companies, I find that of the 145 different models offered for sale, only six rods are potentially suitable for wet-fly fishing on larger waters, or anywhere that maximum line control is required. The reader would do well to seek the advice of reputable tackle companies when seeking a suitable long light-line rod for wet-fly fishing.

All too often, modern carbon rods are designed with actions that are described as 'fast' or 'tip-flex' which is all very well for distance-casting and delivering single nymphs, dries or lures, but is totally unsuited to wet-fly fishing. Many rods, perhaps most, do not comfortably cast short lines, while their quick actions result in a three-fly cast tangling on the back-cast as the loop thrown is too narrow. Tip-actioned rods may also fail to cushion the light tippets required by the wet-fly exponent when fishing a team of small flies. What is required is a rod with an action variously described as 'softer', 'traditional', 'all-through' or 'middle-to-tip', which basically means that the rod will flex easily from the tip and well into the middle section, thus affording the leisurely casting of a short line and a more open loop on the back-cast. Above all, avoid any rods marketed with the claim that they produce 'tighter loops, better wind penetration and greater distance', for as a wet-fly tool they will be found completely wanting.

I count myself lucky that a number of years ago I was able to purchase several models of the original Hardy 'De Luxe' carbon-fibre range. They are softer-actioned carbon rods, yet without sloppiness, and cope well with wet-flies, although they will also deliver dries and nymphs as required. I have rods in this range from 7ft (2.1m), rated for no.3 lines and suitable for the smallest of overgrown streams, up to 10ft (3m), rated for no.6 lines and for reservoir work on windy days. Even the shortest of these rods will roll cast beautifully and is ideal for fishing a team of spiders on small overgrown streams where a longer rod would not be a viable proposition. The longest rod, though it has the power to cast a long line when required, has a mellow enough action to execute short-lining with a team of loch flies and to make it a pleasurable experience without any hint of fatigue.

However, a long rod is clearly not suited to all situations and would certainly be a real encumbrance on the tree-lined upper Derbyshire Wye and similar streams. Personally, I think at least three rods are required to cope with wet-fly fishing in all situations (and in terms of economy they will cater for dries and nymphs as required):

- A rod of 10ft to 11ft (3m to 3.4m) rated for no.4 to no.6 lines for reservoir and loch fishing from bank or boat and also for larger open rivers where wading makes it possible to avoid bankside trees.

- A rod of 8ft 6in to 9ft 6in (2.6m to 2.9m) rated for no.3 to no.5 lines for small lakes and medium-sized rivers.
- A rod of 7ft to 8ft (2.1m to 2.4m) for brooks, small rivers and any streams with lush surrounding vegetation and the overhanging branches of trees.

As discussed above, tip-actioned rods should be avoided when fishing the wet-fly and I therefore find it strange that while Edmonds and Lee sensibly advocated pliant rods for wet-fly fishing, W.C. Stewart preferred a stiffish rod which seems quite unsuitable.

Fly Lines

It is often argued that the line is the most important item of tackle. Choose the wrong line and our effectiveness as fly fishermen certainly diminishes; would you want to cast a no.8 line onto a tiny moorland beck? No, of course not. With the aid of a rod, the line delivers the flies and controls them so that they do what we want them to do. Of course, it is well that the flies are delivered delicately and my view is that this is effectively accomplished by using as light a double-tapered line as conditions will allow and if the front taper of this line is fine and gradual then it will enable us to keep as much line off the water as possible if we are using a long enough rod. On every occasion when it is possible to do so, I prefer a floating line to any other, not least because it facilitates maximum control of the flies.

Horse-hair lines of the past were tapered from the tip of the rod down to the point and the sections of hairs forming the taper were joined together by water-knots. It was customary to have between twelve and twenty hairs where the line was attached to the rod tip, tapering down to between one and three hairs at the fly. One of the great weaknesses with modern tackle is that we have to join a relatively thick fly line to a relatively fine leader and as the two materials have different properties, turnover of the leader

may be impeded. In the days of horse-hair lines there was no distinction between fly line and leader; it was all of a piece and even the fly was generally whipped onto hair when it was made. It is easy to underestimate the strength of a good horse-hair line and although they were light and buoyant they were easy enough to cast short distances because of the steep taper produced during manufacture. Over the centuries a variety of materials for fly lines were experimented with – horse hair and silk twisted together, viol string catgut, silkworm gut – but all of these materials produced relatively light fly lines. Once powerful split-cane rods were developed, these materials were simply too light to get the best out of the cane. A new line was needed and this was really the development that led to distance-casting and a style of fishing quite different from the old wet-fly technique.

Towards the end of the nineteenth century heavy, braided, oil-dressed silk lines were developed in America in order to harness the power of split-cane rods by makers such as Leonard. Now the rod and line combination could combat any wind and deliver a small fly quite a distance, plus the fact that there were larger and lighter reels capable of storing a considerable amount of fly line. The new developments were particularly useful for the emerging dry-fly school, as G.E.M. Skues outlined: 'The things which made the dry fly generally possible were the coming of the heavy American braided oiled silk line and the split cane rod.' However, what now became standard tackle did not really benefit the wet-fly angler.

The oiled silk line encouraged the development of shorter and more powerful cane rods, suited to distance-casting, but this tackle combination was quite unsuited to the short-lining upstream wet-fly technique. Further, even when greased, the new lines rested *in* the surface film, rather than *on* it, which made controlling a team of wet-flies no easy proposition. Being heavier than earlier types of line, the oil-dressed lines also made it more difficult to keep as much line off the surface of the water as the wet-fly exponent would have liked.

My fly-fishing career commenced with cane rods and oil-dressed silk lines. Silk lines were generally available in only three colours, straw, brown and olive-green; my Kingfishers were a beautiful and almost translucent olive-green in colour – I still like olive-coloured fly lines even in plastic. Silk lines certainly facilitated excellent distance-casting, cutting through a wind much better than plastic lines, because they had a finer diameter for their weight. Being much thinner than equivalent sizes of plastic lines, oil-dressed silk lines were also less likely to scare fish. They were also extremely supple and not prone to coiling in the manner of plastic lines, because principally there was no stretch in them. This too was an advantage in terms of feeling the gentlest of takes, although it did not help to avoid breakages by providing any kind of cushioning effect. However, the downside of silk lines was only too evident. They had to be heavily greased in order to float and once the tip absorbed water it would sink and no amount of regreasing would be of any use until the line had been thoroughly dried out. Good for long casts with a dry-fly, they were not so good for drifting a wet-fly close to the surface, although an ungreased line made an excellent intermediate or slow sinker for reservoir fishing on rough days.

In addition, oil-dressed silk lines were the very devil to look after, for they had to be stripped off the reel and thoroughly dried after every outing. A lack of care and the lines soon rotted or became tacky and useless for fishing unless a whole complex procedure was carried out. Nevertheless, oil-dressed silk lines were beautiful and I loved the smell of them, just as I loved the spiked lavender smell of Allcock's line grease. Silk lines were never cheap. I still have a copy of the 1963 *Allcock's Anglers Guide* and find their Glider silk lines running from 43/6 (forty-three shillings and sixpence) up to 72/- (seventy-two shillings) and that was before 'purchase tax' was added! A good silk line cost about half the price of a decent split-cane rod. Finally, in the late 1960s or early 1970s, I forget which exactly, I succumbed to the 'revolutionary' new plastic lines.

I found that plastic lines took a bit of getting used to at first. They certainly floated well but were more difficult to cast in windy conditions, having a greater diameter than silk lines of the same weight. Early plastic lines were also thicker in diameter than the lines available today and somewhat less resilient. Thankfully, rapid improvements were made and the development in coatings now meant that they cast better, lasted longer and required little maintenance, just a quick wipe after use to remove any dirt or grit and an occasional application of line cleaner to counteract any leached-out plasticizer.

Personally, in selecting a line, I look for one that possesses all the advantages of plastic along with some of the clear advantages of earlier lines such as horse hair and silk. Accordingly, my ideal line would be as follows:

- It should be, like an oil-dressed silk line, of as low a diameter as possible and with a gradual taper ending in a fine yet buoyant tip (the fine tips on many lines are apt to sink). Line sizes no.2 to no.5 are suitable for rivers and no.4 to no.6 for stillwaters.

- A good floating line should be very buoyant and should not sit too deep in the surface film, which would make it difficult to lift off or mend.

- It should be as supple as silk and have little coil memory so that when a cast is made it lies in a straight line on the water, or is easily thrown into a wavy line when counteracting drag on rivers.

- It should have minimal stretch in order to keep the angler in touch with a fish.

- It should be resilient, requiring minimum maintenance, and have a smooth surface that slides easily over the rod rings without wearing them. (A new generation of lines has been developed with a quite different surface, composed of ridges or similar micro-textures. Such lines claim to aid presentation and even buoyancy, but they are principally designed to improve the distance of the cast – the jury is still out at the moment.)

- My preference is for a good double-tapered line, but other tapers are equally acceptable performance-wise and we will consider them in due course.

- I prefer drab olive fly lines to brightly coloured lines, but this is simply based on tradition. There is an inconclusive debate as to whether or not brightly coloured lines scare trout and all I will say is that such lines seem out of place on the fisheries I frequent.

Although I have expressed a preference for double-tapered lines, I certainly wouldn't argue that it is the only profile suited to wet-fly fishing and if only a short line is being fished, then there is little difference in terms of taper and presentation between *some* weight-forward lines and most double-tapered lines. I say 'some' weight-forward lines because there are also others that possess a very short front taper and are 'ultra' weight-forward. Such lines should be avoided, for they are definitely suited only to distance-casting and will not achieve a delicate presentation of the flies at short range. Most double-tapered lines possess a long and gradual front taper, making them ideal for delicate presentation, roll casting and line mending. If a weight-forward line is chosen for wet-fly work it too should have a reasonably long and gradual front taper. I still think double-tapered lines have the edge, particularly since you can reverse them on the reel when one end is worn out, which makes them a great deal more economical. Infuriatingly, some of the best olive-coloured lines are only available in weight-forward profile. If economy is not necessarily a concern, then weight-forward lines are a viable proposition for wet-fly fishing and particularly lines with a long front taper and/or long belly. Rio produces olive-coloured lines with this kind of profile, in small sizes too, and they are good for wet-fly work.

Lines with a short head, followed by fine running line, are generally inappropriate, as the fine running line simply does not allow line mending. Lines with this kind of profile are for distance work. However, one line that possesses a *very* fine running line and is still good for wet-fly fishing is the Lee Wulff Triangle Taper, which has an extremely fine tip, a very long continuous tapered body and then thin running line. The running line will not come into use when short casting (yet will allow occasional long casts in the manner of a shooting head), but it takes up little room on the reel, which is an advantage. The long front taper facilitates excellent fly presentation, particularly when rolling out the flies, and makes line mending very easy indeed. This line is available in olive and makes a very good wet-fly line.

I like the dark olive lines produced by Rio and

Cortland, the latter under the name of Clear Creek, but they are only produced in weight-forward profile, although the front tapers are quite long and end in fine tips. However, a pale olive line (described as 'olive dun') is produced by Orvis under the current title of Wonderline Generation 3 and they too are good lines, being available in double-tapered and weight-forward profiles. Tackle dealers often tell me that 'everyone is using weight-forward lines and there is no call for double-tapers', but I use them and I can't believe that I am the only one.

In my opinion, colour doesn't really matter over much; my preference is based on tradition rather than science. If watching the end of the fly line for a take is a consideration and eyesight is not what it used to be, then a light-coloured line may be advantageous. That said, I don't have wonderful eyesight these days but spotting the movement of a darker fly line doesn't seem to be a problem when casting relatively short distances. Over the years I have used olive, brown, white, grey, ice blue, pale green, lime green, mint green, straw, bright yellow, peach and fluorescent pink and orange lines and I am not aware that any of these lines has scared fish and reduced the numbers I caught.

Most trout lines are produced in lengths varying from 25yd to 30yd (22.9m to 27.4m), but this is of little concern when casting a long line is not the main consideration, even on lochs and reservoirs. What is important on stillwaters is to have enough backing on the reel and I am never happy unless the fly line is attached to at least 100yd (91.4m) of backing. It is not often that a trout will take you deep into the backing, but that fish of a lifetime may just run a considerable distance. It is also as well to have a reasonable store of backing when fishing on rivers, although length of fly line for river fishing is often even less of a consideration than on reservoirs. Indeed, it is often the case that a small river allows the angler to use only half of a double-tapered fly line (the other half being stored for future use), which means that a smaller and lighter reel may be employed and/or the amount of backing increased.

It will have become clear that most of my wet-fly fishing is carried out with floating lines and that sinking lines are something of a secondary consideration. That said, there are times when trout are lying deep in the water and refuse to rise up towards the surface, or when the conditions are so rough that a floating line is controlled by the surface waves rather than by the angler. For deeper work I prefer a relatively slow-sinking or medium-sinking line, which allows the flies to be retrieved slowly and I don't feel that there is a place for high-density lines in traditional wet-fly fishing. When it is very windy on reservoirs, a floating line will soon be swept into the bank and therefore does not provide full control of the flies. In rough conditions, a slow sinker will allow the flies to be controlled just below the surface, although there are other lines that will also do that job: intermediate lines which sink very slowly indeed and remain just under the surface, as well as floating lines with various lengths of sinking tips, known as 'sink tip', 'anti-skate', 'wet tip' and so on. These are useful lines allowing good fly control under gusty conditions, although some models are rather more difficult to cast than a standard floating line. Some of the recently developed sinking-tip lines have clear tips and indeed there are also full slow sinkers that are available in clear format. They claim to be invisible to trout; I have not used them so therefore reserve judgement.

Reels

It is usually said that the reel is merely a store for the fly line. Those who hold that opinion often advocate playing a trout by hand (yielding and retrieving line by hand), but I regard this as a bad policy for it means dropping line onto the bank, or into the boat, which leads to the line snagging, tangling or getting damaged. It is far better to get any loose line back onto the reel as soon as possible after hooking a fish, so that the combination of rod and reel provides maximum control over a fighting fish. If trout are to be played on the reel, then it must be a good one, for I once had a cheap reel that seized up when a large fish made a determined and fast run. Needless to say, the cast broke and the fish was gone. A good and reliable reel is a necessity, not a mere affectation! Apart from any practical considerations I admit to simply loving 'classic' reels.

There are an unbelievable number of fly reels available today and a glance at any tackle catalogue reveals a range in price from something like £25 up to £500! Anglers pay what they can afford for a reel, but it needs to be a good and reliable model. Most wet-fly fishing is carried out with light-line rods and it is therefore best to purchase a light reel that will balance the rod when fully loaded with fly line and backing.

I just love classic reels.

All too often, anglers forget that the reel becomes much heavier when fully loaded and that means that a number of modern reels, particularly large arbour reels (or 'arbor' if you prefer), become very heavy indeed. For example, a typical large arbour reel in a catalogue in front of me weighs exactly twice the weight of my Hardy LRH Lightweight, yet has less line capacity and would, I think, be too heavy for the rod I use for that line weight. Though light, a reel for wet-fly fishing needs to have adequate line capacity and must be smooth running. It must be totally reliable when a fish runs, though I am not much concerned with drag mechanisms as I can put pressure on the line by hand.

I have reels that have given good service for forty years, but the current trend is for reels to be seemingly updated and improved each year so that anglers are tempted to buy the latest model in order to keep up with their peers. You can't beat traditionally engineered reels made from high-grade bar stock aluminium and although they don't come cheap the expenditure is worth it. In a number of years they may well become collectable and their value will rise considerably. You may have gathered that I favour traditional, or 'classic', reels and that is for a very good reason – they have never let me down. Reels have gone through a variety of fashions in the last fifty years and the most recent fad is the large arbour reel that one simply can't fish without. There are supposedly two advantages to this design of reel: firstly, the large diameter spool minimizes the fly line forming coils; and, secondly, the retrieve rate is more rapid than a smaller diameter of reel. However, unless you try to squeeze a fly line onto too small a reel, coiling isn't much of a problem. For example, loading a double-tapered no.5 line onto a Hardy LRH Lightweight reel allows plenty of backing and this backing creates an arbour large enough to prevent a problem with coiling, even though the reel is only 3.2in (8cm) in diameter. In contrast, fitting the same amount of backing onto a well-known make of large arbour reel would require a considerably heavier reel with a diameter at least 30 per cent greater. Some large arbour reels are very heavy indeed, even though they have a considerable number of holes drilled into the frame and spool in order to save weight. I like a small reel and if I want a rapid line retrieve I simply wind the reel handle a little faster. I do admit to owning a couple of large arbour reels. One is only 3in (7.5cm) in diameter and takes a weight-forward no.4 line and an adequate amount of backing for river fishing. However, I prefer double-tapered lines for wet-fly fishing and large arbour reels, having reduced capacity, are really made for weight-forward lines, so that I don't consider them generally suitable.

Ultimately, reels are a matter of personal choice and I will take the liberty to refer to my favourites. There are two series of classic reels by Hardy that I would never be without: the Lightweight series and the Bougle series. I use four Lightweight reels, although the largest of them, the Princess, is unfortunately no longer in production. The smallest Lightweight, and probably the smallest fly reel currently in production anywhere in the world, is the Flyweight, with a diameter of only 2.5in (6.4cm) and weighing only 2.75oz (78g), yet is capable of holding a double-tapered no.3 line, or even a weight-forward no.4. The next reel is the Featherweight, with a diameter of 2.9in (7.4cm) and weighing 3.4oz (97g); it comfortably takes a double-tapered no.4 or weight-forward no.5 line and an adequate amount of backing. The LRH Lightweight is 3.2in (8cm) in diameter and weighs in at 3.7oz (104g). It takes a double-tapered no.5 line or weight-forward no.6 and plenty of backing, although a low diameter double-tapered no.6 will still fit on. The LRH has been in continuous production for fifty years and that tells its own story. The great American angler, Lee Wulff, even caught salmon up to 25lb on cane rods fitted with LRH reels and if it's good enough to cope with large salmon, then it's certainly going to cope with wet-fly fishing for trout! As noted above, the Princess is no longer available, although it is an excellent reel for no.6 and no.7 lines. It has the same diameter as the larger of the two large arbour reels that I possess, but while that reel struggles to take a weight-forward no.5 line, the Princess easily accepts a double-tapered no.7 line. All the Lightweight reels that are in current production are constructed from bar stock aluminium, are simple to maintain, very light, reliable and as aesthetically pleasing as any classic reel should be.

The fact that I have a penchant for Hardy reels should not be seen as a denigration of reels by other makers; there are certainly other excellent reels in production. Still, we like what we like, and the other series of reels I favour are the Bougles, which are really lightweight versions of the classic Perfect. I use the Bougle in three sizes. The smallest has a diameter of 3in (7.5cm), weighs 3.6oz (105g) and takes a weight-forward no.4, or even double-tapered no.4 line and plenty of backing. The House of Hardy seems to be very conservative when it quotes the capacities of Bougle reels, which have quite wide spools offering generous capacity. The 3.25in (8.3cm) Bougle, weighing 4.1oz (116g), copes with anything up to a weight-forward no.6 line, while my largest Bougle, at a diameter of 3.5in (8.9cm) and weighing 4.7oz (125g), is ideal for double-tapered no.6 or weight-forward no.7 lines.

The above reels are those I generally fish with and they have never let me down, although I have other Hardy reels and reels by other makers too. I am right-handed and so have all my reels set for left-hand wind, as I require my right hand to hold the rod with when casting and playing fish. I see no point in changing the rod over to the left hand when playing a fish, so that the reel may be wound with the right hand. This does not make much sense to me. However, there are right-handed anglers who have their reels set for right-hand wind, and left-handed anglers with reels set for left-hand wind. If they are comfortable with this arrangement then that is fine by me.

Leaders (or Casts)

We cannot escape the fact that the leader, or cast, is extremely important in terms of presenting the flies. In the days of horse-hair lines there was no such thing as a 'leader', since the whole line tapered in one piece from rod to point. The development of heavier casting lines has meant that we now have to join a finer diameter of material to the end of a relatively thick casting line so that the joint itself potentially interrupts the flow of the line during the cast. The task is to minimize the negative effects of any particular joint in order to extend the taper from line to leader so that the leader turns over smoothly and presents the flies delicately. There are many different types of leaders available, all claiming to produce a smooth turnover, but the ideal has never really been reached. I cannot delve deeply into the technological aspects of leader design and will only assert that I have tried everything available and have now returned to the tried and tested method of nail-knotting a thick length of nylon directly onto the end of the fly line. A tapered nylon leader is then attached to the thick butt. It is as good as anything and will turn the flies over nicely as long as the tip of the fly line and nylon butt are close enough in diameter and the weight difference of the materials is not too great. We are aiming for the kind of continuity provided by a horse-hair line and thus trying to prevent the joint between fly line and leader ruining the momentum of the cast.

I think that I have used just about every type of leader material and made-up leader that is currently available. Polyleaders, braided nylon leaders and woven or plaited nylon leaders are available in floating, intermediate and sinking versions and, being steeply tapered from a thick butt to a fine point, will turn over a fly pretty well. It is easy enough to attach a fine tippet to the end of all three types of leader. Note, however, that I refer to 'fly' in the singular for the big drawback to these leaders is that they will not take droppers. On the other hand, there will be times when only a single wet-fly is being fished – close to a weed bed, for example.

Also available for fishing a single fly are continuous tapered leaders made of nylon, copolymer or fluorocarbon. They are usually steeply tapered from a thick butt to a fine point, but the thick butt makes it difficult to nail-knot the leader to the fly line and it is not possible to thread the butt through the core of the fly-line tip in order to produce a neat finish. Continuous tapered leaders turn over pretty well, but there are too many disadvantages apart from the fact that they will only take a single fly. For example, the tip will often become worn out or broken so that a further length of fine tippet material has to be knotted on, which means that they cease to be continuous tapered leaders. Of the three materials, though thickest in diameter, nylon is by far the most reliable. Just about every continuous tapered copolymer leader that I have bought has been useless. Supplied in a wound coil, they retain the coils and are the very devil to straighten out. The manufacturers seem to overestimate the tippet strength of copolymer leaders and I have suffered more breakages with this material than with any other leader material. Further, fine points are apt to twist after continuous casting and that renders them utterly useless. Twisting at the tippet is also a problem I have found with several brands of continuous tapered leaders made from fluorocarbon and although this material is very fine for its given strength, I have often found that the stated strength is somewhat overestimated.

So far, then, we have not encountered a leader suitable for a fishing team of flies and I am afraid that we must resort to knotting lengths of material together in order to produce a leader with droppers. Having said that, there is a fair argument too for constructing a knotted tapered leader when fishing a single fly, for I am convinced that the weight of the knots actually aids turnover of the leader. It is generally argued that knots weaken the leader, yet this is not much of a problem with good materials and I have not found any continuous tapered leader that is reliably strong. Given that leaders with droppers require knots, it is important that we choose a leader material that accepts knots readily without losing too much strength. I generally prefer good old-fashioned nylon, although I have made good leaders out of Orvis Super Strong, which, ironically, is apparently a copolymer resin material! Leaders made out of recognized brands of fluorocarbon spools are at best adequate. While it is possible to construct a leader with a fine point, knots do seem to weaken fluorocarbon considerably and this material is too limp for my liking. Using a limp material for droppers means that they will wrap around the leader at almost every cast, thus making tangles a frequent occurrence. There needs to be a certain stiffer quality to materials chosen for leaders and this takes us back to nylon.

Nylon may be thicker in diameter than other materials (although so-called 'double strength' nylons are available), but it is stiff enough for the construction of effective droppers and it knots better than other materials. Above all, and no matter what all the 'experts' tend to declare, it is a damn sight stronger, more resilient to abrasion and more reliable than other materials. It has been around for a long time and has proved itself in every realm of fishing. Using nylon, I have experienced far fewer fish breaking me than when using other materials and particularly when a trout takes the fly savagely. If nylon is relatively thick in diameter when compared to copolymer or fluorocarbon, and if this puts a few fish off, then so be it, but I do not think that I get fewer takes with nylon and the percentage that I land certainly increases. The thicker diameter of nylon is definitely not an issue for stillwater wet-fly fishing, or on rough streams where turbulence hides the leader. However, there are clear and shallow streams where fish become leader-shy and where the point needs to be as fine as possible. Although I sometimes drop down to a tippet of 1.7lb (0.8kg) where the trout are relatively small, I have generally found 2.6lb (1.2kg) Bayer Perlon to be capable of dealing with any size of trout. This nylon has a diameter of 0.15mm, but I have also found a tippet of 6X Orvis Super Strong to be extremely reliable and it has only a 0.13mm diameter for a breaking strain of 3.5lb (1.6kg).

Commercially produced knotted nylon leaders with droppers are at a premium, although they are available. I have used the Fog brand of nylon leaders for many years and have found them totally reliable. Fog produces the Wet Fly Cast with two droppers in 3yd (2.7m) and 4yd (3.7m) lengths. There is a loop at the butt end which I snip off so that I can blood-knot the leader directly to the thick nylon that I have nail-knotted to the fly line. Fog leaders have enough stiffness to minimize the two droppers tangling and they are available in various point sizes. I use them in point sizes 2.5lb (1.1kg) up to 6lb (2.7kg). I will continue to use Fog leaders because they are convenient, but there is a downside to purchasing ready-made leaders – expense. Constant changing of flies results in the droppers becoming shorter and shorter until they can no longer be used and for this reason it is useful to produce our own leaders.

Producing your own knotted leaders with droppers is easy enough and a good number of leaders can be made at a single sitting during the dark winter months. A glass of single malt makes the process all the more pleasurable. However, too many glasses of single malt render it impossible! Completed leaders can be wound onto cast carriers (we still have that old confusion between 'leader' and 'cast') and then stored in leader or cast wallets. Leader wallets and cast carriers are readily available, but cast carriers made out of cardboard are certainly good enough. When producing homemade leaders there is a temptation to extend the lengths of the droppers, knowing that they will wear down as flies are changed. This is a mistake, for too long a dropper will only result in it wrapping around the main leader; I would say that a dropper length of 6in (15cm) is the limit. The other solution to this problem is to use leader rings to attach the droppers. These tiny nickel silver rings are attached to two sections of the main leader by tucked half-blood knots and then the dropper is attached to the ring. When the dropper wears down, another length of nylon can be tied on to replace it. Leader rings also have the advantage of allowing the angler to attach any strength or thickness of dropper rather than being dependent on the thicker of the two leader lengths joined together. Currently, dropper rings with external diameters of 1.5mm, 2mm and 3mm are readily available from a number of suppliers (*see* diagram below).

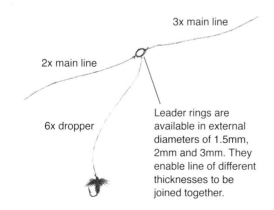

Leader rings are useful when using droppers.

As with most aspects of fly fishing, the construction of a leader with droppers involves elements of personal choice, but I would add that the leader should be as long as the rod will comfortably cope with, given that most casts we make when wet-fly fishing are relatively short. For example, if our average length of upstream casts on a river is only about 7yd (6.4m), then a leader of 5yd (4.6m) means that only 2yd (1.8m) of fly line will be working the rod. It is a tall order. In summary, the leader length should suit the length of rod we are using and the type of water being fished. Thus, while I might only use an 8ft (2.4m) leader on a small river, using a short rod, a 16ft (4.8m) leader will not be a problem on a reservoir when employing a longer rod.

It is my feeling that the modern obsession for avoiding knots is largely a product of the unreliability of many modern leader materials. The knots actually add stiffness to the leader, which certainly helps it to turn over effectively and to deliver the flies delicately. Having used many brands of materials, I now settle for three that I can trust entirely – Maxima, Bayer Perlon and Orvis Super Strong. Maxima I now only use for the thick and stiff butt length of the leader, which is attached by nail-knot to the fly line and I use it in breaking strains from 12lb (5.4kg) to 20lb (9kg), depending on the size of fly line in use. Maxima in these strengths is nice and stiff, so that it has the 'beef' to turn the rest of the leader over. Most of my leaders are made up from several sections, generally 7 or 8 plus the butt of Maxima, and it is therefore possible to produce a gradual taper by stepping down in breaking strains/diameters from butt to tippet. The important thing to remember, however, is that there should not be any joint that steps down too steeply – knotting together lengths that differ greatly in terms of breaking strain and diameter is simply asking for trouble. Knotting 8lb (3.6kg) nylon to 3lb (1.4kg) nylon would result in the finer line being drastically weakened. Most of my leaders are fashioned from lengths of Bayer Perlon, sometimes with Orvis Super Strong tippets, although I have also started to use leaders made entirely from the Orvis material for finer fishing on rivers. Bayer Perlon has been around for a long time and although it is regarded as a line for coarse fishing, it has served me well as a leader material for decades. Unfortunately, I am now experiencing difficulties in obtaining spools of the material.

I will now describe how I might make up a fairly standard stillwater leader of about 14ft (4.3m). A shorter leader for river fishing simply requires a shortening of each section and also a scaling down of the diameters to a finer point. Given that Bayer Perlon seems to be no longer readily available, I will make this leader out of Orvis Super Strong, with the exception of the butt, but the reader may freely use whatever material he or she favours. This leader is made up of eight sections (section one being the butt and section eight the tippet) as follows:

1. a 1ft (30cm) butt section of 15lb (6.8kg) Maxima nail-knotted to the fly line
2. a 1ft (30cm) section of 0X Orvis SS (diameter: 0.011in/0.28mm; strength: 15.5lb/7kg)
3. a 1ft (30cm) section of 1X Orvis SS (diameter: 0.01in/0.26mm; strength: 13.5lb/6.1kg)
4. a 1ft (30cm) section of 2X Orvis SS (diameter: 0.009in/0.23mm; strength: 11.5lb/5.2kg)
5. a 1ft (30cm) section of 3X Orvis SS (diameter: 0.008in/0.20mm; strength: 8.5lb/3.9kg)
6. a 1ft+ (30+cm) section of 4X Orvis SS (diameter: 0.007in/0.17mm; strength: 6lb/2.7kg); this section, when knotted to section 7, should provide a 6in (15cm) 4X dropper
7. a 4ft+ (120+cm) section of 5X Orvis SS (diameter: 0.006in/0.15mm; strength: 4.75lb/2.2kg); this section, when knotted to section 8, should provide a 6in (15cm) 5X dropper
8. a 4ft (120cm) tippet section of 6X Orvis SS (diameter: 0 .005in/0.13mm; strength: 3.5lb/1.6kg).

Made up in this way, whether the leader is made of Orvis Super Strong, Bayer Perlon or any other reliable and 'knot-friendly' material, we have a leader that will turn over well and deliver the flies without causing too much disturbance. It is a leader model that may be stepped up or stepped down, in terms of length and strength, in order

to cope with any water. What is important is that the knots are made with care and it is a good idea to lubricate the knots with a product such as Knot Perfect in order to avoid weakening the line through friction or abrasion.

Other Items of Tackle

It is important to remember that unless you are fishing from a boat, traditional wet-fly fishing involves a great deal of walking; if you are constantly on the move, then too much gear becomes a real burden. Travel light. Whatever you wear must be light and comfortable, though warm enough to keep you happy on cold days, while other items of tackle need to be kept to a minimum even though those pages and pages of 'useful' items in tackle catalogues are quite seductive.

Whenever possible, wading should be avoided, but for comfort, modern breathable stocking-foot chest waders and wading boots are difficult to beat when it is necessary to wade or to walk any distance. They will also enable you to walk through wet vegetation, or to sit on a wet bank, without experiencing the discomfort of wet legs and a soaking bum. In general, the best boot soles for wading are those made of felt, but it is as well to fix a few studs onto the sole or heel in order to avoid slipping on other surfaces such as grassy banks. Unfortunately, the downside of breathable chest waders, even the very best of them, is that they are vulnerable and can easily be torn on broken branches, thorns or barbed-wire fences. I still also use rubber thigh waders, particularly on shallow rivers.

A light, breathable and packable waterproof coat is essential. It should be roomy enough to go over whatever undergarments are worn when the weather is cold and should not impede movement so that casting becomes tiring. Whoever invented the fishing waistcoat, or vest, deserves a medal, for they are a real boon – or should be. There are many excellent vests on the market at the moment, but a good vest is one with a sensible number of appropriately sized pockets. Some vests have too few pockets and silly pockets that won't fit anything in; I recently saw one vest that wouldn't even take any

Always travel light when fishing the wet-fly: the author exploring the stream.

reasonably sized fly box. Unfortunately, there are also vests with too many pockets, many of them so hidden away that it would take years of exploration to find them. If a vest has too many pockets, then there is the temptation to fill them so that the whole garment becomes so heavy that it induces back and neck problems in no time at all. In any case, with all that gear stowed away, how on earth do you remember where everything is? Whatever vest you plump for, make sure that it does have secure inner pockets for valuables (you don't want to drop the car keys into the river!) and large rear compartments that will take a waterproof and/or extra jumper. I would say that the real essentials for any vest would be:

- scissors or nippers
- artery forceps for removing hooks, or an Orvis Ketchum Release tool
- needle-nose pliers for squeezing down barbs (unless all your flies are dressed on barbless hooks)
- a sharpening stone
- fly floatant (for occasional dry-fly fishing)

- Permagrease or Mucilin (red tin) for ensuring that the fly line continues to float
- Fuller's Earth mixture for sinking casts
- polarizing sun glasses (clip-ons if you normally wear glasses); apart from cutting out glare and preventing headaches, glasses will protect the eyes from that inevitable mistimed cast
- fly boxes
- spools of leader material
- ready-made casts in a wallet
- a priest (unless all your trout are to be returned).

These are the bare essentials, but it isn't really necessary to add anything else. Over the years, I have begun to refine my tackle items in order to save weight wherever I can. I have always loved Wheatley aluminium fly boxes and have several, but they add weight to the vest. I now use those excellent C&F boxes because they are light, made of a tough plastic and keep the flies in a better order within a series of foam slits. C&F boxes are manufactured with slots of different

A long-handled landing net is useful for boat fishing and fishing from steep banks.

sizes to take anything from the tiniest spider to the largest loch fly, holding them in place very securely.

So that's the tackle – apart from the landing net. Increasingly, when a river requires wading I find it possible to dispense with a net altogether and to simply release a fish by hand. This, of course, presupposes the use of barbless hooks. However, I still have a liking for the classic American-styled wooden nets, or scoop nets, which are very light and can be carried on the back with a strong elastic or quick-release lanyard. When fishing from higher river banks, or, for most reservoir situations, a landing net with an extending handle is very useful, but it must remain light and should be easy to carry – either via a lanyard over the back or via a belt clip if preferred.

I cannot stress enough times that light tackle should be chosen as well as kept to a bare minimum, yet I usually end up on the bank wondering why on earth I have brought some item or other with me. It is always something 'useful' that never ever gets used!

5 WET-FLY FISHING ON RIVERS

Fishing Up and Across

The focus of the present chapter is on tactics and techniques for river fishing. W.C. Stewart, writing in the mid-nineteenth century, was the first angler to outline wet-fly fishing methods in any kind of detail and it is with Stewart that we will begin. Like anglers before him, Stewart argued that we should cast our line so that 'the flies will fall first upon the water, and as little of the line with them as possible'. This is a first principle of wet-fly fishing and it is also the reason why we should choose a rod long enough to provide us with complete control of the line and flies. Apart from enabling us to keep as much line off the water as possible, the long rod will also allow us to skip or 'dibble' the dropper flies on, or near, the surface of the stream. It is generally agreed that the most effective part of a wet-fly cast is when the flies first alight, so they must therefore land before the fly line. Further, if too much fly line is on the water, then it is at the mercy of the current so that the flies drift unnaturally; even if a fish should then take, hooking it becomes difficult. Stewart is precise in explaining this:

> If you were to fish up a strong stream, and allow the middle of your line to light first, before you could get it straight and prepared for a rise, your flies would be almost at your feet, and should a trout take one of them on their alighting – the most deadly moment in the whole cast – the chances of hooking it would be exceedingly small. It is very different if the flies light first; the line is then nearly straight from the point of the rod to the flies, and the least motion of the hand is felt almost instantaneously. Again, in fishing

nooks, eddies, and comparatively still water, at the opposite sides of strong streams, if any of your line lights in the current it is dragged down, and the flies no sooner touch the water, than they are drawn rapidly away in a most unnatural manner, and without giving the trout time to seize them should they feel inclined.

If the avoidance of drag is a prerequisite of dry-fly fishing, then it is no less important when fishing the wet-fly. Keeping as much line off the water as possible reduces the problems of drag, although it is often necessary to cast a wavy line so that an intervening current has to pick up the slack before drag takes effect on the flies. Mending the line continuously during the drift is also often necessary. It helps to flip the rod tip upstream, which will throw an upstream loop in the line, thus extending the length of the downstream drift; in this respect, a long rod is very helpful and, to avoid scaring the fish, a light line is essential. Some situations call for tricky mends, others for a cast which throws out an amount of slack line so that the current takes a little time to pick up the slack before affecting the drift of the flies. The classic situation, and one of the most challenging, is when fishing a slack eddy against the far bank and having to negate the effects of a strong current between the angler and the eddy. If the eddy is overhung by the branches of a tree, it is almost certain to hold a good trout and therefore presents a problem worth solving. On a small stream, a long rod may enable the angler to avoid much of the difficulties posed by intervening currents by keeping line off the water when fishing the eddy; otherwise a wavy cast must be delivered. On larger rivers, and in order to fish as short a line as possible, wading carefully closer to the eddy may become necessary.

Fishing a short line is the ideal, but longer casts may be unavoidable in some situations. Stewart suggests that the beginner should learn 'the art of throwing a long and light line', but advises 'the angler never to use a long line when a short one will, by any possibility, answer the purpose'. Edmonds and Lee too, writing in 1916, dismiss what they term the 'far off and fine' code, believing that the correct way to fish wet-flies is by short-lining. Stewart also believed that trout are more difficult to hook at range. He writes: 'We have invariably found that the nearer we are to our flies the better we can use them, and the greater is our chance of hooking a trout when it rises'. It is certainly easier both to control the flies and to hook fish at short range and arguably more effective casting upstream rather than down. That said, spotting takes when fishing upstream is not a particularly easy business. Stewart acknowledges the problem when he says, 'In fishing up, the rise of a trout is by no means so distinct as in fishing down. They frequently seize the fly without breaking the surface, and the first intimation the angler gets of their presence is a slight pull at the line'. I am inclined to think that no matter how good an angler Stewart was, if he waited only for a pull on the line he would have missed many fish. Often, we must rely only on signs such as a slight judder or movement of the line, a pause in the drift downstream, or a subsurface boil. At other times, the slightest of underwater flashes, what Skues called 'a little brown wink underwater', is the only sign we get that a trout has taken the fly. In the case of wild trout in rapid streams, a quick reaction to a take is usually necessary, for trout can take and eject a fly in an instant.

Stewart's approach to fishing any river was careful and methodical and I do not think that a modern exponent of the wet-fly needs to fish much differently. For this reason, I make no apologies for quoting Stewart at length:

When you are approaching a pool which you intend to fish, if the water is clear do so carefully; you must recollect that the trout see you much more readily if you are on a high bank than if you are on a level with the water. For this reason keep

as low down as possible, and always, if the nature of the ground will admit it, stand a few yards from the edge of the water. If there is a ripple on the water you may meet with good sport in the still water at the foot of the pools, but if there is no wind, it is useless commencing till you come to where the water is agitated. If you do not intend fishing the lower part, do not walk up the side of it, as by doing so you will alarm the trout in that portion, and they may run up to the head of the pool for shelter, and frighten the others; but always come to the edge of the pool at the place where you intend to begin fishing. If the water is very low and the sun bright, it may be advisable to kneel in fishing a pool, in order to keep out of sight, and you must avoid allowing your shadow to fall upon the water above where you are standing.

First, as you approach, fish the side on which you are standing with a cast or two, and then commence to fish the opposite side, where you are to expect the most sport. For this reason you should always keep on the shallow side of the water, as the best trout generally lie under the bank at the deep side. After having taken a cast or two on the near side, throw your flies partly up stream and partly across, but more across than up, from where you are standing. You should throw them to within an inch of the opposite bank; if they alight on it so much the better; draw them gently off, and they will fall like a snowflake, and if there is a trout within sight they are almost sure to captivate it. In this way your flies will fall more like a natural insect than by any other method.

Of course, Stewart's suggestion that the flies should fall on the far bank and then be twitched gently onto the stream, depends on the nature of the far bank. On my local river they would become firmly stuck on sedge grasses or overhanging branches. That is something I have experienced all too frequently! Stewart continues:

After your flies alight, allow them to float gently down stream for a yard or two, taking care that

OPPOSITE: Far from the madding crowd's ignoble strife – Thomas Gray.

neither they nor the line ripple the surface. There is no occasion for keeping them on the surface, they will be quite as attractive a few inches under water. As the flies come down stream, raise the point of your rod, so as to keep your line straight, and as little of it in the water as possible; and when they have traversed a few yards of the water, throw again about a yard or two higher up than where your flies alighted the previous cast, and so on. Unless the spot looks exceedingly promising, you need not cast twice in one place if you do not get a rise ...

While Stewart would not cast more than once in most spots if he didn't get a 'rise', he would cast 'six or seven times' over a promising spot such as an eddy, or beneath a tree, or close to a boulder and particularly in a rapid current where 'the trout may not see the fly at first'. Rapid main currents are often neglected, but Stewart considers that it is in the main current that 'you will frequently capture the best fish'. This is certainly true of well-mended indigenous trout from late April onwards and it is particularly true in hot weather when the more turbulent currents are richer in oxygen. The main current may require a greater expenditure of energy on the part of the trout, but it will also provide a fairly steady supply of food.

Apart from the main current, Stewart would exercise additional casts in other key locations:

> All quiet water between the two streams, and eddies behind the stones, should be fished straight up, and the flies just allowed to remain sufficiently long to let the trout see them; and in fishing such places care must be taken to keep the line out of the current ... on account of the roughness of the water it is not so easy to see a trout rise.

An almost identical set of instructions are given by Edmonds and Lee in *Brook and River Trouting*, sixty years later. Stewart focused on eddies behind stones and, like many anglers, seems to neglect the fact that large boulders produce a 'cushion' of water upstream of them. If this cushion is big enough, it will provide a good lie for a large trout, which may be observed darting from side to side as it intercepts food items in the bifurcating currents that sweep past either side of the boulder.

W.C. Stewart seems to have fished principally from the bank and while it is true that some streams lend themselves to bank fishing, some require wading in order to control the flies and to reach good lies. Wading can facilitate better line control, particularly where there are

Safely in the net: a lovely brown trout hooked in the rapid central current.

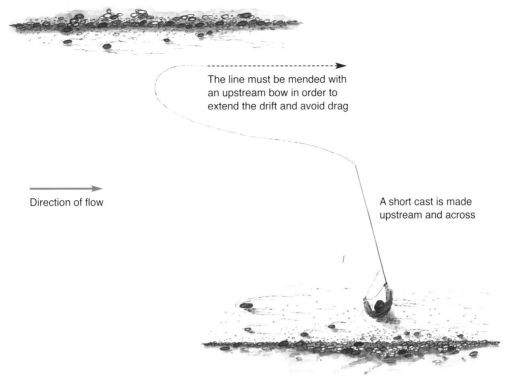

The line must be mended with an upstream bow in order to extend the drift and avoid drag

Direction of flow

A short cast is made upstream and across

Traditional upstream and across wet-fly fishing.

contrary currents to combat. It makes fishing awkward places – pocket water between boulders, channels between weed beds, eddies against the bank, or lies under overhanging branches – a much easier proposition. Some tree-lined streams, of course, may only be fished by careful wading. At the same time, when wading the angler does have a lower profile, which may result in fewer fish being scared under certain conditions of light. Sometimes we overestimate the dangers of scaring fish when wading; more than once in rivers I have experienced trout swimming around my feet when standing in a clear stream.

Edmonds and Lee, unlike Stewart, principally fished rivers by wading, finding it to be the only real way to search an entire stream. However, like Stewart, the authors of *Brook and River Trouting* worked the river by searching the near bank first, then fishing slightly more across, with each subsequent cast being made as they waded across the stream, finally reaching the far bank:

To fish a stream or length of river systematically, crossing and re-crossing, each time a few yards higher up, until the whole has been thoroughly covered, takes time; but it is far better that the angler's flies should be on the water, searching every spot fit to hold a fish, than waving in the air while he moves rapidly on from stream to stream.

It may appear that Edmonds and Lee are enjoying a gentle dig at the chalk stream dry-fly fisherman who walks along the bank, false-casting his fly, until he sees a fish rise and deems it ethically right to cast his fly onto the water. Having said that, there is common ground between Edmonds and Lee and the chalk stream dry-fly man – they fished their flies upstream; so too, of course, did W.C. Stewart.

'Upstream' fishing is sometimes misinterpreted for it is rare that a cast is actually made directly upstream; rather, it is a short cast upstream and across. Indeed, a cast of any length made directly upstream stands a real chance of lining a fish and thus ruining one's chances in the whole pool, as Stewart outlines:

> In casting across, when the flies light, the stream carries them out at right angles to the line, and they come down the stream first, so that the trout sees the flies before the line; whereas, in casting straight up, if a trout is between the angler and the place where his flies light, the line passes over it before it sees the flies and may alarm it.

Fishing Downstream

Most authors on the wet-fly are in no doubt that to persist in fishing downstream is rather foolish and all logic seemingly favours the cast made up and across the stream. The argument runs that it is easier to scare trout when casting downstream and much more difficult to hook them if they take the fly. However, I think it is wise to temper received wisdom with a little circumspection – downstream fishing is often not the hopeless cause that we are led to believe it is. You will recall that at the end of Chapter 2, we mentioned that Viscount Grey was compelled to fish downstream once he had gone blind yet still caught his quota of trout; so downstream fishing, however frowned upon, does work. It is worth considering wise words from John Waller Hills in his *A History of Fly-Fishing for Trout* (1921). In a chapter entitled 'Stewart and the Upstream School', Hills writes:

> All logic favours upstream fishing, at least in clear water, and nothing else is worth talking about. There are not two sides to the argument. And the immense majority of fishing books say the same. But a history of fly fishing would not be complete if it left the matter there. Future students, reading the printed word, would imagine that from Stewart to now everyone fished upstream except some obscure individuals fishing untried waters. But that is historically untrue. Good fishermen, on the shyest of waters, fish downstream and kill fish. Their practice differs from theory, as it often does. Downstream fishing, here and now, in this twentieth century, is better for certain persons and certain occasions.

How cleverly Hills begins the passage by appearing to absorb the received wisdom of the wet-fly gurus before tempering it with his own more liberal viewpoint. When reviewing the logic of upstream fishing it is worth considering what Edmonds and Lee have to say on this subject:

> Upstream fishing is far more difficult than downstream fishing and the initial efforts will prove disheartening. Rise after rise will be missed …
>
> The obvious natural law which causes fish to lie head upstream should convince the reader that no undue stress has been laid upon the importance of fishing upstream, and that the method should be rigidly adhered to on all occasions, except those previously mentioned [i.e. in conditions of heavy and coloured water].
>
> That trout have exceptionally keen eyesight, no one who has ever walked along the bank of a trout stream will deny. How then can the least thoughtful expect to creel decent fish with the river in normal condition, if he stands with the fish below him …?
>
> From these well-known facts it will be obvious, even to the uninitiated, that the best approach for the angler bent on capturing trout in clear water is from behind. Yet, astonishingly as it may seem (and for the simple reason that it is the easier way), many men – we might almost say the majority of men – invariably fish their flies across and downstream, letting the flies sweep right round until they are directly below, where they are often allowed to dangle in the water at the end of a taut line.

Are we to assume that the men derided by Edmonds and Lee never caught trout? If that is the case, then they were foolish indeed to carry on fishing downstream and yet I think they caught their share of fish. Thus, while the up and across method is to be preferred *in most circumstances*, downstream fishing should not simply be condemned with scorn. Of course, Edmonds and Lee did allow the use of downstream wet-flies on those occasions such as cold spring days when rivers are strong-running and tinged with colour. Writing in the *Manchester Guardian* in the 1920s, Arthur Ransome makes a similar case: 'To discuss downstream fishing at all is to assume that there

Chris Fogg hooks a nymph-feeding trout on a Something and Nothing (see Chapter 8) from a Test carrier.

Chris with his trout.

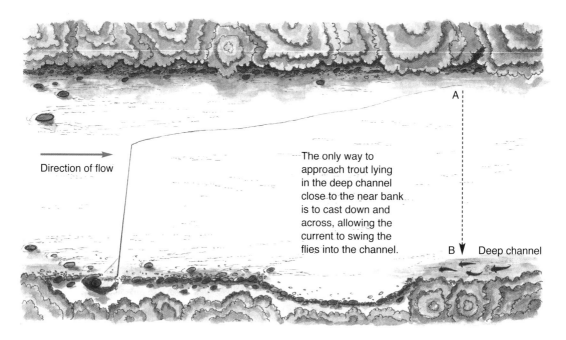

Downstream and across: fishing for trout lying in a deep channel against the near bank.

is more water in the rivers than there was at the beginning of the week.'

Certainly, in heavy water we are generally obliged to fish downstream, for our flies would be swept back in an instant if cast upstream. Stewart, Pritt, Ransome, Edmonds and Lee would all have agreed that a downstream fly had to be fished on a swollen river. At other times, however, they would have it that the upstream technique should be rigidly adhered to, but that is a little intransigent. I wish to make it perfectly clear that upstream and across is generally to be preferred when possible, but there are situations, apart from heavy water, that make it necessary to adopt a different approach. First of all, I will take you to a spot on a river that cannot be fished adequately by casting upstream; it holds good fish and I see no reason to neglect it.

This stretch of tree-lined water, after a series of rapid pools, runs smoothly, is generally quite shallow and is exceedingly clear. It has to be fished from the near bank as the far bank is canopied by low-lying branches and tangled undergrowth. Wading would be a waste of time in water so low and clear and, in any case, the bottom on this stretch is sandy and silty, making

wading inadvisable from the viewpoint of safety. At the point where I am standing, there is a small bay downstream of me; it is little more than an indentation in an otherwise straight and low bank. Just below the bay, there is a deep channel against the bank and this is where the trout lie. It is not possible to fish this deep channel from a downstream position, for three significant reasons. Firstly, the bank is tangled with vegetation so it is not possible to cast upstream close in to the bank when actually standing on the bank. Secondly, and for reasons already cited, it is not advisable to wade this stretch in order to get a better casting angle. Thirdly, even if it were possible to cast parallel and close to the bank from a downstream position, there would be a real chance of lining one or two fish in the channel and thus scaring the entire pod. It's definitely a location that requires a downstream cast and a fine and far off approach.

If we stand upstream of the bay, it is possible to make a long cast downstream and across so that the flies swing across stream and come to rest in the slacker water of the deep channel. The flies do tend to skate across the stream but no matter, this does not scare the trout lying deep against the near bank. In any case, I have taken more than a few trout when the flies have been swinging across the stream, and some good fish too! The first cast is always made so that the flies will swim across to the head of the deep channel where they are left for a few seconds to play in the current. Sometimes they will be taken there and, if not, I retrieve them slowly and occasionally a trout will follow and take upstream of the channel. If the first cast proves fruitless, I then extend the length of line so that the second cast will swing across to a point in the channel a couple of feet downstream of the first cast and so on until either the whole channel has been searched, or I have reached the limits of my casting ability. This location presents a classic case for fishing a downstream technique and I have no qualms about doing so; it really isn't a matter of ethics but merely common sense. It is not an isolated case by any means.

Imagine now, if you will, a long pool ending in a wide and deep section above a weir. Like the deep channel described above, the tail of this pool harbours some very good trout and it is completely tree-lined, making casting from the bank impossible. It is also too deep for wading comfortably and it is not possible to cast from below the weir into the pool itself. In summary, the very trees which provide shelter and shade for the inhabitants of the pool, as well as food in the form of terrestrial flies, beetles and caterpillars, make it impossible to fish from any location save a gap in the trees some twenty yards from the lip of the weir. As luck would have it, there is also a gravel bank adjacent to this gap in the surrounding vegetation and if we wade carefully we are a couple of yards from the bank and in a good position to fish the pool by casting downstream. We draw off line and make a loose cast across and down the stream so that the line lies like a snake on the water. As the current gets hold of the line we roll the rod tip upstream so that the loose line forms an upstream arc; the flies will then drift downstream in a straight line. To extend the drift, and it is possible to drift the flies right to the lip of the weir with this technique, we simply pull more line off the reel, wiggle the rod tip to throw it out onto the water, throw the upstream arc as before and continue the drift. Hopefully, we will get a take from a fish

some distance upstream of the weir and land it without disturbing the rest of the pool, but, if not, we will continue to drift our flies right to the lip. The best trout are often close up to the bank, and under the trees, on either side of the pool so that we can experiment with different lines of drift.

A pool such as this is worth several drifts of our flies but, in order to make even a second drift worthwhile, great care must be taken in retrieving the line once the flies have reached the weir. What is called for is the gentlest and slowest of retrieves and it is surprising how often takes will occur when the flies are being retrieved upstream, though hooking fish will be another matter. There will be plucks and pulls and swirls, but many of them will not result in hooked fish; that is the negative aspect of downstream fishing and something we just have to accept. Generally speaking, a trout that really wants the fly will take a strong enough hold for us to latch onto it; the worst thing is to strike at any little pluck, which may result in a pricked fish and put the whole pool of trout down for some time.

Downstream fishing is said by many to be easy, a good way for beginners to start, but done correctly in the kind of location described above it is far from easy and takes an amount of practice to perfect. It needs to be said that if you are using a three-fly cast and the leader is drifting down the current in a straight line, then it is only usually the point-fly that the trout will see first, thus making the other flies on the cast largely redundant. By and large this does not matter as we will retain the other flies for other stretches of river that we intend to fish upstream and across.

Fishing downstream is necessary in the kind of locations I have described, and I have caught many good trout by casting down and across, or by paying out line to facilitate a direct down-stream drift, but I would not argue that it is an ideal method. It certainly has a number of drawbacks. There is a danger of spooking fish, unless the current is turbulent enough for us to not be noticed and we must take up a position as carefully as possible in order to avoid scaring any trout in the vicinity. We must keep low, use whatever cover the stream affords and fish fine and far off, exercising all our skill to facilitate a good drift without our flies skating unnaturally.

There is undoubtedly a danger that we will prick fish and scare the whole pool and if that is the case the pool may be disturbed for some time to come. Infuriatingly, there will be many little plucks that do not result in firm takes, but if we have not pricked these fish, by striking injudiciously, then the chances are that they will come again. Quite why trout pluck at the fly, or just swirl at it, rather than take it cleanly, is difficult to discern; it could be that they are simply investigating this alien creature in their territory. Spotting takes during a downstream drift is not as easy as anglers might imagine and there are times when the fabled sixth sense seems to come into play. In *A History of Fly-Fishing for Trout*, John Waller Hills writes a good description of the difficulties of spotting takes when fishing the downstream wet-fly. He imagines us watching a skilled downstream fisher at work:

> So minute and various are the indications, that it is often hard for him to say why he struck. Very seldom did he see any sign at the surface. Sometimes a movement under water made a slight, hardly visible boil. Or he may have seen a flash as the fish turned at the fly, or a dim shadow, scarce perceptible in the ripple. Or the line may have stopped for a fraction of a second, or behaved in some peculiar way. Our fisherman, wading out at the head of the stream, could not tell you if you asked why he struck in each case. All he could say was that he knew that a fish had risen.

A further consideration when fishing downstream is that of depth. Now, while traditional wet-fly fishing is, by and large, top-of-the-water fishing, casting up and across does allow the flies to sink a little more deeply on the drift than when casting down and across, or when employing a straight downstream drift. Particularly when flies are on a taut line when fishing downstream, they will remain at the surface and are in danger of skating or dragging. A slack line drift is to be preferred. At the end of a long downstream drift it is obviously necessary to retrieve the flies before recasting and they will remain close to the surface during the upstream retrieve. If the retrieve is too quick they will produce too much surface disturbance, so a very slow retrieve is required. It has often been argued that when fishing downstream the retrieve back at the end of a drift inevitably scares fish. This is not something I have found, although I do make sure to retrieve the flies gently rather than rip them back, or try to lift too much line off the water before recasting. Stewart argued that if the flies are retrieved against the current, then the trout's suspicions will be aroused: 'Trout are not accustomed to see small insects making such gigantic efforts to escape, and therefore it is calculated to awaken their suspicion.'

I think this is crediting trout with powers of thought that they probably do not possess. While it remains true that insects will be borne downstream by the current and are unlikely to swim upstream against it, an artificial fly hovering in the current or gradually working back upstream takes fish rather than scares them. Whether a trout is actually duped into believing that the artificial fly is an actual insect, or is simply being inquisitive when it takes the fly in its mouth, does not seem to be unduly important.

There are other occasions when a careful downstream drift will pay dividends. The cast made down and across, so that the line becomes taut and the flies skate and wiggle across the surface, is not likely to produce success under most conditions. Ironically, however, even this kind of downstream fishing can produce remarkably big fish at dusk, when the light begins to fail and large sedge flies make an appearance. A palmer-dressed fly, skated across the stream, does well at such times!

Nymph-feeding trout are often 'ripe' for the downstream wet-fly. What I now have in mind is when trout are seen bulging to emerging nymphs in a streamy run, glide or gentle current. When you can pinpoint the exact location of the fish, a downstream drift concluding in a form of induced take can prove deadly. Imagine that trout are 'bulging' to emerging nymphs in a nice run some twenty yards downstream and there is a good fish lying in an upstream position of the rest of the pod. We are going to drift a wet-fly down to him and, from this distance, we shouldn't scare him if we are careful. We cast slightly upstream and across, mend the line into

Playing a trout hooked on a Greenwell Spider: it refused all the author's dry-flies.

an upstream arc and then allow the flies to sink as they drift downstream. We will need to strip extra line off the reel, wiggle the rod tip to throw it out onto the water and continually mend the line so that our flies drift downstream in a straight line to the position of the first trout in the group. It is important that we keep a slack line so that the flies either continue to sink, or at least remain a couple of feet down; a taut line during the drift, as will become obvious in a moment, will mar what we are trying to achieve. Then, just before our point-fly reaches the trout's position, we check the line so that it becomes taut and our flies rise in the water just like ascending nymphs. Hopefully, the trout that has been bulging to mature nymphs will be seduced into taking. It is the wet-fly equivalent of the induced take method employed by Frank Sawyer and Oliver Kite, who used weighted nymphs to achieve the same objective. The wet-fly version is generally known as the Leisenring

Lift, although, as we shall see, Leisenring himself carried out the induced take slightly differently from the method described above. Practising the induced take technique with wet-flies assumes that the flow is not too strong so that our flies will indeed sink. In stronger currents, a weighted point-fly becomes essential.

The Leisenring Lift

The Leisenring Lift was named after James Leisenring, who developed the technique on waters such as the Brodheads in Pennsylvania. By trade a skilled toolmaker, Leisenring fished rivers usually worked by dry-fly men, yet he remained an exponent of the wet-fly. He believed too in flies dressed with soft hackles, valuing them for their mobility which created the impression of a hatching nymph or struggling fly. Leisenring published *The Art of Tying the Wet Fly* in 1941, ten years before his death. His most famous pupil, Vernon S. Hidy (known as 'Pete' Hidy) adopted Leisenring's techniques and added further material to Leisenring's book, which was republished as *The Art of Tying the Wet Fly and Fishing the Flymph* in 1971. Hidy coined the term 'flymph' around 1963 in order to make it clear what stage in an aquatic insect's life cycle he and Leisenring were seeking to emulate. A 'flymph' is neither a nymph nor an adult fly; it is that very stage when the adult fly emerges from its nymphal shuck – we would simply call it an 'emerger', but then 'flymph' seems suitably American. Hidy preferred the term 'flymph' to either 'emerging nymph' or 'hatching fly', yet the term never really gained common usage beyond Hidy's coterie in Pennsylvania. Hidy writes that the term 'flymph' accurately identifies 'that dramatic and little-understood interval of an aquatic insect's life: the struggle up to the surface as well as the drift (of some insects) in or just below the surface film'.

Fishing in or just below the surface film has always been a part of the wet-fly tradition, but it is in emulating 'the struggle to the surface' that the Leisenring method comes into its own. Leisenring's original book is principally concerned with tying flies and actually says little about methods of fishing them, but he does describe the wet-fly induced take, which, in his version, is almost a cross between up- and downstream fishing. Leisenring cast his flies upstream and across, allowed them to sink, then just before they reached the position of a marked trout, checked the drift of the flies with the rod so that they rose in the water. He believed that soft-hackled flies were then at their most effective with the hackle fibres fluttering in an animated manner. The trout, attracted by the movement of the fly, and imagining it was an insect about to escape from the stream, made a confident strike. Thus, while most anglers from Cotton, through to Edmonds and Lee, believed that the most killing part of the cast is when the flies first alight on the stream, Leisenring and Hidy thought differently. However, there is room enough for both viewpoints and techniques; it depends on the nature of the stream and the way in which trout are feeding as to which we choose.

Reading the River

Anyone writing about fishing on flowing water has a particular river or stream in their mind's eye and while many of the techniques described in any particular book may be transferable, others may not. Rivers vary enormously. There are tiny, peaty brooks bubbling over barren moorlands and small but lush tree-lined brooks flowing crystal clear through emerald weed beds, bordered by rich pastures. There are medium-sized chalk streams full of plump trout and grayling and limestone streams not far behind them in riches, then there are rapid upland rivers gushing past boulders and harbouring small but eager wild trout. There are wide rivers, such as the Welsh Dee, where an angler must wade deep to get anywhere near his quarry, and tiny streams requiring the utmost care as you creep behind a lone bush in order to avoid scaring the trout you have spotted hugging the far bank. The wet-fly will catch trout on all these streams, although it may be necessary to vary the technique from place to place. For example, the systematic stream-searching employed by Edmonds and Lee, crossing and recrossing the river as they moved upstream, would hardly be feasible on the largest and deepest of rivers. It would take more than a single chapter, probably more than a single book, to cover every possibility, so you will forgive me, I hope, for any generalizations that I make. One thing is common to fishing the wet-fly on rivers, and that is the need to approach cautiously. Having said that, the degree and nature of stealth required of the angler will inevitably vary according to the specific river environment he or she is fishing. For example, trout are less likely to be aware of the angler's presence when they lie in turbulent and slightly coloured water as opposed to a clear and slow-flowing stream. Nevertheless, we should exercise as much caution as possible wherever we fish and whether we adopt the upstream or downstream approach.

I have never really been enamoured by *The Experienced Angler*, published by Colonel Robert Venables in 1662. I think Colonel Venables would have made a rather dour fishing companion and been a bore in the pub; I would much rather have had a pint at Hartington with Charles Cotton! Anyway, no matter how dull Venables often is, there is a deal of good sense too in his book, as in the following passage:

> Fish are frighted with any the least sight or motion, therefore by all means keep out of sight, either by sheltering yourself behind some bush or tree, or try standing far off the River's side.
>
> Keep the Sun (and Moon, if night) before you, if your eyes will endure it … for if they be at your back, your rod with its shadow offend much …

Venables' advice may not have been completely original at the time of writing, but he makes a good point nevertheless and if we tread unwarily, or allow the shadow of our rod to fall on the water, then the game is up. There would be little point taking the trouble to fish upstream if a bright sun is at our back so that our every movement is magnified by a huge shadow on the stream. Equally, bright clothing can be a real giveaway and I cannot understand the recent fashion for wearing orange or red waistcoats and waterproofs. There are times when fishing the wet-fly calls for careful stalking and such caution is not restricted to exponents of the dry-fly.

Extreme caution pays dividends – at least it should do – and it is always wise to fish 'far from the madding crowd's ignoble strife'. Fishing away from the crowds of other pleasure seekers, and other anglers too for that matter, is very important when adopting the systematic stream-searching approach of Edmonds and Lee. However, mindlessly zigzagging up a stretch of river, though it may produce a bag of fish, is not the real essence of fishing the wet-fly. Edmonds and Lee, and Stewart before them, would have agreed that there are key spots where you must concentrate your attention and have a few casts before moving on. This introduces the subject generally known as 'river craft'.

We must learn to 'read' the river, to understand its diverse currents, its deep pools and gravelly runs, and the favoured lies of better than average trout. We need to understand the moods of the river controlled by the weather, conditions of light and atmospheric pressure in particular, as well as the seasonal appearance of natural insects, which has an obvious bearing on the flies we use. Unfortunately, the seasons appear to be shifting; even in 1886 T.E. Pritt wrote that, 'The seasons are given approximately, the actual time of the appearance of each fly being dependent on the mildness of the previous winter and the

Exercising stealth: how close can you get to a trout?

prevailing spring weather.' Thus, flies we may expect to see may already have emerged and disappeared, while others don't seem to appear at all during some seasons. Observation on the day we fish is important, for we cannot rely only on preconceived ideas about what insects should be emerging. Of course, we may observe insects hatching on the surface of the stream, but there are other bankside clues such as flies resting on vegetation or caught up in spiders' webs. While it is true that there are good general wet-fly patterns that will do reasonably well throughout the season, it is equally true that we will do better if we match our patterns to the naturals currently being taken by trout.

Just as predicting the emergence of natural insects can be difficult, so too predicting the best lies in a river may not be as simple as we might imagine. While chalk streams may be fairly consistent from year to year, rain-fed rivers change considerably after heavy winter flood-waters. Deep holes in the river bed appear where once there was an even run, while pools that were once deep become infilled with silt and debris. A real torrent may have gouged out deep holes that will provide excellent lies for trout but a real danger to those who wade the river without caution. The dam we struggled to build only a year ago has been badly breached and several trees have been felled by a particularly violent storm. Sometimes, a tree that has fallen into the river is no bad thing; it may act as a dam and create a deeper pool, while on slower reaches it can act as a groyne, creating a faster current where once the river was lifeless. The branches of the tree offer shelter for trout and some of my best fish have been taken from such a feature. A fallen tree would often make an excellent permanent feature in a river, but the Environment Agency will invariably get twitchy, worrying about flooding, and diligent river keepers or a keen group of club members will remove the offending tree in an instant. Make the most of it while it is still there!

The weather obviously has a great bearing on our sport and always offers us the best of excuses when we do badly. A strong upstream wind can be a real boon as it will hold back the flies and

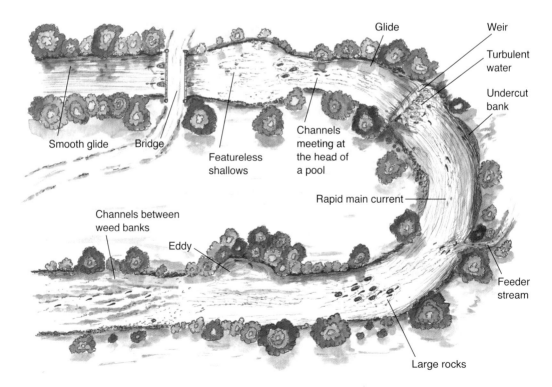

Anatomy of a trout stream.

prolong their drift and it may also make the trout a little less wary. However, I generally find the wind to be blowing down the stream, which makes it difficult to hold back the drift of the flies. Rainfall, or indeed lack of it, obviously affects our sport. Disregarding the evil effects of water abstraction from aquifers, the flow of chalk streams is reasonably consistent, but rain-fed rivers fluctuate wildly and this undoubtedly affects the whereabouts of the resident trout. They may disappear into the cover of undercut banks during a flood, yet the river may also appear empty of fish when, during a dry spell, it is running low and crystal clear. Wading must be avoided when the river is low and we must carefully search every nook and cranny where trout may hide. Trout may be in deeper water, as long as there is a decent flow, yet they are equally likely to lie in shallow and rough water. In the heat of summer, when the oxygen content of the river is depleted, trout are even found in the thinnest of water, hardly deep enough to cover their backs, because it is oxygen-rich.

In spite of the territorial instincts of brown trout (though in general they do not wander around to the same extent as rainbow trout), some fish will move about during the season. Having spawned in feeder streams, they return to the main river and in early spring are likely to be resting up in gentler currents and quiet pools. Some fish may stay there, but as the season progresses they begin to gain condition and often migrate to other parts of the river. The main controlling factor is the weather. Once it warms up, and a greater number of aquatic insects are active, the trout are able to feed greedily and have the energy to expend in pursuit of their food. Even a few warm spells before the season commences may find the trout well-mended and this is an increasing phenomenon given the recent milder winters. Once trout gain strength, some will venture into the stronger currents knowing full well that there will be a constant supply of food; when they were in poor condition after spawning they would not have had the energy to hold position there.

The notion that large trout are always in the most difficult of lies to fish, for example under the tangled roots or branches of a tree, is a myth. They often lie in such positions – but not always.

We may recall that W.C. Stewart warned us never to neglect the main current for 'indeed in it you will frequently capture the best fish'. Particularly when there is a good hatch, flies will often be caught in the main current and attract the attentions of large trout, while the stiller reaches appear devoid of activity. After a dry and dour spell, when trout have been soured off the feed, a little rain may freshen the river and if the main current is not too strong, good fish will then move from their hideaways and feed actively there.

Finding Your Fish

Whatever movement from location to location may occur during the season, brown trout are generally territorial and have preferred lies, the larger fish constantly driving smaller intruders away from their patch. Stocked rainbow trout in rivers are definitely more nomadic and, after stocking, will often instinctively migrate downstream and will congregate in deep weir pools that halt their apparent seaward progress. They will readily take a wet-fly as they rest up in these pools; all too readily at times and that ceases to be much fun. Rainbow after rainbow may fall to the fly without us having to move an inch, but with the brown trout it is different; we must search the river for them and focus our attention on those lies likely to hold the best fish.

A deep even-flowing glide, or 'riffle', against the far bank is a classic lie and it is all the better if it is against a steep bank and overhung by the branches of trees or other vegetation. Trout will feel safe in such a location, will have shade from the bright light of the sun and will be supplied with food both by the current and by the surrounding vegetation. The even flow of the glide creates a good drift for the wet-flies, whether you are fishing up and across, or are employing a downstream drift. Given a smooth and even current, a drift downstream can be extended for quite some distance if you feed out line and constantly mend it using the upstream arc technique described earlier. If there is a rapid current midstream, slack line must be used to counteract the effects of drag. Often, a bend in the river will create a similar lie for trout and an easy enough drift to fish. Cast to an upstream point on the bend and simply allow the rod tip to follow the flies downstream and round the bend. The kind of lie we have described is such an obvious location to try that it might well become overfished on a popular stretch of river. Resident trout become wary and it is therefore well worth fishing classic glides with smaller flies and the finest of leaders, even though there may be a risk of a good fish breaking the leader on an underwater snag. Those trout will undoubtedly have seen a good number of larger flies and coarser leaders; they may have been caught more than once and will therefore be 'educated'.

In contrast to deep glides, extensive shallows will rarely harbour decent fish, particularly if there is little bankside cover, or cover from boulders and weeds. The lack of features in shallows also means that there will not be any points where food items are concentrated. However, the presence of the odd feature may make all the difference, for rapid-running shallows do at least have a high oxygen content when the weather is dry and hot. I know of one wide and shallow pool that often yields a good fish; there is a boulder in midstream and a little run by a bush against the far bank. Either location is capable of yielding a plump brownie while the rest of the pool remains barren. Weed beds in shallow pools can also make quite a difference as they offer some shelter plus a supply of nymphs and shrimps. It is often worth exploring the little channels between weed beds with a single soft-hackled fly; using a team of flies runs the risk of getting caught up, either during the drift, or when a fish has been hooked.

Although there are times when even the largest trout will be in the strong central current of a stream, and particularly where two currents meet to filter food into a single location, good trout are likely to reside near some kind of key feature. A trout's behaviour is controlled by basic needs – primarily focused on food and safety. Small trout are often cavalier; those that remain cavalier either stay small or fall to some predator or other. Of course, to put on weight, a trout requires a certain amount of food without expending too much energy, so that the largest trout are unlikely to enter the most rapid currents unless there is a wealth of food available and they are unlikely to stay there. They will return to a protected lie, one that does not require much energy to hold position, and will drive away any interlopers. If the lie also provides a reasonable supply of food, they will remain there for much of the time. The best lies in terms of safety, energy conservation and a supply of food will obviously hold the largest fish – it is a simple matter of natural selection – but they are also frequently the most difficult of spots in terms of casting a fly. Nevertheless, such locations should be worth the effort.

On rough streams, where most fish are small, prime lies are at a premium. As you work your way up the stream, you will catch plenty of eager little fish, fish that expend a great deal of energy feeding on a meagre supply of food. They take a fly readily, while the larger fish are more wary. Deep holes and pools may hold better fish, but look out also for pockets of water between rocks and boulders; fish such areas carefully, 'picking the pockets' as they say. The tumbling streams of Exmoor and Dartmoor fit this description, streams like the East Lyn, and in the deeper pockets of water between rocks a nice pound brownie may be lurking. When fishing pocket water it really is important that you keep as much line off the water as possible and cast frequently, because the drift through the pocket will be swift. Takes too are often very quick and you must be ready for them. All you may get is a quick pull on the line, a splash, or a yellow-golden flash in the clear but peat-tinged water. Many fish will be missed, but that is the nature of the game and any fish landed represents a minor triumph.

On any rivers where large stones or boulders occur there will be good trout lies worth fishing. Fish will rest behind boulders, where there is obviously slacker water, but the largest boulders also have slacker water at the side of them and even an upstream cushion of quieter water where a fish may lie comfortably. The wet-flies should be cast a few feet upstream of any boulder and then be allowed to drift down the side of it; if a trout lying behind the boulder is feeding, he will undoubtedly move from his position to intercept the flies as they drift past. Even if the water appears at first sight too turbulent to hold trout it should not be neglected. Turbulent water is often deceptive and where it roars, boils and

A good trout lying in shallow water: weeds provide a rich supply of food.

foams around boulders the rough surface water veils the world beneath, where it is often far less turbulent and much easier than we may think for a trout to hold position. Further, we must always remember that this water will certainly be well oxygenated and a very good bet in hot and settled weather. Fishing for trout close to rocks and boulders is tricky and is best executed with a long rod and a light line, most of which should be kept off the surface of the water where it will be at the mercy of complex and fast currents. Generally speaking, if the water is safe enough to wade, then the turbulence is likely to mask your presence so that it is possible to approach close to trout without scaring them.

I do not regard fishing pocket water as imitative fishing, because the speed at which the current carries both natural insects and artificial flies gives a trout very little time to discriminate. The pattern of wet-fly you choose is not of paramount importance. However, a touch of sparkle is likely to add attraction and H.C. Cutcliffe was a great believer in ribbing his wet-flies with gold or silver tinsel when fishing rough water (*Trout Fishing on Rapid Streams*, 1863); an Orange Partridge is a good pattern to use dressed with a rib of gold or silver. Fishing pocket water with a wet-fly offers some exciting and challenging sport and there is really nothing

quite like it. It requires skill, but there is a kind of intimacy with the fish and its environment when you wade close to where a trout is lying.

Just as deeper pockets of water should be sought out on rough streams, deeper pools on any river are likely to hold good trout. Deep water is often fished with a weighted nymph or shrimp, but trout in such water will often rise to wet-flies drifted close to the surface. However, should top-of-the-water fishing prove fruitless, then it is worth replacing the point-fly with a tiny Goldhead or weighted nymph. I also dress some spider patterns with simple bodies of layered copper wire which provides enough weight to sink them a little deeper. When fishing deep water with a reasonably even flow, cast upstream and across, which will allow the flies to sink, then, as the flies drift opposite your position, make an upstream mend and pay out more line so that the drift will continue down the stream. If no takes occur and the drift has been completed, hold the line taut for a while in order to induce a take via the Leisenring Lift, before carefully retrieving at a slow pace. It is surprising how many fish will come at the flies either when they lift in the water at the end of the drift, or when they are actually being retrieved. Takes on the retrieve are generally felt, but at other times all the angler may discern is the slightest of

Playing a fish hooked on a Poult Bloa in a deep pool.

signals from the line. Reading takes when fishing the flies deeper becomes almost an unconscious process after a time; it is almost as if a sixth sense kicks in – something alerted you to the fact that a trout had taken the fly and you tightened instinctively, but could not explain quite why you did so. There is a current fashion for using strike indicators when using weighted flies, but I do not personally think they are necessary.

A deep lie will be all the more likely to hold a good trout if it has the added protection of a jungle of bankside vegetation such as over-hanging tree branches or tangled roots. Such lies may be found where the current has cut into the bank and has perhaps formed a little bay or eddy. Although an eddy is often quieter than the main flow of the river, a current will still circulate round the eddy and supply a constant source of food. A trout in such a location may be able to feed steadily without ever having to move more than a foot or two. If there is an overhanging tree, then the food supplied by the circulating current will be supplemented by terrestrial flies, grubs, beetles and caterpillars which invariably tumble

into the water. Eddies, however, can be quite difficult to fish, particularly when your line has to traverse a rapid main current in order to land the flies in the slacker water of the eddy; all too easily the drag of water on the fly line will whip the flies out of the eddy and they will skate alarmingly. If line cannot be held off the current, then a very slack and wavy line needs to be cast so that the flies have time to drift round the eddy before the main current takes up all the slack. Once drag has been avoided, a trout may take, but there is the added problem caused by slack line. In other words, you may not be in direct contact with the flies and an amount of slack line needs to be gathered up before a clean strike can be made. A long rod will gather up the line much more quickly than a short rod. Trout feeding in eddies can often be spotted clearly enough, which allows the angler to plot their feeding paths. At this point, it is worth noting that the circulating current of an eddy often results in trout facing in the opposite direction to the main flow of the river.

When fishing an eddy, watch the trout for a

time and think carefully about the cast that must be made. It will probably require inch-perfect presentation; the point-fly will perhaps have to land on the edge of the current entering the eddy so that it will be swept naturally into and around the little bay. Without doubt, there will be a branch overhanging the very spot where you need to cast and perhaps even a couple of dangling flies. Do not add yet another hazard to wildlife. A point certainly worth noting is that trout in eddies often have a different feeding pattern from those stationed in the main river. For example, trout in the main river are clearly rising to dark olives at the surface, whereas that good two-pounder in the eddy is not rising at all, though he does appear to be feeding. He may, of course, be taking a different insect in the micro-habitat of the eddy, but on this occasion he is actually feeding on the same dark olives but under the surface. This is what is happening: emerging duns, and even duns that have fully emerged but not freed themselves from the

water, are swept into the eddy by the current and disappear under the surface as they enter it. Look at the current where it leaves the eddy, a couple of duns are bobbing to the surface again but others have already been eaten. A wet-fly is clearly the best bet in this location.

Bridges crossing the stream are always a good bet. If it is a substantial bridge, then the bridge piles may create a cushion of water in front of them comfortable enough for a trout to lie out of the main current. Before seeking to fish under a large stone bridge, search around the piles first. Neglecting to do this runs the risk of not only missing a potential fish, but also lining it so that it shoots under the bridge and puts every other trout down. Casting to fish lying under bridges is difficult and fishing upstream under a bridge is often pointless; not only is it a difficult cast and impossible to control the drift fully, but there is every chance of lining fish. It makes much more sense to employ a downstream cast and control the flies so that they drift naturally under the

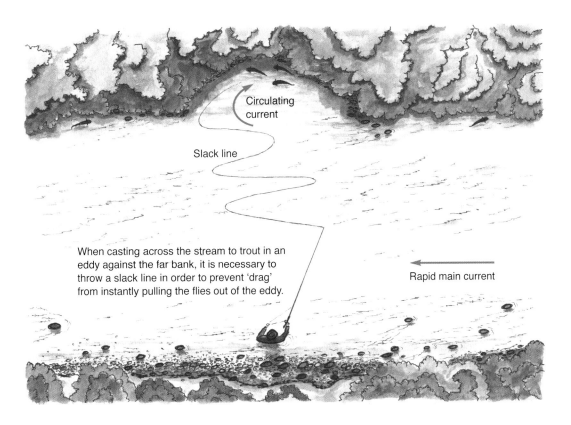

Fishing an eddy.

bridge. Bridges provide trout with shade and shelter; they simply wait for food to drift down to them, although they will make frequent forays into the water above the bridge before drifting back into its shade.

Trout stationed under bridges will be well known to most anglers; everyone has had a crack at 'Old Charlie' and he is as wary as any trout can be. Nevertheless, a careful downstream drift with soft-hackled flies may just tempt him, but once he is hooked the fun really starts. The worst situation arises when there is a weir on the downstream side of the bridge – a hooked trout invariably makes for it and if he succeeds then you are really in trouble. If the bridge is merely a narrow footbridge then it might be possible to pass the rod underneath and to set off in pursuit, but a reasonably sized stone bridge probably means that you will have to battle it out where you stand. I caught a large and memorable 'wild' rainbow from under a little stone bridge. Above the bridge the river tumbled over a shallow rapid, then entered a deep pool under the bridge itself; the shallow rapid run fell steeply into the pool and a hooked fish would have had difficulty getting up it. Only a short distance downstream of the bridge there was another rapid run; a hooked trout could easily have swum down it. So, having hooked my trout I fully expected him

to head off downstream and that would have led to a catastrophe, but he didn't. Powerful though he was, he simply charged around the pool under the bridge and eventually tired enough for me to ease him out of the pool and to net him at the foot of the upstream rapids. Sometimes, you are just lucky!

Another feature worthy of a few additional casts is where any water enters the river, be it from a sizeable feeder stream or a mere trickle. Even water falling into the river from a drainage pipe may attract trout. Water entering the river oxygenates it and may just carry extra items of food; I recall seeing a number of trout congregating around a drainage pipe on one occasion. From time to time there was a real commotion in the water and it was clear that some tempting food item was entering the river via the pipe. On closer inspection it became clear enough; every so often a tadpole came wriggling down the pipe and fell into the river. I didn't have any tadpole imitations with me but I took a fish on a Black and Peacock Spider. Towards the end of the season, brown trout gather close to significant feeder streams, which they will shortly ascend to spawn and some big fish may fall to the flies. However, there is perhaps an ethical issue raised by their potential condition and it may well be best to leave them horny and

Weedy rivers should be fished only with a single fly.

in peace. It is surprising how small some breeding streams actually are and I have often seen large fish in streamlets no wider than two feet and hardly deep enough to cover a decent trout's back.

While deep weir pools usually hold good trout it is a mistake to ignore the foamy water at the foot of the weir, which is a great deal more turbulent at the surface than underneath. Such water will be rich in oxygen, making it an excellent trout-holding location in hot weather, and various creatures that have been tumbled over the weir will churn around in the water beneath, thus providing a ready larder for trout. At the foot of a significant weir pool on the Derbyshire Wye there is another tiny weir pool no larger than the size of the average kitchen. The water is turbulent indeed and it is such a small pool that it might easily be neglected. However, it often holds some impressively large fish and I never cease to be amazed each time I hook one.

The neck of any pool, just at the point where the rapid current meets slack water, is always worthy of a few additional drifts. It is possible to cast up into the current and then to make an upstream arc so that the flies drift naturally into the deeper and slacker water of the pool itself. Land the point-fly right in the current and then mend the line as necessary to achieve a lengthy downstream drift. However, you may expect a take from a fish quite quickly if the flies are presented delicately. The neck of a pool offers a prime lie for trout and the largest trout are likely to be upstream of any pod of fish so that they get first choice of any food items entering the pool. However, if no fish takes close to the neck of the pool, the flies should be allowed to continue their drift some distance downstream; if they are lifted off the water too close to the point where most trout are likely to gather, then the commotion will undoubtedly scare the fish and set them charging for cover. The whole pool may then be disturbed for some time to come. Even where the neck of a pool is relatively shallow and rapid, and considerably shallower than the main body of the pool, it is likely to yield surprisingly good fish from time to time. Although a fish taking up a position in the current entering a pool has to expend more energy than a trout lying in the slacker water of the pool, it has first pick of any food items, although it will only stay there when food is plentiful. Thus, during a good hatch of fly, many of those that are either drowned after emerging, or are washed downstream during the process of emergence, will enter a pool at the neck. Such food items are more likely to be underwater rather than floating on the surface, so that the wet-fly is often a better bet than the dry-fly. While the neck of a pool is always worth focusing attention on, there will also be trout at the tail of a pool, but I always find that the tail is better fished with a downstream drift.

Alkaline rivers, such as the chalk streams of Hampshire, Wiltshire and Dorset, or the limestone rivers of Yorkshire and Derbyshire, often have abundant weed growth and it is always worth fishing the channels between weed beds with a single soft-hackled spider pattern (if the rules of the fishery allow it), for a team of wet-flies is intended for open water. Fishing more than a single fly around weeds is asking for trouble, for the dropper flies will invariably get caught up. Luxuriant weed growth provides trout both with cover and an abundant supply of food in the form of shrimps and nymphs. Lying in the channels between weeds, or under rafts of weeds, trout feed voraciously under water and a 'nymphy' spider pattern, such as the Poult Bloa, will often outfish a dry-fly. Of course, the trout will rise from time to time and engulf both floating duns and artificial flies, but a great deal of their food will be taken sub-aqueously, which thus makes the wet-fly a sensible choice. Even F.M. Halford recognized the fact that the bulk of a trout's food was eaten underwater and he outlined this in a chapter entitled 'Studies in Fish Feeding' to be found in *Dry-Fly Fishing* (1889), so I fail to see why many alkaline rivers are the sole preserve of the dry-fly. Soft-hackled spider patterns are similar to the unweighted nymphs used by G.E.M. Skues a century ago and the battle he fought then to legitimize them has clearly still to be won. There is little difference in casting a Poult Bloa to a chalk stream brown trout actively feeding on nymphs, to casting a floating mayfly pattern to a fish occupied by Ephemera danica; both methods, it seems to me, are legitimate.

Wet-fly fishing on rivers is a sophisticated branch of fishing and I have tried to provide an overview of the theory and practice. Whether you are systematically searching the stream, or exploring just those key locations most likely to hold the best trout, skill will be required in controlling the drift and avoiding drag, but there is also the skill required to land the flies just where you want them. Casting is an important aspect of wet-fly fishing, particularly when using a team of flies as opposed to a single fly. A stiffish rod designed to throw a narrow loop will run the risk of tangling a team of flies, for the required backcast loop when fishing the wet-fly must be more open. This calls for a longer and more pliant rod, but it also entails slowing the cast a little in order to avoid a narrow loop and an annoying tangle. I am an intuitive type of caster and certainly no expert in that respect. I still manage to tangle the flies or land them in the branches of a tree, so I am certainly not going to pontificate about the technical 'dos' and 'don'ts' of casting. There are good books on casting and DVDs too, while several fly-fishing journals run regular articles on various casting techniques. Of course, there are also qualified professionals who will iron out all your casting faults. When I read about casting in magazines I often find that casts I have adopted, or developed as I went along, are accepted standard techniques with fancy names. It is satisfying to know that I can perform a 'steeple cast' or 'side-cut', even though I didn't know what those names meant before I saw the diagrams accompanying the articles.

The word 'casting' is itself of comparatively recent origin, for, browsing through the classic books of old, you will find that you are simply advised to 'throw your flies' upstream and across. It was perhaps assumed that the reader knew how to 'throw' the flies and therefore enough said. I do not feel that I am qualified to say much more and attempting to describe the detailed steps required to make a difficult cast is certainly beyond my scope. However, I must provide a little amplification. When short-lining, it is really only necessary to hold the rod out to your side, at a 45-degree angle, and to flip the flies out in front of you in a very relaxed manner. There is no straining for distance and it is hardly a cast as such. If there are trees behind, learning to carry out a simple roll cast is extremely useful. Imagine that you have cast upstream and across, and your flies have drifted a little downstream of your position. You simply raise the rod up towards the vertical, gathering up line as you do so, and then roll the tip of the rod upstream; the flies should alight in line with the direction that the rod tip is pointing. It's as simple as that – I hope. Alternatively, the backcast can be made sideways, or in a lateral plane downstream, before a forward cast is made in a lateral plane upstream. This is rather more difficult than the simple roll cast, but it is possible to achieve a greater distance once it is perfected. The main problem with side-casting is that the application of too much force widens the loop of line, which is good for avoiding the flies tangling, but bad in that it runs the risk of catching in bankside vegetation. Conversely, too little force during the side-cast may result in the flies tangling anyway.

One cast that is absolutely essential is the slack-line cast – throwing a wavy slack line into the main current so that the flies themselves drift naturally before the current produces drag. Naturally, on a small stream, a long rod will enable you to keep as much line as possible off the water in order to avoid drag, but there will be plenty of occasions when the slack-line cast is required. The simplest way to create a slack line is to move the rod tip from side to side when making the forward cast. For example, if you are facing upstream and casting upstream and across, make an overhead cast and then, as the line unfurls, move the rod to the right (that is, downstream); then, as the line falls, move the rod tip back upstream to point at the position you are aiming at. The line will then have a good curve on it. Alternatively, when making a quickish forward cast, if you stop the line just before it falls on the water, it should produce a wavy slack.

Well, I suppose I have just proved the point I made earlier – I am an intuitive caster and not the person to offer technical instruction on casting! Just enjoy experimenting and your repertoire of casts will become extensive. Each location you fish will demand a cast being made in a specific way and, as they say, necessity is the mother of invention.

ABOVE: A fish hooked on the last cast of the day.

RIGHT: A cracking brown trout to end a perfect day.

6 WET-FLY FISHING ON STILLWATERS

Introduction

In a single chapter it is impossible to cover every aspect of wet-fly fishing on stillwaters, but I can at least outline the principles of traditional techniques. New ways of fly fishing on lakes and reservoirs seem to be developed annually, but that does not mean that the old ways will no longer catch fish. Traditional wet-fly techniques have stood the test of time and, in addition to their effectiveness, can add a pleasurable dimension to catching trout that I would argue is rather lacking in some of the modern methods.

It may be an old adage that stillwaters are never still – but it is a truism nevertheless, for there are times when the surface is as rough as the sea and even when it is flat calm at the surface, the influence of prior winds and temperature changes will have induced circulating currents. However, 'stillwater' is about as good a term as we can coin to distinguish lakes and reservoirs from rivers. Stillwaters are as varied as rivers and even the large expanses of water – Welsh lakes, Irish loughs, Scottish lochs and English reservoirs – require the angler to adopt different flies and techniques to suit each location. English reservoirs differ considerably from one another, so that fertile lowland waters may be as different from barren upland reservoirs as chalk streams are from peaty highland burns. Lowland reservoirs are often relatively shallow and food-rich, whereas deep upland reservoirs often have a limited supply of aquatic life so that the trout have to forage for whatever they can get and may depend on terrestrials being blown onto the water.

As with the term 'reservoir', the word 'lake' encompasses so many different types of fisheries, from small, artificially constructed put-and-take fisheries to the mountain lakes of Wales and the large waters of the English Lake District. Cumbria itself offers variety enough given the contrast between lakes such as Windermere or Ullswater and the tiny tarns high up in the hills. Quite a few of the high Cumbrian tarns, or mountain lochans of Scotland for that matter, hold trout and are similar in size to commercial put-and-take fisheries, but surface area of the water is the only conceivable similarity. Thus, I cannot hope to cater for the uniqueness of every type of stillwater, although I can guarantee that wherever trout swim, traditional wet-fly tactics and flies will catch them.

We may say that we are wet-fly fishing whenever our flies sink beneath the surface – whether they be nymphs, lures, loch flies, soft-hackled spider patterns or whatever – and 'beneath the surface' may encompass anything from a few inches down to trailing a high-density sinking line as far down as it is possible to get. However, when I use the term 'wet-fly' I am thinking about spider patterns, small traditional winged wet-flies, palmers and, above all, traditional loch patterns, and thinking about fishing them in a fairly leisurely manner, principally in the upper layers of water. Fishing in the upper layers generally means using a floating line, although, as noted in the chapter on tackle, there will be times when it is necessary to use a sink-tip, intermediate or slow sinker. Having stated the categories of flies that I consider to be 'wet-flies', it needs to be made clear that artificials excluded from that category, principally nymphs and dry-flies, are not excluded because I reject them, but simply because they are not what this book is about; for example, there is certainly a place for combining a dry-fly on the top dropper with two wet-flies on the cast.

Unless it is really rough, which may require the use of a sink-tip, intermediate or slow-sinking line, I prefer to use a floating line at all times on lakes or reservoirs. A floating line facilitates efficient line control and provides visual take detection, since all takes do not register with a felt pull on the line. Naturally, the floating line is at its most effective when trout are feeding in the upper layers of water, yet if the water has reasonable clarity, trout feeding deeper down will rise to take the flies closer to the surface if the 'food' item has enough appeal. As a last resort, when trout will not rise to the flies, which happens when the water is quite coloured, then it may be necessary to use a sinking line, but I have found this to be fairly rare.

There was a time when traditional wet-fly fishing, generally with loch flies, was the dominant method on Scottish lochs, Irish loughs, Welsh and English lakes and even English reservoirs. When I began reservoir fly fishing in the early 1960s, most of the anglers I encountered fished with traditional loch flies supplemented with a few spider patterns borrowed from rivers and the odd dry-fly for a good evening rise. We assumed that the same flies were in use throughout Britain and were unaware that in other parts of England quite

different flies were used and had been for some time. Indeed, what had happened many years before on some of the lowland English reservoirs paved the way for quite different flies and different ways of fishing them.

The opening of Blagdon Lake in Somerset for trout fishing in 1904 provided the platform for a few innovative anglers to develop new patterns rather than rely on traditional flies. Blagdon played host to individuals such as Dr Howard Alexander Bell, who rejected standard patterns and preferred to start from scratch. Bell's approach to Blagdon was akin to the imitative approach adopted by river fishers such as Skues, which meant that he observed natural insects and then made his own copies of them. Thus, in the 1920s, he dressed bloodworm imitations, a Black Buzzer (chironomid pupa), Amber Nymph (sedge pupa) and a good number of other imitative patterns. At the time, his approach was unusual, although others such as J.C. Mottram also developed specific stillwater patterns. For example, in *Fly-Fishing: Some New Arts and Mysteries* (1915), Mottram introduced a floating midge pupa with a body fashioned from a slip of cork. Thus it was that anglers such as Bell and Mottram introduced an embryonic imitative approach to reservoir fishing which established a separate branch of the sport from the loch fly technique. The flies were different, but perhaps the methods of fishing them were

Local knowledge is always useful: sharing a joke with Stephen Cuthbert at Arnfield Reservoir, Derbyshire.

similar, for Bell was not a man to cast a long line. Bell moved around a great deal and preferred to cast a short line, allowing the three flies on his leader to sink a little before retrieving them slowly. It was still a recognizable traditional wet-fly technique that Bell employed when fishing his new nymphs.

Alongside traditional loch-styled fishing and the imitative nymphing approach, a third style of fishing emerged during the twentieth century – lure fishing. What really gave impetus to lure fishing was the introduction of large trout, and particularly rainbow trout, to new reservoirs around the middle decades of the twentieth century. Perhaps the single most significant event that led to the popularity of lure fishing was the opening of Grafham Water, near Huntingdon, which was first stocked with trout in 1965.

When Grafham opened for fishing in 1966 I was eighteen years old but didn't have a car. It was a long way from home and I couldn't afford to get there by public transport, with the additional cost of an overnight stay somewhere. I felt that I had really missed out. The angling press was dominated by stories of anglers catching great numbers of huge trout, mainly on lures, from the newly stocked and fertile water. However, a book I then acquired made me wonder if perhaps Grafham was not quite the idyllic water I had imagined it to be. In 1952, T.C. Ivens published *Still Water Fly-Fishing* and it was one of the first books to promote a new way of fishing reservoirs using powerful rods that would cast great distances, particularly when coupled with the new shooting-head fly lines. Ivens was pretty catholic in his taste for flies and used a mixture of loch flies, nymphs and lures, with the odd dry-fly thrown in. However, he did pave the way for the 'new wave' lure approach, catalysed by the opening of Grafham, via his technological approach to tackle and long casting.

Ivens fished Grafham, yet in the enlarged third edition of *Still Water Fly-Fishing* (1970), he gives a somewhat different view of the early years on that reservoir to the picture painted in the popular angling press. In summary, while bank fishing at Grafham was initially relatively easy, it became less so as hordes of anglers ploughed up the margins, destroying marginal weeds and feeding grounds, and driving the trout farther out. Evening rises within casting distance soon became a thing of the past. It is still a typical scenario on many English reservoirs. 'Herons' stand side by side and hurl large lures as far out as they can, while the boats beyond the ploughed-up margins and all the thrashing and splashing, do rather better. It need not be like that and indeed things are beginning to settle down a little. The development of numerous small lake fisheries has taken some of the pressure off the larger waters, while the increased use of smaller flies, particularly nymphs and dries, has lessened the impact of fishing with powerful rods and heavy lines. However, on large waters, unnecessary wading is still a factor that drives trout away from the margins and it is the margins that should supply the richest supply of food. If the food is there, trout will feed very close in, particularly towards dusk, and a stealthy approach will result in their capture. Of course, waters vary considerably and I acknowledge the fact that wading may be required on the extensive shallows of a lowland reservoir, while an upland water may be quite deep close in and even dangerous to wade. Injudicious wading destroys marginal flora and fauna, which in turn means that trout have no reason to visit the margins as there is simply no food there for them. The subsequent effect of this is that trout may only be reached by anglers who are able to cast long distances, or by those fishing from boats. Unfortunately, on waters where trout do feed close in those who fish from boats often invade the margins and interfere with the sport of bank anglers. Etiquette is an essential ingredient of fly fishing and I sometimes feel that it is in short supply.

Boat Fishing

I am not going to say a great deal about boat fishing because I am only an occasional boat fisher. There are good books on boat fishing for trout and the reader could do far worse than consult an excellent recently published book by Dennis Moss (*Trout From a Boat*, 2007). The fact that I rarely fish from a boat is simply because

It is always wise to play a trout from a sitting position when boat fishing.

I am something of a landlubber and clumsy in boats. There is no doubt that fly fishing from boats is a pleasurable activity as long as the angler is competent in handling a boat (and it is always best that there are two anglers fishing together in a boat), takes the necessary safety precautions and shows respect for other boat anglers and for bank anglers in particular. All too often, however, ethical considerations are ignored: boats cut across one another; jostle for positions close to rearing cages; or ruin the sport of bank anglers. Equally, while most of us might agree that our society has become too health and safety obsessed, there are still too many boat fishers who take little care of their personal safety. The most common error is to stand up to cast from a boat in alarmingly rough conditions, so that the boat rocks from side to side and is in danger of taking on water.

There are as many ways of fishing from a boat as there are from the bank: dry-flies; wet-flies; nymphs; lures; on the surface; just below the surface; deep down; with a static fly; slow retrieve; fast retrieve; and so on. The boat may be anchored, or the angler may prefer to drift in order to cover a greater area of water. Traditional wet-fly fishing from a boat is a pretty specific technique, as it implies fishing close to the surface with traditional wet-flies and from a slowly drifting boat. The fact that traditional wet-fly fishing is practised on the drift means that the angler must ensure that the chosen drift does not interfere with the sport of other anglers.

I don't know quite why, but there was a spell in the 1960s when traditional wet-fly fishing from boats seemed to get a lot of stick in angling literature. One author accused boat fishers of a lack of imagination, suggesting that they always used the same few flies no matter what the conditions; hardly a crime I thought. The other principal criticism levelled at boat fishers was that they practised a very dull and repetitive method during a drift. The description would run something like: 'as they drift along they mindlessly make repeated casts in front of themselves, drawing their flies back across the water, and then when they reach the end of the drift they row all the way back to start the monotonous process all over again'. I assure you that the above criticism was not unusual and it is little more than a paraphrase of a passage written by a well-known angler.

The author's ideal boat fishing conditions.

To be fair, the suggestion that wet-fly fishing from a drifting boat is somewhat boring has been around for a long time and I am sure it is a criticism generally made by those who have not tried it. Even as long ago as 1924, when R.L. Bridgett published *Loch Fishing in Theory and Practice*, the author found it necessary to counter the idea that traditional boat fishing was unscientific and monotonous, writing:

A very serious reproach has been cast against the loch fisher. It has been declared that loch fishing is only a game of chuck-and-chance-it, not at all entitled to the dignity of the name of sport. In many cases the charge is deserved, but loch fishing is not necessarily such a poor game, any more than river fishing must needs be scientific.

In the above passage, Bridgett is referring specifically to the boat fisher when he uses the term 'loch fisher' and he then proceeds to refute the accusations levelled at loch fishing in an illuminating and erudite manner.

The fact that I only fish occasionally from a boat has nothing to do with the belief that it is boring and everything to do with an overdeveloped wariness of boats. I enjoy boat fishing when there is a nice ripple and when my son, Christopher, handles the boat! A gentle breeze prolongs a drift without the need for a

drogue and facilitates pleasant fishing – but rough conditions are simply not for me. Bridgett, however, provides some advice for boat fishers faced with rough weather:

'... when gales are out and the loch is very wild, the lee of a wood, besides being the only comfortable part, is capable of making the hours pass pleasantly. Flies and caterpillars are blown off the trees, and the trout soon learn that something is being provided for their sustenance. The boat moves quietly along the calm belt; the angler is sheltered from the gale; the flies search the edge of the troubled waters, and not in vain.'

How comforting it all sounds, yet I am left wondering what unpleasantness there was to be experienced in voyaging towards 'the lee of the wood' and how Bridgett got back to shore again after passing his hours so pleasantly! Thus, as a realist, I remain very cautious about boats and shudder when I see white crests of waves on the water. For me, it has to be settled weather and a gentle ripple at most, before I will venture forth and yet, in spite of my wariness of boats, I view traditional wet-fly fishing from boats in a rather romantic way. I remember being on holiday in Scotland once as a boy, I cannot recall where it was, but we sat by a crystal clear river a short distance from where it tumbled into a loch. Although it was a warmish spring day there was drizzle in the distance and a rainbow arching over a shroud of mist that covered most of the loch. It was a scene that Turner would have relished painting. A boat materialized out of the mist. Two anglers were drifting broadside to the gentle waves and taking turns to cast short lines from long rods with a rhythmic grace that was as hypnotic as it was aesthetically pleasing. As one of the anglers raised his rod and held it aloft, there was a splash and he had a fish on. It was perhaps the most evocative angling scene I have imprinted on my memory. Observing those anglers on that unnamed loch, the last thing that came to mind was that they were practising a boring 'chuck-and-chance-it' method.

As an occasional boat fisher I do not count myself competent to talk of technicalities such as oars, petrol engines, electric motors, drogues and other equipment. Suffice it to say that I would hardly ever require a drogue when only fishing on pretty calm days. My approach to boat fishing is therefore to offer some general principles and those too of a personal nature. The first principle is that I regard boat fishing as fishing the wet-flies close to the surface, which even lends itself to the inclusion of a dry-fly on the top dropper. Using a long rod and floating line, casts are generally short and made downwind so that the team of flies unfurls gently in front of the boat and is then retrieved a little quicker than the drift of the boat. As the flies near the boat, the rod is lifted and the top dropper fly dibbled on the surface before recasting. The flies are on, or in, the water for most of the time, so that the chances of catching trout are maximized. It is a straightforward enough technique, though a little amplification will not go amiss.

It may be thought that fishing close to the surface is very limiting. When trout are rising all around the boat confidence is obviously boosted, but for much of the time trout also lie close to the surface without actually showing themselves and it is psychologically important to believe that they are there. Once a fish has been hooked, or even felt, then belief is reinforced. On the other hand, even when obvious rises are not in evidence, there may be signs that trout are present and the observant angler will read these signs. There may be, for example, a slight bulging in the water, or a flattening of the surface in a ripple and these are sure signs that trout are feeding on nymphs, pupae or drowned flies just under the surface. In open water, the presence of numbers of birds may also help to locate fish; where, for example, swallows and martins swoop low over the water to take hatching flies, there may be trout close to the surface feeding on ascending nymphs or pupae. If fishing close to the surface with a floating line proves fruitless, then a slow-sinking line may be employed so that the flies fish a little deeper. This may require a rather longer cast in order to ensure that the flies sink before they are brought back again with a figure-of-eight retrieve.

Bridgett was of the opinion that the flies used for surface fishing should be changed when fishing a little deeper down, because flies 'cannot represent surface insects and subaqueous creatures equally well', but I feel he overstates the case. A cast with a Peter Ross or Butcher on the point, a Mallard and Claret, Teal and Green,

A good rainbow trout taken on a Peter Ross.

Teal and Yellow, or Connemara Black on the middle dropper, and an Invicta, Palmer or Black and Peacock Spider on the top dropper, will work at any level in the water, as will other combinations of flies. Where I do agree with Bridgett is in his assertion that a boat fisher should not fish at anchor but should cover as much water as possible. While river trout are able to hold a position because their food will be swept down to them by the current, trout in lakes and reservoirs are compelled to search around for their food. Even when a chosen drift yields not a single take, it is always worth covering the same line again – what might have been a fishless area can suddenly become fruitful as the trout move into it. The fact that a drift does not produce a fish close to the surface does not automatically mean that they are feeding at a greater depth; it could simply be that they are feeding close to the surface somewhere else. The generally nomadic nature of stillwater trout sometimes makes them difficult to locate and this may be daunting on great expanses of water where local knowledge becomes invaluable. On small lakes and reservoirs it is easy enough to cover all the water and to be assured that fish are never very far away.

There are, however, features on lakes and reservoirs that will regularly hold fish. These features are often close to the shore and may be fished comfortably from the bank, although a drifting boat provides a different approach to the ways in which they may be covered. Any drift close to the shore should not be at the expense of bank anglers fishing in that location. A drop-off, where the marginal shallows fall away to deeper water, is an attractive feature and this is the attraction of islands as well as the main shoreline. Shallow and rocky shores hold good supplies of food, such as caddis larvae or shrimps, or insects that have drifted there and collect between the boulders, but it may be dangerous to drift the boat too close and there is always a good chance that the flies will become snagged. Tree-lined shores, often difficult or impossible to fish from the bank, are good areas to drift along, for the trees may supply a constant source of terrestrial insects for hungry trout. On breezy days, calm lanes form near the shore and are among the best of drifts. To the annoyance of

the bank angler, calm lanes are frequently just out of casting distance, but are an easy target for the boat angler. Flies collect in calm lanes, particularly on the edges of them, and trout are attracted in numbers; it is usual to see rises and bulges all along the length of the calm lane. However, these trout can be easily scared by an injudicious and clumsy cast.

There are plenty of other features where more than a single drift may be called for. Drifting alongside weed beds on broad shallows may be lucrative as the vegetation holds great supplies of food. Shallow and silty bays, unless they have been denuded by careless wading, are worth focusing on at certain times of the season, because they may be home to legions of chironomids and even mayfly nymphs on some waters. It is likely, however, that when such areas are consistently producing good numbers of fish they will be the occupied by legions of bank anglers. Feeder streams are worth a number of casts and any decent stream will form a strong current well out into the lake or reservoir. While the current sweeps items of food out into the main body of water it also provides the advantage for trout of more oxygenated water during hot spells of weather. It may thus provide activity when other areas of the lake or reservoir seem dormant and is a good bet in July and August.

The basic mechanics of traditional wet-fly fishing from a boat are simple enough, but it is worth considering them again lest this technique should be confused with other methods of boat fishing. Unless a boatman is employed, two anglers sit side by side in the boat and drift broadside with the wind at their backs; of course, the boat may require occasional adjustment to maintain the drift. Short-casting in front of the boat, or a little to the left, or to the right, the anglers take care not to tangle one another, which necessitates casting alternately. Boat partners who become used to one another develop a fluent and rhythmic sequence. Casts made to the left or right across the wind at a 45-degree angle are generally more effective than casts made straight downwind, for the ripple brings the flies round in a most attractive manner. The use of a long rod and light line allows the flies to be gently unfurled in front of

This trout swirled at the top dropper, then took the point fly.

the boat and provides maximum control of the flies. Once a cast has been made, the flies are retrieved slowly after a slight pause and the retrieve should be made just a little more quickly than the drift of the boat. During the retrieve, it is important to gather the line bunched in the hand, for line that is simply dropped into the boat will undoubtedly tangle and usually when a fish has just taken.

A trout may take when the flies first alight on the water (or shortly afterwards, which is why it is best to pause before starting the retrieve), or at any point during the retrieve, yet the deadliest point may well be at the very end of the retrieve. As the flies approach the boat on the retrieve, the long rod is raised so that the flies themselves rise in the water, not that they will have been fishing very deep anyway, and the top dropper fly is dibbled on the surface rather after the manner of a hatching aquatic insect or struggling terrestrial. There is a swirl and the rod may almost be ripped from your hands. It is exciting stuff. Clearly, it was the movement of the top dropper fly at the surface that attracted a trout's attention, but, perhaps more often than taking the top dropper, a fish will swirl without taking and then turn to take one of the other flies on the cast. The top dropper fly will have still have done

its job in attracting a fish, but this kind of short rising emphasizes the fact that if the top dropper fly is not taken cleanly, then it is wise not to whisk the flies from the water and thus risk missing a potential take to the other flies.

While the disturbance caused at the surface is useful in attracting a trout's attention, there are anglers who prefer to allow the top dropper simply to rest statically on the surface at the end of the retrieve and this technique too is often successful. In this case, however, a buoyant dry-fly is preferable to a wet-fly. This is often termed the 'hang' method and as the top dropper remains at the surface the other two flies will hang down in the water. When using a long rod and short line it is possible to bring the top dropper fly to the surface at some distance from the boat, yet it is surprising how close to the boat a fish may be prepared to take. Of course, the boat angler is at liberty to take this to the extreme by practising the ancient art of dapping – but that would call for at least another chapter and we would be wandering too far from the art of the wet-fly.

Maximizing the length of time that the top dropper remains at the surface is extremely useful when sedges (or caddis flies) are in evidence and scuttling around on the surface.

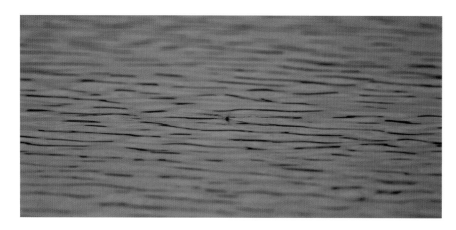

Sometimes a static bob-fly is taken: any second now!

This may well be on a summer's evening when trout signal their interest with the most obvious of slash takes. At such times, an Invicta, Green Peter or Red Palmer (Soldier Palmer) pays dividends on the top dropper. Flies tied with grouse, woodcock and bronze mallard wings, and in a variety of body colours, may be used on the point and middle dropper. An alternative approach is to combine wet-fly and dry-fly techniques by using a buoyant dry-fly on the top dropper. In this role it is difficult to better a G & H Sedge, or even a small Muddler, for the wake emanating from these flies emulates the disturbance caused by skittering naturals and attracts the trout's attention.

While boat anglers develop a smooth rhythm when fishing their wet-flies – cast, pause, retrieve, dibble or hang, recast and so on – it is important that the process does not become too mechanistic. For example, at any point during the retrieve the angler must look for trout showing in a different direction so that they may be covered quickly. The long rod and light floating line provide a further advantage here, in that they enable the angler to lift the line smoothly from the water and to recast in a different direction. As the flies are fishing close to the surface it is easy to lift the line from the water, but it would be rather more difficult when using a sinking line.

Repeated casting can become tiring and a heavy rod will soon make the wrist ache. A light and traditionally actioned wet-fly rod allows the angler to flip out the flies in a relaxed manner, with the minimum of effort, and it does not bear

comparison with the use of stiff and powerful reservoir rods and heavy sinking lines. It is often said that the most exciting thing in fly fishing is seeing a trout rise to take a dry-fly, but the swirl to a wet-fly close to the surface, or to a top dropper fly dibbling at the surface, is no less exciting and can certainly make the pulse race. Naturally, there will also be times when the take is signalled only by a pull during the retrieve, or even a quick movement of the line, but then I find this exciting too.

It is obviously worth casting a team of flies to any trout that shows itself, but, after an initial refusal, this must not become an obsession and begin to take over from the rhythm of the traditional technique. All too often, we cast towards the ring of a rise, a splash, or boil in the water yet nothing happens and this is generally because the trout has already moved on. Sometimes it is easy enough to spot the feeding path of a fish and to cast a little way ahead of it, yet trout can move quite quickly when searching for food in lakes and reservoirs. It is wise not to get trapped into 'trout chasing', for it is rarely a productive pastime. A couple of refusals from a fish that has been spotted may indicate a lack of interest on the part of the trout, although it is more likely to be the case that it has simply moved on. When trout are on the move, it is far better to target a general area of activity from a drifting boat than to waste too much time targeting individual fish. Patience is required, but if trout are in the general vicinity they will find the angler's flies eventually. If they do, yet the angler witnesses only a swirl rather than a solid take, it pays not to be too hasty in lifting the flies off the water. As we have seen previously, a trout may rise short to the top dropper fly yet take other flies on the cast, but it is not unknown for a fish seemingly to refuse the top dropper more than once before actually taking it. Trout often swirl at large natural insects in order to drown them before taking them cleanly underwater and the same process may occur with respect to large artificial flies employed on the top dropper. On the other hand, we may possibly overestimate both a trout's eyesight and its ability to aim its rise accurately at all times. An apparent refusal could therefore be little more than a clumsy miss and this was the opinion of R.L. Bridgett when he wrote:

> Sometimes it will miss the fly altogether; in fact that is a frequent occurrence on the loch, and it need occasion no surprise, for the play of light,

the vagaries of the lure influenced by the wind and wave, and the length of the journey all tend to make it difficult for a trout to locate its prey unerringly.

In clear water I have seen trout rise from the deep and miss the fly, only to take it a second time once they are already close to the surface. Bridgett may well be right and this emphasizes the fact that we should never be too hasty in removing our flies from the water.

Boat fishing is a pleasant pastime in fairly clement weather, but, personally, I wouldn't set foot in a boat if there was the slightest chance of a squall. It is not very pleasant in a boat either during torrential rain, even when the angler is wearing the best foul-weather gear that money can buy. I enjoy boat fishing when the conditions suit me, but it is now time to step onto dry land.

The all-through fighting curve of a good loch rod.

Bank Fishing

The lessons learned from boat fishing will stand us in good stead when we fish from the bank. It is still a matter of using a long rod and light line, of short-casting our flies close to the surface and of covering as much water as possible. Further, the kind of productive locations identified as good boat drifts will also be promising areas to explore from the bank and this certainly necessitates being on the move. There is much to recommend traditional wet-fly fishing from the bank; it may be practised in the roughest weather when even the most confident boat fisher thinks twice before setting out. As far as possible, loch-styled bank fishing amounts to an attempt to replicate the techniques of the boat fisher, so that it is far removed from the use of heavy lines and powerful rods. For this reason, it is best that we emulate Dr Bell and seek quieter banks away from the crowds of anglers ploughing up the shallows. Where it is quiet and there is food enough in the margins, short casts will often find trout feeding close to the bank, particularly at first light or in the evening. We will undoubtedly make a few longer casts to reach trout we have spotted feeding further out, but distance-casting will certainly not dominate the way we fish.

Where the banks of a stillwater are overgrown, and casting is only possible from little pockets between bushes, then I would probably choose to use a single nymph or dry-fly for such waters do not lend themselves to the kind of wet-fly technique I have in mind. My ideal location for fishing a team of traditional wet-flies would be a long stretch of bank providing easy access to cast and walk, and a gentle to stiffish breeze blowing along it so that I can flip out the flies and drift them round – if there is a calm lane then so much the better. As I progress along the bank I will encounter fairly uniform stretches that may be covered relatively quickly but other features may entice me to linger a while. On upland reservoirs and lochs the water can be quite deep close to the banks which, being barren of trees, allows the angler to cover the maximum amount of water, forever casting and moving, casting and moving. Being constantly on the move means travelling light. Too many anglers encumber themselves with so much gear that they become rooted to a single spot; travelling light allows the angler to explore a much greater area of the banks.

A Perfect Day's Fishing

It is rare for us to encounter perfect fishing conditions and this is why we have so many excuses for poor catch rates and blank days – it was too hot or too cold, there was no breeze, or it was far too windy, and so on. However, it is time that I treated myself to a perfect day. I am

The long and pliant wet-fly rod also cushions fine leaders: no need to grimace when playing a good fish!

Not quite ideal conditions: not much of a breeze but an inky sky might produce a decent day.

right-handed and as I stand by the water there is a nice breeze blowing from right to left along the bank so that I can cast easily over my right shoulder. I like it that way. I prefer to use a light floating line, fish the flies slowly, and keep them close to the surface. The sky is a little overcast, but there are a few rays of sun peeping through and although there is a breeze, it is quite warm. Before fishing, I treat the leader with a thin smear of Fuller's Earth so that it sinks a little and doesn't glint on the surface when the sun shines through the clouds.

It ought to be a day when insects hatch in numbers, but there isn't much evidence of this and only the odd terrestrial has been blown onto the water. I will begin fishing with a standard trio of flies and make changes when any natural insects are in evidence. At the moment, the game seems to be to attract a bit of interest from a trout or two and to make a reasonable start to the day. I am going to commence fishing with a size 16 Peter Ross on the point, a size 14 Black Pennell on the middle dropper and a size 12 Black and Peacock Spider on the top dropper. The theory behind the choice of three flies for my initial cast is simple enough if not very scientific. The Peter Ross has been chosen essentially as an attractor, not only because of the flash of silver but also because black and red seem particularly attractive colours to trout. The Black Pennell, while generally attractive as a

pattern, also suggests emerging midges and I would expect them to be in evidence at some time during the day. Alternatively, a winged Blae and Black, or a Bibio, could have been used in this position. Finally, the Black and Peacock Spider just looks like it ought to be a natural creature, a beetle maybe, and a very juicy food item at that. At the moment, there is a fresh breeze and a nice ripple. However, if I had been faced with only the slightest ripple, or even calm conditions, I would probably have used a cast made up entirely of spider patterns and a good starter would be a Snipe and Purple on the point, a Greenwell Spider on the middle dropper and an Orange Partridge on the top dropper. Spider patterns are certainly not restricted to use on rivers.

It is now time to make my first cast and it will be short, no more than a rod's length or so. As I look along the bank, with the wind at my back, the cast is made at between 45 and 60 degrees from the bank, so that the line will swing round nicely and I won't start the retrieve until the flies are quite close to the bank. It is surprising how close in trout will lie. If I were to cast at anything close to a 90-degree angle, with the wind blowing almost parallel to the bank, then the line would soon crumple into a series of curves and the flies land back at my feet in no time at all. Casting along the bank means that the flies fish effectively as the line bows round and they will

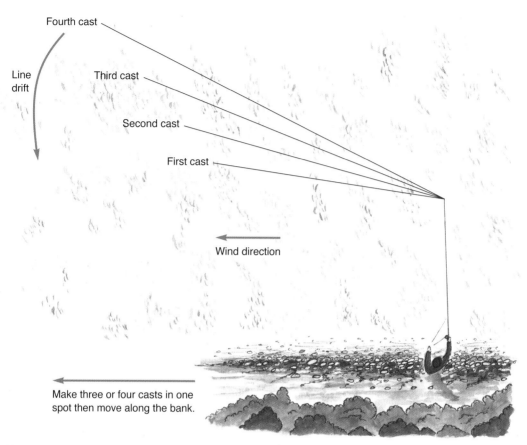

Fourth cast

Line
drift

Third cast

Second cast

First cast

Wind direction

Make three or four casts in one
spot then move along the bank.

Searching the bank with a team of loch flies.

swim for a longer period of time without the need to retrieve, although a very slow retrieve may be employed if desired.

So my first cast is made and I watch intently for a take as the flies swing slowly round, but there is no sign of a fish and once the flies have drifted within a few feet of the bank I begin a slow figure-of-eight retrieve and then raise the rod high so that the Black and Peacock Spider dances around on the surface. There is a swirl at the top dropper so I leave it there for a while, but nothing else happens. There are obviously fish around so I try the same short cast a couple more times, but without avail.

It is now time to extend the length of the cast before moving along the bank. I pull more line off the reel and make a similar cast to the first, but a little further out, and repeat the process, yet no fish shows this time. Stripping a little more line off the reel, I cast at 45 degrees from the bank, but this time, instead of allowing the flies to swing round with the breeze, I begin to retrieve as soon as the flies touch the water – slow retrieve, pause, a few little erratic pulls, pause, slow retrieve and so on. Because the retrieve was begun as soon as the flies alighted they will remain close to the surface and sometimes, when trout ignore flies on the drift, a little movement will stimulate action. And that is what happens. There is a swirl on the surface and the line is pulled from my left hand; tighten, and the first fish of the day is on. It has taken the Black Pennell and fights well enough, though it proves to be only a small rainbow of a pound or so. Nevertheless, it is bright and silver, felt like a fish twice the size, and soon recovers and shoots away once it has been released.

Moving slowly along the bank I repeat the same process, beginning with short casts and then extending the length of line, but no more than three or four casts are made in any one spot. This morning, the action seems a little slow, even though the fish are in the upper layers and occasionally show at the surface. If I thought that they were lying a little deeper and were not prepared to rise up in the water, then it might have been useful to allow the flies time to sink, or even to have experimented with a weighted fly on the point, but I know that they are close to the surface and therefore decide to replace the Black and Peacock Spider with a buoyant Red Palmer. The theory behind using a dry-fly on the top dropper is that it will not only keep the other flies close to the surface, but will also cause maximum disturbance when retrieved and when dibbled at the surface at the end of the retrieve. Further, when the flies are allowed to drift, the dry-fly provides a good indicator of a take. On this occasion I have chosen a Red Palmer because of its buoyancy, but if there were natural flies very much in evidence then I might have chosen a fly appropriate to them; for example, a black Klinkhammer would have been a good choice if black chironomid midges were emerging.

The change of fly does the trick and I catch two further fish, one to the Peter Ross on the point and one to the Black Pennell, but on each occasion the fish swirled at the Red Palmer before taking one of the other flies. Thus, the dry-fly had done its job in attracting the trout's attention, even though it may not have caught a fish in its own right. However, the fourth fish, and the heaviest so far, does fall to the Red Palmer and it takes just as I raised my rod to dibble the fly at the surface before recasting. This trout followed the flies for most of the length of the cast but did not take until the last second, presumably thinking that its prey was about to escape from the water. When it did eventually take the fly it actually hooked itself, which was perhaps as well since my concentration had wandered and I was glancing at a curlew wheeling around above. Its mournful cry had grabbed my attention and it is usually the case that trout take when the attention wanders. It is relatively rare, however, for trout to hook themselves and even when using wet-flies concentration is required to spot a taking fish. Occasionally, there will be a strong pull but takes may be gentle too, especially when the flies are

being allowed a free drift. There may be a slight draw of the line, hardly discernible, a splash, or swirl, or a mere glint of silver or gold. On several occasions I have noticed the line simply appear to sink a little, yet tightening the line has resulted in the solid feel of a fish. At other times, a sixth sense seems to kick in and I tighten into a fish without being able to explain quite why I did so. When retrieving the flies, it is not uncommon to experience an infuriating sequence of little plucks which do not seem to result in a positive take; at best, striking when you feel a pluck results in pricking a fish but that is all. The trout is clearly investigating the fly but is uncertain about it. Ignore the plucks and fish out the cast; the fish may take just as the flies are about to leave the water. If not, a change of fly is a good tactic and this is exactly how my next fish comes to the net.

Having experienced a series of plucks I am unsure as to whether the fish were nipping at the Peter Ross or the Black Pennell, or even both. They certainly weren't nipping at the top dropper fly, which would have been very evident. Thus, I decide to replace the Peter Ross with a small Mallard and Claret, with the Black Pennell being left in place for the moment. If the plucks continue, I will replace that too. On the very next cast the Mallard and Claret is taken firmly so the change of fly worked, as it often does. Anglers often change their flies too frequently, rather than their techniques, yet there are definitely times when the flies should be changed. I do this automatically each time a trout has either been pricked or lost after being hooked.

Having worked along the bank I have settled into a good rhythm and have caught a few fish. I have experimented and made a few changes as the situation dictated, but now I have reached the end of the long and fairly uniform bank and the nature of the landscape changes. Some waters are uniform and open around the whole perimeter so that we can explore the entire water systematically, but others are much more varied. When a bank is uniform we are constantly on the move, searching the length of it, but there are various features on most waters that are particularly attractive to trout and encourage us to linger a little longer; at the same time, the lack of a uniform bank may also make it impossible to move along quite so freely. I will now consider some of the features that are worthy of the bank angler's attention, though we have already made reference to them when fishing from a boat. The main difference between fishing features from the bank, rather than a boat, is that we can remain longer in one spot while fishing from the bank and therefore explore it with changes of fly, retrieve, depth and so on. Even a slowly drifting boat does not allow us to focus for long on a limited area of water.

Any feature that provides trout with shelter, or shade, and a ready supply of food, is worth special attention. While I might move quite quickly along an open bank, I will devote more time to exploring tree-lined banks, or banks bordered by gorse, bracken or shrubs and bushes. When there is a breeze terrestrials are often blown onto the water along such banks, which may also be more shaded than more open reaches. The time of year is, of course, important when fishing areas of water bounded by vegetation or trees. At different times of the year, terrestrials such as beetles, ants, caterpillars, daddy long-legs and a host of other creatures will have their significance. I particularly look forward to windy days in late April and early May, when the ungainly hawthorn fly (*Bibio marci*) can appear in great numbers and, being a poor flier, inevitably ends up on the water. In America it is known as the 'black dance fly', which is eminently appropriate given its erratic flight and long, gangling hind legs. The Black Pennell is a suitable fly to use at this time, the pheasant tippet tails suggesting the natural's long legs, although a Black Palmer fished as a top dropper creates a better impression of the fly's buzz and struggle when it lands on the water.

It would be foolish to move too quickly away from a bank where terrestrials are providing a meal for the trout and fish are showing everywhere. It may seem that a dry-fly would be the order of the day but the wet-fly works just as well, perhaps better, because terrestrial flies are easily drowned. A wet-fly retrieved just under the surface often provokes more response than a static dry-fly. Heavily vegetated banks don't make for comfortable and easy fishing and there must be an expectation that the flies will occasionally tangle in bracken on the back-cast,

or end up in a branch of a tree. Where the banks are tree-lined close to the water, a roll cast is useful, as the line can be unfurled over the water without the need for a back-cast, although this presumes that there is enough clearance for the long rod to be raised vertically. If not, a variety of side-casts are possible, whereby the back-cast is actually made parallel to the bank.

Beyond the tree-lined stretch of bank there may be a small promontory and this too is a good spot for a few extra casts and a good location to observe patrolling fish. There could be a bay at the other side, while in the lee of the promontory will be calmer water. Where the calm water of the bay meets the ripple is the most attractive area and, standing on the edge of the promontory, it becomes possible to cast out into the rippled water so that the flies drift round towards the calm water. It is likely that fish will show around the edge of the ripple as natural flies are gathered there. Let us imagine that there are great numbers of small black midges in evidence and trout are rising regularly. We are tempted to fish a small dry-fly, a Black Gnat perhaps, and it may result in a fish, yet it will have to compete with the legions of naturals and that is a tall order; the odds are quite lengthy. Often, the tiny dry-fly will be ignored, whereas wet-flies, gently twitched close to the surface, offer a contrast and attract the trout's attention through their movement. When trout are feeding on small black flies I have had success with larger black wet-flies, or even loch flies such as the Butcher and Peter Ross. That said, there are certainly occasions when trout are preoccupied and it is generally when they are swimming very close to the surface to sip in their food that they will not look at a contrasted fly. A couple of seasons ago, there was a massive fall of tiny black beetles on a local reservoir; the trout went mad for them and the only fly that stood any chance of catching a fish was a floating beetle pattern made out of black foam. Patience was certainly required in order to wait for a trout to select the artificial and spotting a take was no easy business. Many times I would strike, only to find that a fish had risen to a natural beetle close to my artificial. I am not so obsessed with the wet-fly that I do not recognize that there are times when only the dry-fly may work. It certainly pays to be flexible.

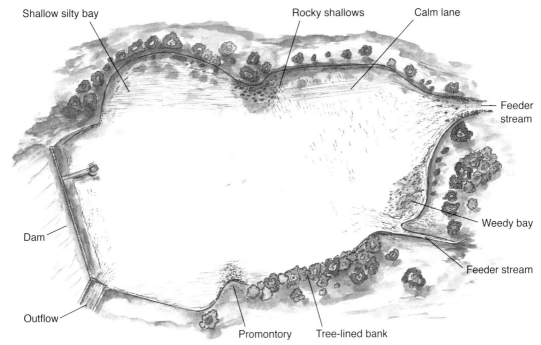

Shallow silty bay   Rocky shallows   Calm lane

Feeder stream

Weedy bay

Feeder stream

Dam

Outflow

Promontory   Tree-lined bank

Anatomy of a reservoir.

Fishing the Shallows

Shallow areas of lakes and reservoirs are often ignored, though they may be productive enough and home to a variety of aquatic insects, shrimps or corixae – providing they have not been ploughed barren through careless wading. I know of one shallow silted bay so full of bloodworms that any red fly is likely to do well, although it is also plagued by perch that tend to grab a fly before the trout have chance to react. Shallows often produce excellent weed growth and weed beds are more effectively fished from the bank rather than from a drifting boat; a boat only allows the angler to search along the edge of the weeds, whereas the bank angler can explore all the little pockets of water between the weeds. I would not choose to argue that weed beds are the exclusive domain of the wet-fly because they aren't; nymphs and dry-flies are effective too, but the wet-fly does have an advantage. While a dry-fly remains at the surface and cannot explore the deeper pockets of water between weeds, weighted nymphs easily become snagged in the weeds. It is possible, however, to sink a wet-fly, but to control it so that it doesn't sink too deeply and become snagged.

Whatever the advantages of a team of three flies in open water, the use of more than one wet-fly is not a good idea when fishing weed beds. When a trout takes a fly, the other trailing flies are almost bound to snag the weeds and even when a trout takes a single fly, keeping it away from the weeds is no easy task. Small spider patterns, such as the Orange Partridge, Snipe and Purple, Snipe and Yellow or Greenwell Spider are effective wet-flies for weed-bed fishing and also have the advantage that they will sink slowly. Nevertheless, I have also done very well when using a tiny Peter Ross or Teal and Yellow and this was a discovery I made in the early 1960s when these were among the few flies that I owned at the time. Quite why these flies should work so well around weed beds I cannot say, but they do. The weed beds I fished were full of ephemeroptera nymphs, shrimps and corixae and it would be difficult to argue that my traditional loch patterns imitated them. Nevertheless, I still think that small versions of the flies cited above are worth fishing in and around weeds. It is by no means unusual for trout to lurk right in the weeds so that fishing over the top of weed beds can also be an effective

Hooked in shallow water this trout was loath to enter the net.

method. As there may be little depth of water above the weeds, a greased leader will keep the fly close to the surface and it is less likely to scare fish than it will in open water. A stronger leader point is also recommended, as a hooked fish will inevitably plunge into the weeds.

Although I have spent time focusing on weedy areas of water, they are not the only shallows worthy of our consideration. Silted, muddy and sandy shallows may well provide plenty of insects to interest trout, although if such an area is pitted with the boot prints of wading anglers it is best ignored. Productive shallows may hold fish during the day, but these fish are likely to be very wary; however, their sense of security seems to increase as the light falls and that is when we are most likely to catch them. When the water level was dropped to repair the dam on my local reservoir it exposed a muddy expanse littered with stones of various sizes. There were also channels and gullies so that the shallows had key features and were not uniform. Being able to explore the area just after it had become exposed was very illuminating, for it was rich in feed. There were caddis larvae by the millions, the mud oozed with writhing bloodworms, while isolated pools of water in the gullies held quantities of larvae, pupae, nymphs, corixae and small fish.

I have found trout to be far less wary where there are rocky shallows strewn with protruding boulders, features common on loughs and lochs and on a number of upland reservoirs. Such marks are often quite difficult to fish from the shore and a little careful wading may be required in order to reach pockets of water between the stones, but they are often more difficult to fish from boats as there is the constant danger of crunching into an underwater hazard. Wading rocky shallows runs less of a risk of destroying the fauna than it does where there is a soft bottom rich with insect life and it is often necessary to wade in order to cast in the likeliest of spots. Trout feel relatively safe where there are boulders for cover, but the angler must still move slowly and cautiously. Shallows strewn with stones may not be as fertile as weedy shallows, but there will probably be lots of caddis larvae, small fish, beetles, corixae and even shrimps in more alkaline waters. Stoneflies, usually associated with rivers and streams, are also present on some stillwaters, particularly if there is a feeder stream nearby. When there is a good wave on the water, insects will also be washed into the rocky shallows where they collect between the stones. Those stones provide food for trout, and shelter too, but also plenty of snags to test the angler's tackle once a fish has been hooked and indeed even when one has not been hooked.

Whatever the risks, I particularly enjoy the challenge of fishing rocky shallows on rough days, when the risk of snagging the flies is high yet the trout seem less cautious. A greased leader is useful so that the flies fish close to the surface and in rough conditions a greased leader is unlikely to scare the fish. Favourite flies for fishing rocky shallows include a Butcher Spider (a wingless version of the Butcher), Orange Partridge, Snipe and Purple, Peter Ross, Black Pennell, Black and Peacock Spider, Connemara Black, Mallard and Claret and Teal and Green. I fish one rocky area of water which is extremely shallow close in and full of hazards, though it shelves away into deeper water. During rough weather it is a very productive mark and seems to attract some of the water's native brown trout, probably descendants of the original fish which inhabited the river before it was flooded to create a chain of reservoirs. The trick when fishing this mark is to cast to the deeper water and then to bring the flies over the shelf and into the hazardous shallows. Takes occur near the drop-off and in the shallows, but it is never easy to avoid snagging and it is necessary to accept that flies will be lost. I do, however, catch plenty of brown trout and the odd rainbow from that mark and although most of the 'wild' brownies are small I did have one beautiful fish which weighed just short of 2lb. It took a Connemara Black.

Dam Walls

Dam walls are known to be good fishing spots on reservoirs, but if they attract hordes of other anglers, as they often do, they lose their appeal for the mobile wet-fly fisher. The appeal of dams is that they often facilitate easy access to deep water, which means that they are usually fished with sinking lines regardless of the fact that trout often feed close to the surface. Trout are more likely to feed in the upper layers as the season warms up and may be deeper down early in the season. However, given the topsy-turvy weather we have experienced recently, a warm spell just before the start of the season may result in trout feeding close to the surface as early as March. I have even seen trout rising to hatching midges on a mild day in February. Even if trout are

feeding deep down, a team of wet-flies will catch fish when a sinking line is used and traditional wets have the advantage of fishing effectively when retrieved slowly, whereas large lures often need to be positively ripped back. I find lure stripping quite tedious and tiring. In contrast, smaller loch flies can be fished in a more leisurely fashion with a variety of slow retrieves; the flies themselves stand up to the trout's scrutiny, providing more of an impression of something edible, so that the trout takes the fly because its feeding instinct has been stimulated. I admit that I am generalizing and that there are lures that do stimulate a feeding instinct by emulating an escaping item of prey; a Muddler, for example, is a pretty good imitation of a minnow, while various streamers suggest other small fish or leeches. That said, it still remains true that lures generally have to be fished more quickly than traditional loch flies. When fishing dams, and trout are not evident at the surface, nor are obliging when we retrieve the flies soon after they alight, the flies should be allowed to sink and be timed as they do so. Takes 'on the drop', which are quite likely, will then identify the feeding depth, so that each subsequent cast may be timed before beginning a retrieve. However, trout do not always feed deep down off dams.

When a strong wind blows onto, or along, a dam, food items are washed onto it and trout may well feed close to the bank and near to the surface. The traditional wet-fly does well under such conditions, although it is not necessarily comfortable fishing; casting can be tricky, calling for a heavier rod and line than we would normally use, and the droppers may tangle with infuriating regularity. Conversely, a wind blowing over the top of the dam can produce ideal wet-fly conditions. When the water close to the dam is calm and sheltered, so that the wind produces rougher water a little way off the dam, then the edge of the ripple is where wind-blown insects will collect and adult flies emerge. It is a key feeding zone and ideal for fishing our flies if it is within casting range of the dam wall. With any breeze at our back, casting at distance is relatively easy and we should leave our flies to drift around the edge of the ripple for as long as possible before retrieving them. As we want the flies to remain close to the surface, it is a good idea to use a dry-fly on the top dropper, which may be taken in its own right, but also acts as an indicator of takes to the wet-flies.

When fishing fairly statically in this manner, winged loch flies are less effective than other designs of fly. Soft-hackled spider patterns are a good bet, particularly the Snipe and Purple, Black Spider and Greenwell Spider, as are hackled patterns such as the Black and Purple Pennells and palmers dressed with cock hackles such as the Red Palmer (Soldier Palmer) or Bibio. Of course, when trout are rising, a single dry-fly may be used, but the combination of dry-fly and wet-fly hedges our bets. While palmers are good top dropper dry-flies, Klinkhammers are also effective, but for rougher water I would choose a really buoyant dry-fly such as a G & H Sedge or even a Mini-Muddler.

I suppose that my favourite situation is when a gentle to medium-strong breeze blows along the dam so that I can work along it in the same manner that I would fish any straight stretch of bank. If the breeze is stiffish and from right to left, I work systematically along the bank, casting short and gradually increasing the length of the cast, letting the flies drift round and then retrieving them again. After a few casts in one spot, I move along the bank until the whole of the dam has been covered, or, as is usually the case, I get nearer to another angler. However, if the breeze is only gentle, and it is possible to cast into the wind as well as cast with the wind at my back, then it is worth experimenting with the 'fan' method. The fan method involves thorough coverage of water from a single spot on the dam. A short cast is made to the right (into the breeze) and the next cast a little to the left of that and so

The edge of the ripple is where wind-blown insects collect and adult flies emerge.

A good ripple along the dam: this trout took a Muddler Palmer on the top dropper.

on until the whole fan of water to the right of us, directly in front and to the left of us has been covered. Each cast allows a little experimentation with styles of retrieve. Once the first fan has been completed, the process is then repeated with a longer length of line and repeated again until the limit of casting distance has been reached; each 'fan' will thus have covered a greater area of water. A series of fans is perhaps executed with the flies fishing close to the surface and then further fans with the flies fishing a little deeper down, so that eventually a large area of water will have been searched at different depths and with a variety of retrieves.

The fan is the antithesis of the mobile method of fishing, for it takes some time to fish a single spot, but it is a useful ploy on crowded walls when it is impossible to walk the length of the dam. Mobile fishing involves moving along to find our quarry, but it must be remembered that stillwater trout move about, so that what may be empty water one minute may hold fish the next. Thus, when exploring a single spot with the fan method it may seem initially fruitless but there should always be the expectation that a fish or two will soon show up. Recently stocked trout often move up and down the dam wall in shoals, but there isn't much fun fishing for them. It is amusing, however, when the dam is lined with anglers, to see rods bending in sequence as the shoal of stockies moves up and down the dam, presumably becoming a smaller and smaller shoal by the minute.

Dam walls are not always uniform and there are often key points that consistently yield the best fish, sometimes in the corners of the dam, sometimes near an outflow, or sometimes where there is a deeper hole. The hole may be a product of a dam wall that is beginning to break up, a not uncommon feature of some upland waters, and I once marked such a spot with a little stick and caught a number of good trout from that position, whereas most of the trout caught elsewhere along the dam were considerably smaller. Holes in the bank and cracks between stones also harbour fish fry, minnows and sticklebacks and there are times when good trout will come very close in to feed on them; at these moments, a cast including flies such as the Peter Ross, Butcher and Teal, Blue and Silver should be brought into play. Finally, dam walls must be fished with care for they can be steep, slippery and uneven.

Feeder Streams

Feeder streams are among the most lucrative features and even the smallest of them will attract fish, especially in warm weather when it provides more oxygen-rich water. I recall one small feeder, not much more than a trickle really, that always held a good trout at the point where it entered the reservoir. Larger feeder streams will carry a current well out into the main body of water and will also form a deeper fish-holding channel, and while the extremity of the current may only be reached from a boat, the channel may be fished well enough from the bank. Indeed, large feeder streams may allow the bank angler to fish some way up them in addition to being able to cast into the current entering the lake or reservoir, thus adding the variety of river fishing to loch or reservoir fishing. A feeder stream should be regarded almost as a river micro-habitat, for it may produce insects, for example stoneflies or reed smuts, that do not occur in the main body of water. The stocking of sterile fish no longer means that feeder streams are plagued by black and out of condition rainbows early on in the season, although towards the end of the season spawny browns may be hanging around before they enter the stream to breed. Fishing for them is then a matter of ethics.

One of my favourite feeder streams produced such a strong current that it could be seen flowing strongly into the reservoir for quite some distance before arching to the right and dissipating. Standing at the point where the water entered, flies could be cast into the strong current and as it took hold; a strong pull was felt and more line was paid out so that the flies were swept out into the reservoir. This meant constantly stripping line from the reel and waggling the rod tip to pay it out into the current, all the while being prepared for a wrenching take from a big trout and some of them were very big. If there was no slack line, it was impossible to miss a take, for the line would simply rip away and the rod tip lurch over as the fish hooked itself. If a fish didn't take during the drift, it often took as the flies were being retrieved back against the current and it was a rare day when this feeder stream didn't produce a few fish. It is not difficult to guess that this became a very popular spot and in the end I only fished it very early in the morning when no other anglers were around and it was still dark. In the darkness the current foamed phosphorescently

into the reservoir and there was something very eerie and unsettling about it. I caught some of my largest rainbows before dawn, but then wearied of the ease with which these fish succumbed and went off to look for more of a challenge.

Feeder streams do not always provide easy fishing, but it is wise not to neglect them during the dog days when the hot weather may sour the appetite of most fish. Broken water absorbs more oxygen than relatively static water, so that during warm weather the area around a feeder stream will be oxygen-enriched and trout require oxygen as well as food. When the water is oxygen-depleted they are unlikely to feed. The feeder stream thus provides trout with the oxygen that makes them physiologically able to feed and provides a source of food too. A stream entrance effectively produces a different eco-system from the rest of the stillwater and while this may include insect species normally associated with rivers, it will also produce an enriched habitat in the loch, lake or reservoir. The stream washes silt deposits into the main body of water and these build up alongside the channel formed by the current. Weeds begin to grow in the silt and these weeds provide a home for several species of nymphs and other aquatic creatures. Thus, feeder streams offer extremely attractive features – although to the extent that they may become too popular, too easy, or both.

The Calm Lane

Unless there is a severe drought, feeder streams offer permanent features for us to focus on, but another key feature of stillwater fishing, the calm lane, is transient and when it does exist it may be infuriatingly beyond the reach of the bank angler. Often, a calm lane will drift in and out of casting range, and the trout with it, and there is nothing more frustrating. This may be where the boat fisherman scores. A long calm lane, parallel to the shore, and that shore a great expanse of accessible straight bank, is something we dream of yet rarely encounter. Calm lanes form under windy conditions, even when it is quite rough, and there may even be several calm lanes parallel to the bank. Trout congregate in the calmer water of these zones in order to feed on the food items which collect there, terrestrial and aquatic flies alike, and fish usually reveal their presence with rises and boils as they patrol up and down these zones. Apart from any insects that are blown into calm lanes, emerging insects often become trapped in the meniscus of the calmer water. While it may still be possible to catch a fish away from the calm lane, it is likely that most takes will occur either within it or close to its edge. That is where the trout are. The most sensible approach to calm lanes is to adopt a kind of dead-drift technique whereby you cast into the zone and, as the flies begin to drift, move slowly along the bank to keep pace with them; it has sometimes been referred to as 'walking the fly'. Occasionally, depending on the wind and surface drift, it may be necessary to recast, although it is often possible to drift the flies for some distance with a single cast. Trout will be in the calm lane somewhere, so it is important to resist the temptation to cast and recast repeatedly; this may simply scare the fish and ruin our chances. Even though it may be generally quite windy, trout in the calm lane are easily scared, so that presentation of the flies needs to be accurate and delicate.

I would argue that standard loch flies are inappropriate for calm lanes and it is better to fish them with tiny soft-hackled spiders and a fine leader; a small Bibio is a good choice for the top dropper as it has enough buoyancy, dressed with cock hackles, to keep the other flies close to the surface. The Bibio also has enough 'buzz' to suggest a struggling insect, yet it is still a small fly and unlikely to scare easily spooked fish. Flies such as the Black Spider, Snipe and Purple or Greenwell Spider are good choices of wet-flies for calm lanes and they should be cast into the calm lane with the Bibio on the top dropper resting right on the edge. I am not saying that a dry-fly will not work when fishing calm lanes – it will – but I think that I hook more fish on spider patterns than on dries. When fishing either wets or dries I never see a problem with greasing the cast in rough water, but this is definitely not a good idea when fishing a calm lane. The trout will not be more than a couple of feet down,

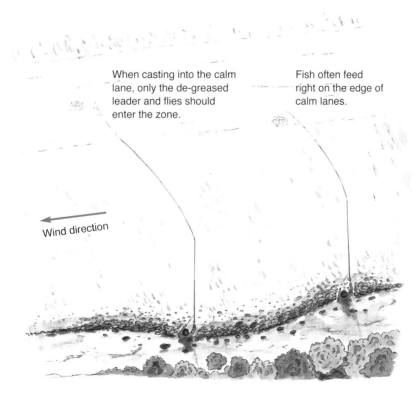

When casting into the calm lane, only the de-greased leader and flies should enter the zone.

Fish often feed right on the edge of calm lanes.

Wind direction

Fishing calm lanes.

often even closer to the surface, and a fine degreased leader is essential if we are to avoid scaring wary trout. Of course, the portion of leader above the top dropper may be greased, since it will be out of the calm lane and in the ripple; greasing this part of the leader will prevent the top dropper from being dragged under and will aid line control. When it is necessary to recast, the flies must be inched gently out of the calm lane before the line is lifted off the water, otherwise the disturbance may ruin our chances of a fish.

Calm lanes can provide excellent sport from the bank if the right approach is adopted. However, the cynic in me believes that some supernatural force designed them to torture anglers. Just when you think you have cracked it, and will undoubtedly take your limit of trout, the calm lane inevitably drifts out beyond your reach. I hate calm lanes!

Small Lake Fisheries

In the present chapter I am aware that I have made no references to the many small lake fisheries that exist throughout Britain, but traditional wet-fly techniques are no less effective on commercial fisheries. It depends on the size of lake, but experience suggests that small flies are best – soft-hackled spider patterns and scaled-down loch flies. I do not think that a team of three flies is necessarily appropriate for small fisheries and, in any case, more than a single fly is usually contrary to the rules, essentially because of the risk of multiple hook-ups. Searching for trout on large waters can sometimes be challenging, whereas small lakes provide the angler with a psychological boost – you know that there are fish pretty close to you wherever you stand on the banks. I have neglected small lakes in recent years, probably because of my aversion to the growing obsession with stocking huge rainbows and bizarre strains of trout. The alchemist's pursuit of golden trout holds little appeal. However, commercial lakes which have that 'natural' feel to them are pleasant enough places to fish with the wet-fly.

7 SOFT-HACKLED FLIES (NORTH-COUNTRY FLIES, OR 'SPIDERS')

Introduction

The wet-flies featured in the present chapter are variously referred to as 'soft-hackled flies', 'north-country flies', 'north-country spiders' or simply 'spiders' and it is difficult to decide on a single title. They are called 'north-country flies' because most of them originated in the north of England, but these wet-flies have gained increasing popularity in North America where they are appropriately termed 'soft-hackled flies'. The term 'spider' is perhaps the oldest name for this type of fly and I imagine that it originated because the long-fibred sparse hackles had a spidery appearance. Perhaps the term 'soft-hackled flies' is the most appropriate and I will *try* to adopt that term, yet I will inevitably lapse into calling them 'spiders' for the simple reason that it has become a habit.

It is easy enough to recognize this style of fly dressed with a slim body of plain silk, or silk tinged with fur, and a couple of turns of hackle, either from a game bird or from poultry. There is no wing and no tail; indeed, no fly could be of simpler design yet commercially dressed patterns often bear little resemblance to the originals. They are inevitably too large and overdressed, lacking the delicacy of original dressings and hardly suggestive of natural creatures. As W.H. Aldam's *Quaint Treatise* informs us, the task is to imitate 'thoes small beautiful tender dellagate and nate water bred Duns that ought to be the Anglers coppiing'. Thus soft-hackled flies, seemingly so simple and easy to dress, are just as easy to get completely wrong, yet when tied correctly are among the most effective wet-flies ever developed. Their effectiveness is by no means confined to river fishing – some of them are excellent stillwater patterns.

It would be easy enough, like Pritt, or Edmonds and Lee, to devote a whole book to soft-hackled wet-flies and indeed I have done just that in *A Handbook of North Country Trout Flies* (Old Vicarage Publications, 1988). In a single chapter it is therefore only possible to cover the essentials of materials and dressing techniques, while offering a small selection of flies chosen from the hundreds of patterns developed over the centuries. However, I believe that the flies selected here are among the best tried and tested patterns. It is likely that a limited number of names come to mind when soft-hackled flies are discussed, names such as Jackson, Theakston, Pritt, Edmonds and Lee (with the addition of Leisenring and Nemes in America), but many of the patterns made famous by these authors had their origins centuries before. The dressings were passed from generation to generation, often by word of mouth, and it would be impossible to trace their originators. With some notable exceptions, the flies made famous by nineteenth-century writers were not original and had been in circulation for some time. When T.E. Pritt published *Yorkshire Trout Flies* in 1885 he inadvertently perpetuated the myth that soft-hackled flies emanated from a single county of England, whereas they were used in most counties of the north, over the border in Scotland and definitely as far south as Derbyshire and Staffordshire.

In past centuries, birds and animals killed for the pot would provide the raw materials for dressing trout flies, yet while most fishermen only made use of local game, as early as the seventeenth century, anglers with a little more brass began to use more exotic feathers and furs imported for the clothing and millinery trades. Reference back to Chapter 2, and the materials used by James Chetham in 1681, emphasizes this point. Nevertheless, wet-flies from the north of England were most commonly fashioned from furs and feathers obtained locally. Fly dressers of bygone days past were somewhat indiscriminate in their killing of birds and animals, so that the necessary conservation of protected and rare species has put many of the traditional hackle feathers off limits to the modern fly dresser. While grouse or woodcock feathers are easy enough to come by, we are hardly likely to dress flies with feathers from an owl or dotterel. There are, thankfully, good alternatives, yet in spite of renewed interest in soft-hackled flies, it is still relatively difficult to obtain all the materials required via mail order, while most fly-fishing shops now only seem to stock synthetic fly-dressing materials. Effective soft-hackled flies cannot be dressed unless we have the right materials and that is a matter we need to consider in some detail.

Materials for Soft-Hackled Flies

The materials required for tying soft-hackled spider patterns will form the basis of a tying kit that will cater for other styles of wet-fly treated in the present book.

Hooks

I will begin with hooks, because even if we obtain the appropriate materials for dressing spider patterns, wrapping them around the wrong kind of hook will create a quite different kind of fly. In providing the dressings of soft-hackled patterns I will quote appropriate sizes of hooks, but to quote a size 14 or 16, for example, is meaningless unless the reader has some idea of the hook I have in mind. There are a bewildering number of makes and types of hooks on the market today and one manufacturer's packet of size 16 hooks

may contain much larger hooks than a packet from another maker. The weight of wire, length of shank and width of gape all have a bearing on what the hook will look like. Thus, a long-shanked, wide-gaped size 14 hook, fashioned from heavy wire, will be much heavier and larger than a size 14 hook with a short shank, narrow gape and made out of fine wire.

The first thing required of a hook for soft-hackled flies is that it should be made out of fine wire, which not only produces a light fly but encourages us to dress a slim body. The shank of the hook should be short, or medium-short, and the gape should be about average: too wide a gape and the fly is unbalanced, while a very narrow gape impairs the hooking qualities. Wide-gaped hooks are also inappropriate because the point of the hook will get caught up with the hackle fibres. Some hooks are curved for most of their length, useful for pupae and shrimps but not for soft-hackled flies, which require a straight shank and a neat round bend. I prefer straight-pointed hooks and although hooks with offset points are said to provide better hooking qualities, I have not found this to be the case and such hooks seem to break easily or bend out of shape. Today, barbless hooks are to be preferred for river fishing, although barbs can be closed quite easily with needle-nose pliers without damaging the hooks. It is actually cheaper to de-barb hooks than to purchase barb-less hooks, which are, quite ludicrously, dearer. Given that we are increasingly encouraged to catch and release, would it not be a good idea to sell barbless hooks cheaper than barbed hooks? There is, however, a theory that barbless hooks are more likely than barbed hooks to create a tear in a trout's mouth during the fight. I think that there is some truth in this, so that barbless hooks with arrow head points (produced by Partridge) are a good idea, as they provide a better purchase and are less likely to work backwards and forwards, thus producing a tear. Hooks are a matter of personal choice and once you have found a hook to your liking buy a good stock of them, because you can guarantee that they will no longer be in production when you need a new supply.

I have a liking for hooks with straight eyes, although they are not easy to come by. Hooks produced specifically for fly dressing usually have up-eyes (for dry-flies), or down-eyes (wet-flies), but I found a number of excellent coarse-fishing hooks that had straight eyes, were fine in the wire and were just the right shape for soft-hackled flies. Among them were Aiken Specimen hooks (code 1234), Drennan (code 1532) and Drennan Barbless (code 1542) and similar hooks are still available. Partridge Limerick hooks (code J1A) are suitable for soft-hackled flies, as are the Partridge Captain Hamilton International series, although I often struggled to acquire the latter hooks in small enough sizes. If they are available, Mustad also produces suitable hooks (codes 9479, 9578A, 3904 and 38943) and I have a store of these patterns that I purchased many years ago. There are new makes on the market and I am sure that many of them are very good; the fact that I omit to refer to them should not be taken as criticism of these brands, it is simply that I have not tried them.

I have experimented recently with a number of other hooks and quite like Partridge hooks made out of high carbon steel and labelled as Surehold, Upwing, Dry, Barbless; while they are intended principally for dry-flies, they don't make a bad hook for soft-hackled wets. They are fine in the wire and strong, although the shank is just a little on the long side. Turrall produces a good wet-fly profile with its Barbless Sproat Wet Fly/Nymph hooks, although they are a little thick in the wire and more suited to very rapid streams, or when fishing a little deeper; a finer-wired version is marketed as Barbless Extra-Fine Dry and although they are intended for dry-flies they are suitable for soft-hackled wet-flies. I also have some very good Kamasan hooks of different sizes in a plastic box, but, unfortunately, have lost the packaging and therefore do not know the codes. The reader would do well to learn from my mistake and to label all stored hooks so that they can be replaced like for like.

Hackle Feathers

I may be careless when it comes to hooks, but I do label my hackle feathers with great care because it does not take a great leap of the imagination to guess that the right choice of feather is fundamental to soft-hackled flies. With the exception of hen feathers taken from a cape and feathers such as the speckled back feathers used for dressing the Orange Partridge, most soft-hackled feathers are taken from the wings of birds. It is therefore much better to purchase pairs of wings than bulk-buy packets of feathers.

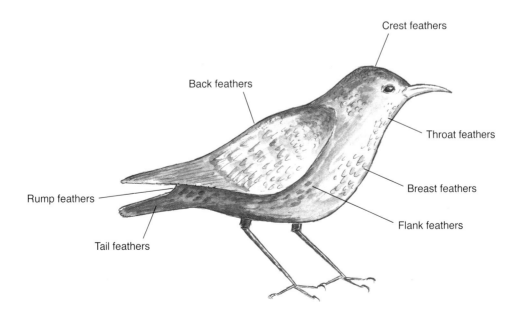

Feathers from a bird's body.

Packets of feathers may come from different parts of a bird and there aren't likely to be many small feathers of the right size, shape and colour. While grouse, woodcock, partridge and other feathers may be obtained from those who shoot, great care must be taken in cleaning, preserving and storing these feathers, so that mites do not ruin them and the rest of your fly-dressing materials.

Even when I purchase whole wings I pluck off the required hackle feathers carefully, wash them and then store them in labelled containers with a few crystals of naphthalene. (Incidentally, many of the feathers left on the wing after removing the hackle feathers will be used for other purposes; the primary and secondary wing feathers, for example, will be required for dressing winged wet-flies.) The labelling I use informs me where the feather came from and even what size of fly the hackle is suited to, as in the following examples:

- **Moorhen**: dark grey, marginal covert, top of wing (size 18)
- **Moorhen**: dark grey, lesser covert, top of wing (size 16)
- **Moorhen**: paler mid-grey, undercovert, underside of wing (size 14).

The smallest hackle feathers are usually to be found in the marginal coverts around the edge of the topside of a wing, or on the bow of a wing, although there will also be small feathers on the underside of a wing. Feathers on top of a wing are generally darker and more marked than those on the underside. The position of a feather on the wing is critical in terms of size, shape, colour, shade, patterning and even the degree of softness.

Unfortunately, there are many traditional patterns that we cannot perfectly replicate because the specified feathers are no longer available – feathers such as corncrake (or

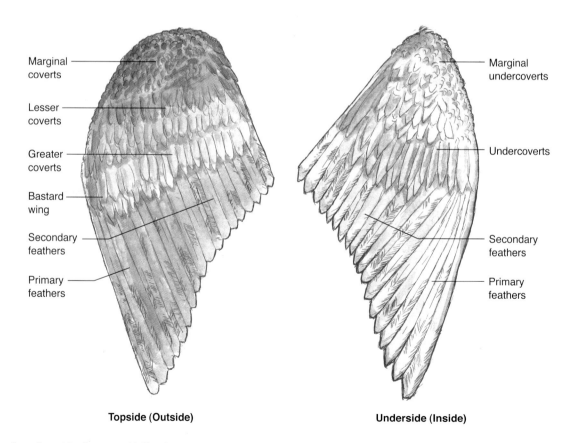

Topside (Outside)   **Underside (Inside)**

Location of feathers on a bird's wing.

landrail), dotterel, godwit, tawny owl and so on. As far as possible I will endeavour to suggest substitute feathers and in many cases they will produce just as effective a fly as the original. The wings and body of a starling supply a whole array of substitute feathers and if you do not already have a supply of fly-dressing materials this should be your first purchase. Of course, it is also possible to dye a substitute feather to the shade required, but this does tend to add a little stiffness to the fibres. Acquisition of the following feathers is recommended with the proviso that not all the wings will be readily available from suppliers.

Cock starling Obtain a whole skin if you can. The starling, or, as it was once called, the 'shepstare' (or 'shepster'), has figured in fly patterns for centuries. The value of the cock starling is not only that it provides substitute feathers for several other birds, but that it also possesses unique feathers in its own right such as the glossy dark feathers, shot through with hues of green or purple, which make excellent hackles for Black Spiders. The range of feather colours possessed by the wings and body of a starling is enormous and there are excellent marginal and lesser covert hackles, pale undercovert feathers and plenty of other good hackles to be found on the back, neck and elsewhere on the wings. The primary and secondary feathers provide good winging materials for smaller flies, while any of the small and paler feathers may be dyed as substitutes for the feathers of rare birds such as the corncrake (or landrail).

Coot A pair of coot wings may be difficult to acquire, but it is worth the effort for the sooty black feathers in the marginal coverts.

Golden plover I still have a couple of pairs of wings purchased years ago, but golden plover wings may now be hard to come by. The marginal covert feathers on the topside of the wing are among the most beautiful of hackles – mousey-coloured but with golden-yellow blotches around the edges. There is no direct substitute, although any starling feathers with paler patches may be used at a pinch. It is also possible to colour the pale tip of a jack snipe feather yellow with a Pantone pen and when this is wound around the hook it provides a similar effect.

Grouse The red grouse provides dark brown feathers with orange speckles from the marginal coverts on the top of the wing, mottled feathers from the base of the neck, reddish-brown back feathers and smokey-blue undercovert feathers used for hackling the famous Poult Bloa.

Hen blackbird A hen blackbird's wing contains some useful marginal covert feathers that may be used as substitutes for other hackles, while the primary wing quills may be used later for winged wet-flies (for example, the Greenwell's Glory).

Hen hackles It is worth stocking up with hen feathers. Some of them will be used to dress soft-hackled flies, but they will also be required for the dressing of traditional winged wet-flies and loch flies. Natural capes supply good quantities of small feathers, although there are many poor capes on the market at the moment and good quality capes are quite pricey. Dyed feathers too will be required for the different styles of wet-fly and most packets of dyed hen feathers usually contain enough small feathers to make the purchase of expensive dyed capes unnecessary. I have natural capes containing feathers in various shades and patterns, including greenwell (ginger with black centre), coch-y-bondhu (red-brown with black centre), furnace (deep red), black, blue dun, brown, ginger, honey dun and badger (cream with black centre). However, an initial selection of greenwell or coch-y-bondhu, black, brown and ginger will provide capes to cater for most soft-hackled flies and other styles of wet-fly. To supplement the natural colours, dyed hen hackles catering for the soft-hackled flies that require them, and for other wet-flies, may be obtained in colours such as crimson, claret, yellow, green, orange, pale blue and various shades of olive.

Jackdaw The smokey-grey throat hackles of a jackdaw, though a little long in the fibre, are excellent hackles, though acquiring them may be something of a challenge.

Step 1   **Step 2**   **Step 3**

 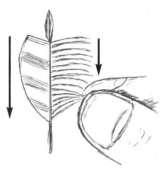

Remove the fluffy
flue from the base of
the feather.

Moisten the tips
of the feather and
stroke together.

Gently pull the fibres
so that they are at right
angles to the stalk.

Preparing a feather for a soft-hackled fly.

Partridge If possible, obtain a whole body skin, for you will need brown speckled back feathers and speckled grey breast feathers. It is also worth obtaining a pair of wings from a French partridge; there are some superb dirty olive-grey hackle feathers in the marginal coverts.

Snipe Snipe wings are invaluable (even though the starling provides fairly good substitute feathers), but a whole body skin is preferable. For example, the mottled brown rump feathers provide attractive hackles, although the most commonly used feathers are those from the marginal coverts and undercoverts. The Snipe and Purple is tied with spoon-shaped feathers from the marginal coverts of a jack snipe's wing, which are an overall grey in colour with a little whitening towards the tips.

Waterhen (or moorhen) Many soft-hackled flies originating in the north of England were dressed with waterhen, or moorhen, feathers and perhaps the most famous of all these flies is the Waterhen Bloa. The preferred hackles are the dark grey feathers from the marginal coverts, although there are similar feathers from the lesser coverts and undercoverts. When moorhen feathers are unavailable, it is possible to use the darkest of starling feathers.

Woodcock A pair of woodcock wings will supply many small hackles suitable for spider patterns, while the larger wing feathers (primaries and secondaries) will be required when winging traditional loch flies. The marginal coverts and bow on the topside of the wing provide rich brown barred hackle feathers, while the feathers from the undercoverts (underside of the wing) are paler and barred buff-brown.

Body Materials: Furs, Herls and Silk
The bodies of many soft-hackled flies are simply made out of plain tying silk or floss silk. Where a fur dubbing is called for, it should be applied very lightly indeed and should be little more than a 'tinge' of fur over the tying silk so that the colour of the silk shines through and blends with the colour of the dubbing. Many of the dubbing furs in use a century ago are now difficult to obtain, but this need not worry us unduly for they can be replaced by other furs.

The following furs will be found useful when dubbing the bodies of soft-hackled spider patterns.

Fox fur The red fur from the ear of a fox is called for in a number of traditional patterns and it is useful to mix with other furs. You can't obtain fox fur? Never mind, any soft red-brown synthetic fur or wool will suffice.

Hare's ear There is no more useful and flexible dubbing material than hare's ear, both because it provides a variety of colours from white, through fawn and brown, to black, and because it blends so well with other furs. Hare's ear also provides a range of textures from soft hairs to spikey hairs which provide extra 'kick' and movement.

Mole fur Mole skins are readily available in the natural dark blue dun (or iron-blue dun) colour, bleached white, or dyed in a variety of other colours. Mole fur is extremely soft-textured and can be blended easily with other furs or synthetics in order to emulate furs that are no longer available. Being very soft, mole fur absorbs water readily, so that it is best to use it sparingly as a dubbing material unless you intend to produce a fly that will sink a little deeper.

Natural blends A recent commercial trend has been to produce packets of blended natural and dyed furs, most of which seem to use hare's ear as the base fur. A whole range of colours is available and there are some interesting shades of olive. Some of the blends include strands of synthetic sparkling material, but I am not convinced this adds a great deal to the effectiveness of the dubbed body of the fly.

Rabbit fur Different shades of rabbit fur are readily available and may be used on their own, although one of their best attributes is that they mix well with other furs; blue rabbit under fur is particularly useful in this respect.

Red squirrel You must be joking! Once highly prized as a dubbing fur, the rarity of our native red squirrel makes it abundantly obvious that this fur is no longer available and, of course, the demise of the red squirrel was not brought about by fly dressers but the introduction of that delinquent relative, the grey squirrel. A mix of red-brown seal's fur, a pinch of rabbit fur and a touch of mole will provide a substitute.

Seal's fur Seal's fur, or indeed several of the excellent synthetic substitutes (*see* below) is often thought to be too coarse a material for dubbing small hackled patterns. However, the slightest dub of seal's fur just behind the hackle, as a kind of thorax, will add a little sparkle and help the hackle to 'kick'. When using spider patterns for stillwater fishing a dub of seal's fur, no more than a 'glaze', produces a most attractive fly; a touch of purple seal's fur may be added to the Snipe and Purple or a touch of hot orange to the Orange Partridge.

Synthetics On the whole, I still prefer to use natural furs for dubbing the bodies of soft-hackled spiders, although synthetic materials may be required as substitutes for rare furs, in which role they are often blended with available natural furs. My favourite synthetic dubbing is Partridge SLF (SLF stands for 'synthetic living fibre'), which is soft and has fibres that seem pretty natural. It may be used on its own, but it mixes very well with natural furs and is available in around fifty colours.

Water rat (vole) fur Several traditional patterns call for a dubbing of 'water rat', but it is unlikely that the natural fur will be readily available. However, a good substitute may be produced by mixing mole fur with any brown fur or synthetic material.

Wool It is all too easy to forget that wool is a natural material. For centuries, wool was a staple ingredient for tying trout flies and the angler would dye the wool to whatever shade he required and it is rather strange that it has been a neglected material in recent years. As a dubbing material, wool should always be used sparingly, but it looks most attractive when a tinge of brown wool is sparingly dubbed over primrose tying silk.

Fur was not the only material used for dubbing the bodies of traditional flies. In attempting to copy the exact body colour of an insect, the old fly dressers would also dub various herls over the tying silk, although it must be said that herl bodies are quite fragile. Herls can be used in four ways: to cover the entire body of the fly; in open turns so that the tying silk shines through; to form a small thorax behind the hackle; and to produce the fly's head in front of the hackle. The following herls may be required:

Heron herl Bodies were often made of dubbed heron herl, either in its natural grey colour or dyed shades of olive. Heron herl may be difficult to obtain, but there are reasonable substitutes available.

Magpie herl Some of the old patterns call for bodies dubbed with magpie herl, or even heads fashioned from it. Magpie herl is black, with a purple tinge, and running finger nails along it will help the flue to stand out.

Ostrich herl Although ostrich herl is available in several dyed colours its long flue is generally inappropriate for small wet flies. Nevertheless, a thorax of black ostrich herl added to a Black Spider is useful when imitating insects such as the hawthorn fly.

Peacock herl While natural green peacock herl is most commonly used, a beautiful bronze colour can be produced by dyeing the herl in magenta dye. Stripped peacock herl makes a very realistic segmented body, although it is very fragile and soon becomes shredded. It is easy enough to strip the flue from the herl by placing it on a hard surface and then stroking a rubber gently along its length. The flue may also be removed by drawing the herl through the nails of your thumb and forefinger.

While the bodies of soft-hackled spiders were produced from furs or herls dubbed over the tying silk, they were just as likely to be made out of floss silk or plain tying silk.

Floss silk The bodies of soft-hackled spiders may be constructed of floss silk wound over the same shade of tying silk and Pearsall's Marabou floss silk is available in the same shades as the tying silk. The theory behind using floss silk is that, when wet, it provides an impression of translucence, but it is easily damaged by a trout's teeth so that it shreds and unravels. There is also the danger that the body of the fly will become rather bulky when floss silk is wound over tying silk and it is certainly inappropriate for the smallest flies. I prefer bodies of plain tying silk which does not seem to impair the performance of the flies in the least.

Tying silk Fly dressers often go to great lengths to construct the body of a trout fly, but it is surprising how effective a body of plain tying silk can be. There are many reliable synthetic tying threads on the market at the moment, most of them very fine and strong, but traditional wet-flies require traditional tying silk. The reason for this is that we are able to guarantee that we are using the exact same colour that Pritt or Edmonds and Lee used. Pearsall's Gossamer tying silks may not be as strong as some synthetics, but they retain consistent colours when dry, wet, waxed or blended with furs. When constructing bodies entirely made from tying silk, at least two layers of silk must be wound along the body, so that the colour of the hook shank does not show through when wet. This is clearly important when using lighter colours of silk. While the reader is free to use whatever type of tying thread he or she prefers, I recommend Pearsall's Gossamer tying silk and will be quoting the following shade reference codes when giving the dressings of wet-fly patterns: white (1); straw (2); primrose (3); yellow (5); amber (6); light orange (6a); purple (8); black (9); grey (9a); ash (10); scarlet (11a); crimson (13); claret (14); mulberry (15); olive (16); brown (17); green (18); hot orange (19); and light olive (20).

Traditional spider patterns are simple and drab on the whole, but no less effective for that, so we rarely use ribbing materials such as tinsels and wires though they do occasionally have their uses.

Tinsel We will require a good supply of tinsels, particularly fine oval embossed tinsel in gold and silver, when tying loch flies, but there is little call for the material when we are dressing spider patterns. H.C. Cutcliffe was of the opinion that a ribbing of flat gold or silver tinsel added more attraction when fishing the rough and tumbling streams of Devon and there are those who share his opinion. The Orange Partridge often has a rib of flat silver tinsel added to it, which may improve its performance in rough water and when fishing for grayling. Flat tinsels are apt to tarnish and it is better to use a material called Mylar, which does not discolour and is available in silver, gold and copper. Mylar is usually supplied in the form of a woven tubing, but it is easy to separate the strands with a needle and it works out much cheaper than using little bobbins of tinsel.

Wire Fine wire is available in the standard colours of gold and silver, but also in a range of other colours as well such as copper, green and red. While I don't find a great use for wire as a ribbing material, it may occasionally be used to protect a delicate body. For example, a copper, or even red, wire rib over the body of the Black Snipe will prevent the peacock herl from being easily torn. Where I do find a use for wire is in the construction of underbodies, so that a soft-hackled spider may be sunk more deeply. An underbody of copper wire, or the finest grade of lead wire available, will add enough weight to sink the fly into a deep pool, or to prevent it from being swept too quickly downstream in rapid water.

Tools

The two words to remember when tying a soft-hackled fly are 'slim' (body) and 'sparse' (hackle). Spider patterns are the ultimate minimalists of the trout fly world! Minimalism, too, is the order of the day with reference to fly-dressing tools. There are some incredibly overcomplicated and expensive vices on the market and gadgets galore, most of which are simply not necessary. Just remember that at one time even a vice wasn't used and anglers dressed their trout flies in the hand employing a pair of sharp scissors as their only tool. Actually, it isn't that difficult to tie a fly without a vice and it is worth trying it as an experiment. Nevertheless, we will accept the comforts of modern life so we will require a vice capable of holding small hooks firmly, but it ought to be a simple vice uncluttered by additional gadgets that only serve to get in the way.

A sharp pair of scissors with fine points is essential and a good bobbin holder will facilitate the construction of neatly wound tying silk bodies. If you are using genuine silk then a bobbin holder with a smooth ceramic tube is useful in order to avoid breaking the tying thread. Small hackle pliers will make hackling easier. They must grip the hackle firmly, but you will still need to take care when winding because soft hackle feathers are easily torn. A dubbing needle will be required for picking out the dubbing fibres and for applying a drop of varnish to the head of the finished fly; actually, I have never bought a dubbing needle and simply use a large needle from my wife's sewing kit.

A bottle of clear varnish will be needed for finishing the head and I have always used Veniard's Cellire Varnish No. 1. A couple of neat half-hitches, well-varnished, make a satisfactory enough head and I have never experienced the tying silk unravelling. Apply a whip-finish if you prefer, but I have dressed effective flies for over forty years without feeling the need for a whip-finishing tool. That nearly completes the kit, save for a lump of fly-dresser's wax and tweezers. Tweezers are very useful for picking up hooks, feathers and other bits and pieces and I wouldn't be without them.

Tying a Soft-Hackled Spider Pattern

The Waterhen Bloa

We are going to practise tying a soft-hackled fly by dressing one of the best-known patterns, the Waterhen Bloa. 'Bloa' is one of those strange dialect terms (akin to the Scottish 'blae') that is not easy to define precisely. The closest we can get is to say that it describes the dark bluish-grey colour we see in the sky when it looks certain to rain. In the case of the Waterhen Bloa, the word 'bloa' aptly describes both the colour of the hackle and body. In order to dress the Waterhen Bloa we will require the following materials given in the summary dressing notes:

- **Hook**: 16 – 14
- **Thread**: primrose tying silk (Pearsall's shade 3)
- **Body**: a fine dubbing of mole fur over the tying silk so that the primrose colour shines through. In order to create a thorax, the dubbing may be a little heavier just behind the hackle

- **Hackle**: one or two turns of a small waterhen (moorhen) marginal covert feather, or a dark grey feather from a starling's wing as a substitute

We have our vice, tools, materials, wax and varnish ready so we can now start to dress the Waterhen Bloa; it might take a few attempts to get it just right but it will be worth it.

Step 1
Fix the hook in the vice, test it, then run the waxed tying silk onto the hook behind the eye. (The primrose silk should have been waxed before use. Actually, as an alternative, an application of line grease provides the primrose silk with a beautiful olive-yellow hue.)

Step 2
Wind the silk in tight, close and touching turns to a point just before the bend of the hook begins. This single winding of silk should be all that is required to cover the hook. If the silk has been well waxed, then the hook shank should not show through the silk and darken it when the fly is wet.

Step 3
Wind two or three returning turns of silk over the first layer of silk near to the bend of the hook in order to produce a small olive-yellow 'tag'.

Step 4
Take the smallest pinch of mole fur, spread it out thinly, and then spin it between the fingers onto the tying silk as sparsely as possible. The fur is teased along the thread and twisted so thinly onto it that the best description I can give is that the primrose silk is 'glazed' with mole fur.

Step 5
Wind the dubbing in open turns along the shank, ensuring that the primrose-olive silk is clearly visible through the fur. Leaving room for the hackle, form a tiny 'ball' of fur close to the eye of the hook to act as a thorax. (This will help the hackle to stand out and provide it with 'kick'.) Tie off the dubbing and scrape off any excess.

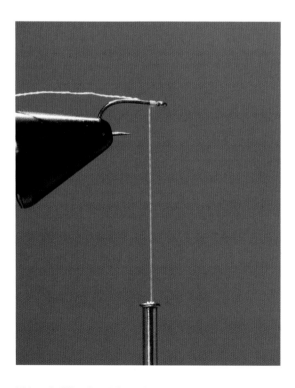

Tying the Waterhen Bloa – Step 1.

Step 2.

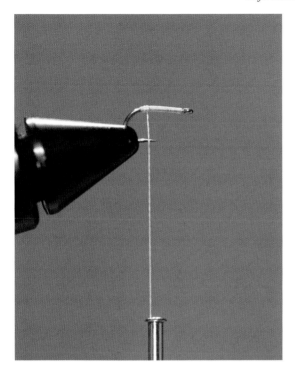

Step 3.

Step 4.

Step 6
Select a nicely shaped waterhen (moorhen) feather, or starling substitute, and strip off the fluffy flue from the base of the stalk. The selected feather should provide fibres that are just a little longer than the hook shank. Originally, a waterhen undercovert feather was used, although I prefer a darker feather from the lesser coverts. It is usual to pull the feather fibres gently parallel to the stalk before moistening the tip of the feather into a little tuft, which may then be attached to the hook – in other words, the feather is attached upside down, although this does not matter with small feathers (as in the step-by-step photograph). Attaching the feather upside down does ensure that the shortest fibres are wound around the hook and the base of the stalk is easier to grip with hackle pliers without tearing.

Step 7
Fix the feather to the hook so that it stands vertically from the shank with the top side of the feather facing the eye. The feather should be very

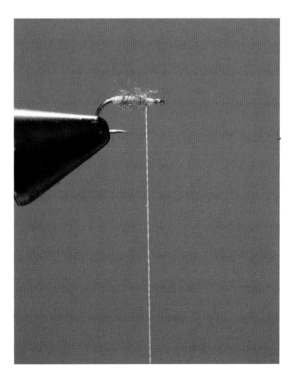

Step 5.

Step 6.

Step 7.

Step 8.

Step 9.

close to the eye (in order to avoid a large and unsightly head) and also close to the fur thorax. When the feather has been fixed in, the tying silk should hang down behind the feather.

Step 8

Wind between one and two turns of hackle around the hook and then carefully work the tying silk through the hackle fibres to the eye. Make sure that no fibres remain trapped by the tying silk, for this will create an ugly and unbalanced fly. The hackle fibres should now be firmly in place and any excess feather may be snipped off with fine-pointed scissors.

Step 9

Complete the fly with a small, neat head and apply a drop of varnish, ensuring that no varnish soaks onto the feather fibres. The hackle should be trapped between the thorax and head so that the fibres stand out nicely and have a slight backward inclination. If the completed head overlaps the base of the hackle fibres it will incline the hackle at too sharp an angle backwards.

It is vital that the fly remain very slim and sparse. Don't worry if the hackle appears very thin, as the fly will probably increase its effectiveness once it becomes a little chewed and ragged.

A Note on Herl Heads

Some traditional patterns call for a tiny head of herl, rather than varnished tying silk, and although I think it unlikely that it adds much of anything to the killing properties of the fly, purists may choose to add this embellishment. Some fly dressers, for example, add a head of magpie herl to the Waterhen Bloa and others use peacock herl. The head may be constructed after hackling, but this is a very fiddly process. There are different ways of doing it, but I will describe what I find to be the easiest process.

After dubbing the body, and before attaching the hackle, tie in the herl close to the thorax, wind it to the eye and back, fix in and snip off the excess herl. The hackle is then attached in front of the thorax and wound over part of the herl, but leaving enough exposed near the eye to form the head of the fly. The tying silk is then taken

through the fibres and the fly is finished off with two half-hitches that bite into the rear part of the exposed herl and should lie hidden. For security, the tiniest drop of varnish may be added, but it is no easy task to achieve this without ruining the herl head.

A Selection of Soft-Hackled 'Spiders'

The following selection of patterns is arranged in groups according to the chosen hackle, so that the reader is able to fashion a number of different flies from the same feathers before purchasing further materials.

Woodcock and Hare's Lug Spider

- **Hook**: 16–14
- **Thread**: well-waxed primrose tying silk (Pearsall's shade 3)
- **Body**: sparsely dubbed hare's ear with a thorax of fur behind the hackle. Pick out a few thorax hairs so that they merge with the hackle fibres
- **Hackle**: barred rich brown feather from the marginal covert of a woodcock's wing

Two versions of this fly can be made – a light and a dark version. The dark version is dubbed with a mix of dark hare's ear and a marginal covert feather; the lighter version requires a lighter coloured mix of hare's ear dubbing and a paler undercovert feather. The Woodcock and Hare's Lug Spider is a good all-rounder and is particularly useful as an emerger pattern, but I have also found it effective when any of the dark olives are hatching. The darker version is preferable at the start of the season and the lighter version from late spring onwards.

Woodcock Spiders

A series of flies, useful when imitating sedge pupae and emerging sedges, can be produced by varying the body colours of flies hackled with a rich-brown marginal covert feather from the woodcock.

- **Hook**: 16–10
- **Thread**: tying silk to match the chosen colour of body – yellow (Pearsall's shade 5), amber (shade 6), olive (shade 16) and brown (shade 17)
- **Body**: yellow, amber, olive-green or fiery brown seal's fur (or Partridge SLF) dubbed over the same colour of tying silk
- **Hackle**: well-marked barred red-brown feather from the marginal coverts of a woodcock

This is a particularly 'sedgey' looking fly. Although the Woodcock Spider may resemble traditional spider patterns, seal's fur was rarely used as a traditional dubbing material. However, seal's fur is appropriate when imitating the plumper bodies of sedge pupae and emerging sedges so that the dubbing should be applied in close, rather than open, turns. Although Woodcock Spiders are good river patterns, they also make excellent reservoir flies and are particularly effective on summer evenings when sedges (or caddis flies) may be emerging in numbers. Sedges cause quite a disturbance when emerging; these patterns therefore work well when retrieved erratically just under the surface. Dressed on a small hook and with a slimmer body, the brown version is also a good imitation of the many brown-bodied stoneflies that are common on rough streams and it may be dressed with waxed hot orange tying silk (Pearsall's shade 19) instead of brown. In this

Woodcock Spider.

case, the dubbing should be applied lightly so that the hot orange silk shines through.

Early Brown

The Early Brown is a traditional stonefly pattern not dissimilar to the Brown Woodcock Spider described above.

- **Hook**: 18–14
- **Thread**: well-waxed orange silk, either light orange (Pearsall's shade 6a) or hot orange (Pearsall's shade 19)
- **Body**: waxed orange silk lightly dubbed with red-brown wool (or Partridge SLF shade 35 or 37)
- **Hackle**: small barred brown undercovert feather from a woodcock's wing (this is a paler feather than the hackle used in Woodcock Spiders)
- **Head**: peacock herl (use only the fine tip of the herl)

As its name implies, the Early Brown is intended to imitate the many small stoneflies (plecoptera)

Early Brown.

encountered on rain-fed rivers at the start of the season. A similar pattern appears under different names in old books. Michael Theakston called it the Early Brown in *British Angling Flies* (1853), W.H. Aldam knew it as the Orange Brown (*A Quaint Treatise on Flees and the Art of Artyfichall Flee Making*, 1876), while to Pritt and Edmonds and Lee it was the Winter Brown. Most writers agree that it is an excellent early season stonefly pattern, although in his *Angler's Manual* (1836) John Turton regards it as a grayling fly to be used in October and November!

Many of the early season stoneflies possess reddish-brown bodies and grey wings folded over the body when at rest. Not every species emerges in the water, for the nymphs of some species crawl onto dry land where the adult breaks out of the nymphal case. In the water, nymphs are more active prior to the emergence of the adult fly and trout feed on them avidly at times. Adults blown onto the stream on windy days provide a good meal for trout, as do females returning to the stream in order to lay their eggs.

Old Master

This is a fly I decided to include largely for historical interest (not illustrated):

- **Hook**: 16–14
- **Thread**: ash-coloured or pale grey tying silk (Pearsall's shades 10 or 9a)
- **Body**: ash-coloured or grey tying silk wrapped over with open turns of undyed heron herl (or substitute)
- **Hackle**: small barred woodcock undercovert feather

Pritt regarded this fly as a 'capital killer' throughout the season, particularly on warm days or in the evening. He informs us that the pattern was invented by a Mr Bradley from Otley, who may have been the eponymous 'old master'. The Old Master is intended to imitate upwinged flies of the ephemeridae and Pritt rather strangely suggests that it is a similar fly to the Greenwell's Glory. Pritt's Yellow-Legged Bloa (dressed with a well-waxed primrose silk body and ginger hen hackle) seems a much closer pattern to the Greenwell's Glory than the Old Master.

Black Game

- **Hook**: 20–14
- **Thread**: purple tying silk (Pearsall's shade 8) waxed until it darkens to almost black
- **Body**: well-waxed tying silk with a thorax of bronze peacock herl behind the hackle
- **Hackle**: small marginal covert feather from the wing of a male black grouse; the correct feather should be almost black but with a bluish tinge to it. If such a feather is not available, a dark cock starling feather with a purple tinge will suffice

'Black Game' is another name for the black grouse and thus this pattern is named after the chosen hackle. This pattern may be regarded as a darker version of the Snipe and Purple. I also like this pattern as an alternative to various Black Spider dressings intended to imitate insects such as midges and gnats. On close inspection, many 'black' natural flies radiate other colours such as green, purple or blue and are anything but simply black. The Black Game will take fish on

Black Game.

rivers, lakes and reservoirs at any time when trout are feeding on black flies and it may be tied in different sizes in order to imitate anything from tiny reed smuts to large hawthorn flies. It is a particularly good fly to use when black gnats (*Bibio johannis*) are swarming over the water and this might be at any time from late April to September. Trout gorge themselves on black gnats and it is often the case that a wet-fly, fished just under the surface, will do better than a dry-fly.

The Black Game is also a good fly to use on lakes and reservoirs during the early part of the season when any black chironomid midges emerge, and in late April and May, tied on a size 14 hook, it may be used to imitate the hawthorn fly (*Bibio marci*). When imitating the hawthorn fly a thorax of black ostrich herl is better than peacock herl. Dressed on the tiniest of hooks, size 20 and smaller, the Black Game offers as good an imitation of reed smuts as you will find, yet these flies are so infuriatingly small, and trout can become so preoccupied with them, that catching smutting trout is no easy matter. Sometimes a complete contrast works better when attempts at imitation fail.

Dark Moor Game

This is another pattern hackled with a feather from a grouse but a red grouse this time:

- **Hook**: 16–14
- **Thread**: hot orange silk (Pearsall's shade 19) waxed to a dark shade
- **Body**: a slim body of dark orange silk tinged with water rat's fur (a good substitute being a mixture of mole fur with brown seal's fur, or Partridge SLF shade 36)
- **Hackle**: very dark brown feather, freckled with orange-brown, from the 'knuckle' of a red grouse's wing
- **Head**: peacock herl

The grouse was often called the 'moorgame' (or 'moorcock') in the north of England. Grouse are subject to colour variations and the fly dressers of old would have sought out the darkest red grouse in order to select the correct feather for the hackle of the Dark Moor Game. John Turton provides this fly in *The Angler's Manual* (1836) and it was also on Pritt's fly list of 1885/6. Michael Theakston also includes the same pattern in *British Angling Flies* (1853), although he calls it the Freckled Dun (reflecting the

Dark Moor Game.

orange-flecked hackle patterning), while other old books refer to it as the 'Orange Grouse'. Pritt actually gives the name Freckled Dun as an alternative to Dark Moor Game, suggesting perhaps that he borrowed the fly from Theakston. It was also sometimes dressed with the addition of wings made from slips taken from the tail feathers of a red grouse. In summary, whatever name was given to it, the Dark Moor Game was valued by most of the classic writers on the soft-hackled fly and it is certainly a most attractive pattern capable of catching trout throughout the season.

But what was it originally intended to imitate? The name 'Dun' suggests that it represents one of the ephemeridae and perhaps whoever invented it had the dark olive or even march browns in mind. It certainly takes fish feeding on any of the darker duns and feeding on stoneflies too, but it may best be regarded as a very effective general fly. Pritt is not very helpful in terms of what the Dark Moor Game imitates and simply informs us that it is 'a goodly fly during March and April, particularly in a brown water, when the river is clearing after a flood'.

Poult Bloa

The Poult Bloa, one of the most famous and heralded of north-country patterns, is dressed as follows:

- **Hook**: 16
- **Thread**: primrose yellow tying silk (Pearsall's shade 3)
- **Body**: waxed primrose silk lightly dubbed with red squirrel fur (substitute). Pick out a little dubbing at the thorax to merge with the hackle
- **Hackle**: small slate-blue or 'bloa' feather from the undercoverts of a young grouse (any similarly coloured feather should suffice as a substitute)

As red squirrel fur may no longer be used, a substitute dubbing is required and in mixing my dubbing I prefer to tone down the red a little. My preferred mix is fiery brown Partridge SLF (shade 35), mole fur and pale blue rabbit underfur, although I still have a supply of red fox fur which may be used in place of the synthetic

Poult Bloa.

material. As in the case of most spider patterns, the dubbing should be applied very thinly. The Poult Bloa is regarded as an excellent imitation of the blue-winged olive (*Ephemerella ignita*) nymph and emerging adults of the same species, but it is also an excellent general emerger pattern. Blue-winged olives are pretty widespread and may be encountered throughout the season, although their maximum period is in the summer, especially in the evening. The adult dun has a dull olive-brown body and blue-grey wings, the latter perfectly suggested by the grouse poult feather ('poult' being a reference to a young bird). The blue-winged olive nymph, or 'bwo' as it is often simply called, is only really active just prior to emergence and spends most of its time creeping around in the stream's moss and weeds; it is usually termed a 'moss creeper' for that reason.

While I think that the Poult Bloa is an excellent 'bwo' imitation, I have a feeling that it was first dressed as an imitation of the pale watery olives (*Baetis bioculatus*), which are as widely spread across the country. If so, I can only think that the original fly would have been dubbed with a grey rather than a red fur body.

Pale watery duns have pale grey bodies tinged with olive and pale grey wings. Pale watery nymphs, unlike the nymphs of the blue-winged olives, are very active and are classed as 'agile darters'. Adults may emerge at any time during the season, although the heaviest hatches usually occur during the summer months. Other species are so similar that, to all intents and purposes, we may regard them as the same fly. Large spurwings (*Centroptilum pennulatum*) and small spurwings (*Centroptilum luteolum*) look very similar to pale wateries, but have tiny spurs protruding from their hind wings.

Brown Shiner

- **Hook**: 16–14
- **Thread**: light orange tying silk (Pearsall's shade 6a)
- **Body**: waxed light orange tying silk with a peacock herl thorax
- **Hackle**: light brown mottled grouse feather from the base of the neck
- **Head (optional)**: peacock herl

Brown Shiner.

This pattern appears in John Turton's *The Angler's Manual* (1836) and is probably a precursor to a number of similar and later imitations of small stoneflies including the very slim and aptly named needle flies. Turton actually recommended it as a fly for August, although it will take fish from the beginning of the season to the end, both as a stonefly imitation and as a general attractor.

Dark Dun

The Dark Dun was dressed in both winged and hackled versions, but it is the hackled spider pattern which I find preferable (not illustrated):

- **Hook**: 14–12
- **Thread**: brown tying silk (Pearsall's shade 17)
- **Body**: well-waxed brown tying silk (or floss silk if preferred)
- **Hackle**: any small dark feather from a grouse or dark brown hen

I like to use the orange-brown flecked feathers from the marginal coverts of a red grouse wing when employing this fly as a general pattern. It is a drab-looking fly but it catches fish and

that it what counts. The winged version was usually hackled with a brown hen feather and winged with slips from the darkest of grouse feathers. The Dark Dun first appears in Michael Theakston's *British Angling Flies* (1853), although it was Pritt who listed the hackled version as the 'Sandy Moorgame' and commented that 'it is probably identical with the dark dun of Theakston'. For the hackle, Pritt chose a dark, reddish-brown feather from the back of a grouse. Both Theakston and Pritt say that the Dark Dun (or Sandy Moorgame) is an imitation of 'Ephemeridae', though neither is specific as to the exact species; Pritt simply recommends the fly from May to the end of July and says that it is 'not to be neglected in a brown water clearing after a flood'. Hackled with a brown hen feather, or even Pritt's reddish-brown grouse back feather, rather than an orange-freckled grouse feather, the Dark Dun provides a good imitation of the sepia dun (*Leptophlebia marginata*) and even its close relative, the claret dun (*Leptophlebia vespertina*). Both natural flies are quite common in some areas of the country, on lakes and the slower reaches of rivers, although they are not present on the chalk streams. For some reason, the sepia and claret duns are rather neglected flies, but I think that Theakston's pattern is probably intended to imitate them. The claret dun would perhaps benefit from a dark claret silk body rather than the brown body specified in the tying notes (although it was also specifically imitated by the Dark Bloa and Broughton's Point described in Chapter 8).

Reffit's March Brown

J.W. Reffit was an angling friend of T.E. Pritt and advised him during the writing of *Yorkshire Trout Flies*. In that book (republished as *North Country Flies*), Pritt gave alternative dressings of the natural march brown, including the following pattern devised by Mr Reffit:

- **Hook**: 14
- **Thread**: hot orange tying silk (Pearsall's shade 19)
- **Body**: hare's poll fur dubbed on hot orange silk and dubbed 'full' at the thorax where hairs are picked out with a dubbing needle
- **Hackle**: small mottled brown feather from a snipe's rump

Apart from his friendship with Pritt, Reffit also corresponded for many years with G.E.M. Skues and it is clear that Skues took a great interest in the soft-hackled wet-flies of the north, which effectively became the prototypes for his series of nymphs. Skues thought Reffit's dressing was a very good imitation of march brown nymphs. There were, however, other march brown dressings similar to Reffit's including an old fly described by Aldam in 1876, which had a body constructed from fox ear fur spun on orange silk. The blending of silks and furs to form the bodies of flies has always been a hallmark of spider patterns originating in the north of England.

The march brown (*Rhithrogena haarupi*) is more commonly found on the stone-strewn streams of hilly areas, although it is by no means as common as it once was. Accordingly, artificials are often more successful as general patterns rather than copies of the naturals. The nymphs of march browns are flat and broad, which equips them well to crawl on stones in rapid water and has led to them being categorized as 'stone clingers'. March brown

Reffit's March Brown.

nymphs only become active prior to the emergence of the adult between March and May, although there is a very similar species called the autumn dun (*Ecdyonurus dispar*), or 'late march brown', which emerges towards the end of the season. Adult march browns are very distinctive flies; their bodies may be a fairly drab brown, but their wings are spectacularly mottled in fawn and brown.

March Brown (Edmonds and Lee)

This pattern, offered by Edmonds and Lee in *Brook and River Trouting* (1916), is probably based on Reffit's original, but it is worth including as an example of the care the authors took in imitating the body of the natural fly.

- **Hook**: 14–12
- **Thread**: light orange tying silk (Pearsall's shade 6a)
- **Body**: orange silk dubbed with fur from the nape of a rabbit's neck lightly tinged a red spinner shade. The body may be ribbed with gold wire or the finest gold tinsel
- **Hackle**: mottled brown feather from a snipe's rump

March Brown (Edmonds and Lee).

While red spinner dyes are still obtainable, and it is also possible to tinge furs with Pantone pens, it is easier to mix a red synthetic fur with the natural rabbit fur when recreating the March Brown pattern developed by Edmonds and Lee.

Snipe and Purple *et al.*

If I were to be limited to the use of only one soft-hackled spider pattern, for both river and reservoir fishing, then I would choose the Snipe and Purple – but I would probably cheat by also tying flies with yellow, green and orange silk bodies. The Snipe and Purple is dressed as follows:

- **Hook**: 18–14
- **Thread**: unwaxed purple tying silk (Pearsall's shade 8)
- **Body**: either plain purple tying silk or floss silk. An optional peacock herl thorax may be added
- **Hackle**: spoon-shaped marginal covert feather from a jack snipe's wing; the correct feather is dark grey, with a slight brownish tinge, and becomes a lighter fawn or cream at the tip; similar feathers from a cock starling may be used as a substitute

The Snipe and Purple is such a simple fly that there is always the temptation to overdress it. I much prefer to tie it with a very slim and plain tying silk body, rather than a body of floss silk, and leave the silk unwaxed so that it will darken in the water. The hackle too should not be bushy, but a mere wisp of a thing and the fly remains effective even when the hackle becomes ragged and worn. While the Snipe and Purple is often dressed with a substitute starling feather taken from the undercoverts of the wing, snipe wings are fairly easy to come by, so that it is better to dress the fly with genuine snipe feathers. The origins of the fly and what it was tied to represent are a little obscure, yet it remains one of the best general river patterns, particularly at the start of the season, and is also a very useful lake and reservoir pattern that does surprisingly well as a chironomid midge imitator. It is the kind of fly that will save a cold and bleak day from becoming a 'blank', but will also take a trout on a hot and still day in July when nothing else moves a fish. I invariably fish the Snipe and Purple on the point of a three-fly cast.

Pritt called the Snipe and Purple the Dark

Snipe and Purple.

Snipe and wrote that it is: 'A splendid killer on cold days in the early part of the season, and is a favourite on the Ribble. In some districts it is not dressed until June, but the angler will find it too good to be neglected as a spring fly.'

It is sometimes suggested that the Snipe and Purple represents the little iron-blue dun (*Baetis niger* or *Baetis pumilis*) and since the maximum emergence period for this fly is around June, that would explain Pritt's comment that in 'some districts it is not dressed until June'. Although a widely distributed fly, the iron-blue dun was undoubtedly more common in Pritt's day than it is today, so that the Snipe and Purple now earns its reputation as a general pattern rather than a specific imitator of a natural insect. Nevertheless, the Snipe and Purple can be used effectively when iron-blues are being taken and also when imitating the purple dun (*Paraleptophlebia cincta*), which is often confused with the iron-blue. Trout can't tell the difference so why should we? The purple dun tends to emerge in May and June but is not as widespread as the iron-blue, preferring fast-flowing alkaline rivers with a good growth of weed.

Over the years, there have been many variations on the Snipe and Purple theme. The Little Black, for example, was a pretty similar fly, although it was hackled with a starling feather while the purple silk body was wrapped with magpie herl. Whatever its origins, the Snipe and Purple is one of our very best wet-flies and we should be grateful to its inventor, whoever he was. In addition to the Snipe and Purple, the Snipe and Yellow (which is similar to the Snipe Bloa) is also a good pattern, although I regard it more as a late spring and summer fly. Dressed with a plain yellow tying silk body (Pearsall's shade 5), or floss silk if preferred, it is a good general nymph or emerger and is particularly good as an imitation of the pale watery olives.

Hackled with the same snipe feather and a body of hot orange tying silk (Pearsall's shade 19), we have a fly to imitate small stoneflies, which will also give the Orange Partridge a run for its money as a general pattern. Finally, snipe spiders dressed with bodies of either green tying silk (Pearsall's shade 18) or olive tying silk (shade 16) will work when trout are feeding on nymphs, small sedge pupae, green chironomids,

Snipe and Yellow.

or when they are simply 'turned on' to the colour green as they sometimes are.

Snipe Bloa

The Snipe Bloa is a close relative of the Snipe and Yellow.

- **Hook**: 16–14
- **Thread**: yellow tying silk (Pearsall's shade 5)
- **Body**: yellow tying silk with a sparse dubbing of mole fur so that the silk shines through
- **Hackle**: small snipe undercovert feather

The Snipe Bloa may also be dressed with a darker marginal covert feather or even a starling feather. Its origins may well have been rooted in the old Blue Dun theme, making it a possible alternative to the Waterhen Bloa. The dressing given above is identical to that listed by Pritt, who regarded it as a good all-rounder through-out the season and a particularly effective fly on cold and wild days. Pritt thought that the Snipe Bloa was the same fly as Theakston's Bloa Brown

Snipe Bloa.

Needle Brown.

and Jackson's Light Bloa and this tends to underline the problem with old patterns – the same fly appears under a variety of names. When the fly is dressed with a paler snipe undercovert feather it provides a good pattern for the pale watery olives. It is a good general nymph and emerger pattern.

Needle Brown

Another stonefly imitation, illustrating the importance of the plecoptera on rain-fed rivers.

- **Hook**: 16–14
- **Thread**: well-waxed hot orange tying silk (Pearsall's shade 19)
- **Body**: hot orange silk waxed to almost a brown colour with a thorax of grizzled hare's ear. A few fibres should be picked out
- **Hackle**: small dark snipe feather from the marginal coverts wound sparsely

This is an attractive fly and was originally given as a winged pattern by Theakston in 1853. It seeks to imitate the small and slender stoneflies known as needle flies (for example, *Leuctra*

fusciventris and *Leuctra hippopus*); trout often gorge themselves on the egg-laying females. At such times, the artificial fly may be fished effectively by twitching it close to the surface. Imitations of needle flies are legion and Pritt used a similar fly, the Dark Spanish Needle, which had an orange silk body, peacock herl head and was hackled with a feather from 'the darkest part of a Brown Owl's wing'. Pritt also used a Light Spanish Needle hackled with a snipe feather, a body fashioned from crimson tying silk and completed with a peacock herl head.

Black Snipe

The Black Snipe is a brilliant general pattern for both rivers and lakes and is clearly a forerunner of the Black and Peacock Spider.

- **Hook**: 16–12
- **Thread**: either brown tying silk (Pearsall's shade 17) or mulberry (shade 15)
- **Body**: two or three strands of green or bronze peacock herl
- **Hackle**: either a dark snipe marginal covert feather, a paler undercovert feather, or jackdaw

When dressing the body of this fly it is wise to moisten the herl before twisting it around the tying thread; the thread will give it strength and will prevent it from unwinding or breaking easily. Of this fly, Pritt says: 'This is an old Yorkshire fly, quoted in many manuscripts on angling, still in existence, although it is not generally dressed. It will kill well almost all the year round, and my own experience has proved it is a good general fly'. It certainly is and the only difference between the Black Snipe and the Black and Peacock Spider is that the latter is generally a bigger and bulkier fly and hackled with a black hen feather. The Black Snipe may suggest a variety of nymphs, beetles and other aquatic creatures and it seems to become more effective as the hackle gets ragged and worn.

Orange Partridge

Who has not heard of the Orange Partridge? Strangely, what has become one of the most famous general soft-hackled patterns started life as a 'mere' stonefly imitation.

Black Snipe.

- **Hook**: 16–12
- **Thread**: hot orange tying silk (Pearsall's shade 19)
- **Body**: either plain hot orange tying silk or floss silk (I prefer plain tying silk which creates a slimmer body, although floss silk over tying silk provides a nice impression of translucence)
- **Hackle**: brown speckled partridge back feather, not too long in the fibre and at most given two turns about the hook; the correct feather has brown speckles on a creamy-buff background and should not have brown bars or blotches on it

As a stonefly pattern, the Orange Partridge originally went under a number of different names. For example, while Edmonds and Lee list the fly as the Orange Partridge, Pritt called it the 'Brown Watchet'. It is likely that the Orange Partridge began life as an imitation of the February red stonefly (*Taeniopteryx nebulosa*), but it has become one of the most used general soft-hackled flies. While a good all-rounder on rivers, I have had a great deal of success with the Orange Partridge on reservoirs when the weather

Orange Partridge.

has been hot and the trout rather dour. At such times it can succeed, either on the point or middle dropper, when all else fails. I consider the Orange Partridge an 'expensive' fly, because brown speckled partridge back feathers, small enough for small hooks and of the necessary patterning, are at a premium. When hackling the Orange Partridge, it certainly pays to tie in by the tip of the feather, so that the smallest fibres are wound around the hook.

While I still believe that the Orange Partridge began life as an imitation of the early February red stonefly, Pritt was of the opinion that it was best used 'from April to September, on warm days', which may suggest that the Orange Partridge had become a general pattern as early as 1885–6. It was also one of the few northern wet-fly patterns to be adopted by chalk stream anglers and was used regularly by Viscount Grey and John Waller Hills among others. The Orange Partridge works well enough when dressed as in the prescription given above, but it is often subjected to embellishments. E. M. Tod, who published *Wet-Fly Fishing* in 1903, gave the body a rib of stripped peacock herl, which does make a very attractive fly. Other anglers add a rib of narrow silver or gold tinsel and use the Orange Partridge principally as a grayling pattern.

'I can't believe it's not a March Brown'.

Edmonds and Lee used a ribbing of gold tinsel or wire. For reservoir fishing I also dress a variant with a very thin dubbing of hot orange seal's fur over the tying silk and this makes a good sedge pupa pattern.

'I can't believe it's not a March Brown'

As you may gather, I had a real problem naming this pattern, for it might have begun life as one of the many imitations of march browns but I now use it as a sedge or caddis pattern. The original fly was dressed with either orange or brown tying silk, but I have changed the colour to suit my purposes. Over the years, a great number of trout that have never seen the naturals must have been caught on artificial flies called March Browns. My March Brown sedge pattern is dressed as follows:

- **Hook**: 14–10
- **Thread**: green tying silk (Pearsall's shade 18)
- **Body**: A mix of various shades of hare's ear fur dubbed in slightly open turns so that the green tying silk shows through. The fur should be picked out with a dubbing needle to create a rough and spiky effect. A rib of fine gold tinsel is optional
- **Hackle**: well-speckled brown partridge back feather

To create additional 'buzz', suggestive of an emerging adult sedge, the hackle may be wound semi-palmered after the manner of W.C. Stewart's famous spiders.

Welsh Partridge

Strictly speaking, this is not a soft-hackled spider pattern, although I have included it because it is a very good fly and, anyway, it is hackled with soft feathers! I could also argue that it was only right to include a fly from Wales, as the present book includes plenty of flies from England, a good number from Scotland and a few from Ireland too.

- **Hook**: 14–10
- **Thread**: claret tying silk (Pearsall's shade 14) or mulberry (shade 15)
- **Body**: either purple or dark claret seal's fur ribbed with fine gold oval tinsel

Welsh Partridge.

Grey Watchet.

- **Hackles**: a double hackle of brown speckled partridge back feather and purple, dark crimson or claret hen; the partridge hackle should be at the eye of the hook

This is a fancy pattern and I have used it to good effect, both on the middle and top droppers, when fishing reservoirs on bright and breezy days. The Welsh Partridge has caught a great number of fish, yet it tends to be the kind of fly knotted onto the cast when I am running out of ideas. It may also prove its worth as a grayling fly, although I have never used it on rivers.

Grey Watchet
The Grey Watchet has also been called the Grey Partridge or Yellow Partridge and although I find it a rather anaemic pattern there are those who swear by it.

- **Hook**: 16–14
- **Thread**: pale yellow or straw-coloured tying silk (Pearsall's shade 2)

- **Body**: plain tying silk with the addition of a peacock herl thorax
- **Hackle**: greyish speckled feather from a partridge's breast

Pritt thought this a very good fly for 'cold days, and in the evenings during June and July', yet Edmonds and Lee considered it a fly to use from May to the middle of June. As a general pattern, a Yellow Partridge dressed with a tying silk body of deeper yellow (Pearsall's shade 5) and hackled with a brown speckled back feather is a much better fly. It makes a pretty good summer fly for lake and reservoir fishing.

Olive Bloa
There is no single fly called *the* Olive Bloa because old books offered many alternative dressings. Pritt, for example, gives two dressings, one hackled with an olive hen feather and one with a plover (or lapwing, or 'peewit') feather. Olive Bloas are intended as imitations of the common dark olives and for this purpose the

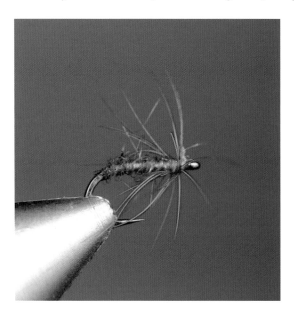

Olive Bloa.

grey wings and bodies that may vary from a drab grey-olive, through dark olive-green, to dark olive-brown. However, I have also seen specimens with much paler bodies and even brighter green bodies, so that there are great variations of colour. There is another fly (*Baetis atrebatinum*), simply called the dark olive, which is to all intents a smaller version of the large dark olive, although it only tends to emerge towards the end of the season. Finally, there is the small dark olive (*Baetis scambus*), also known as the 'July dun', which is again likeliest to emerge from mid-July to the end of September.

Waterhen Bloa

Greenwell Spider is as good as any other pattern, but I also like the following dressing:

- **Hook**: 18–14
- **Thread**: primrose yellow tying silk (Pearsall's shade 3) or a deeper yellow (shade 5) impregnated with line grease, which turns it a beautiful olive shade
- **Body**: tying silk dubbed very thinly with an equal mix of hare's ear, olive-green seal's fur and olive-brown seal's fur (Alternatively, a body of stripped peacock herl dyed olive)
- **Hackle**: dirty grey-olive marginal covert feather from the wing of a French partridge

The above dressing and many of the Olive Bloas listed in the old books are intended to imitate the dark and medium olives common on many rivers throughout the season. At the beginning of the season, only the dark olives may appear to represent the ephemeridae. The large dark olive (*Baetis rhodani*) and medium olive (*Baetis vernus*; *B. Tenax* and *B. Buceratus*) are widespread and can occur throughout the season, even as early as February. The nymphs are very active and are thus classified as 'agile darters', so that a wet-fly may imitate nymphs as well as drowned flies and emerging duns. Emerging duns have

The Waterhen Bloa, a version of the ancient Blue Dun, was the fly we dressed towards the beginning of the present chapter. It is a standard traditional pattern representing the dark olives, blue-winged olive and other similar flies. I will give the dressing again:

- **Hook**: 16–14
- **Thread**: primrose yellow tying silk (Pearsall's shade 3)
- **Body**: a thin dubbing of mole fur over primrose tying silk, dubbed a little fuller at the 'thorax'
- **Hackle**: one or two turns of waterhen (moorhen) marginal covert feather or starling substitute

A whole series of good flies, with different body colours, can be tied with moorhen feathers – if you can get them. Often, the paler grey undercovert feathers are favoured, but I much prefer feathers taken from the marginal coverts or lesser coverts on top of the wing. Moorhen wings possess quite a number of dark grey feathers suitable for small flies and there are also attractive feathers tinged a brownish-olive shade.

Black Spider

As with Olive Bloas, there is no single standard dressing of the Black Spider, which, apart from its use as a general purpose fly, may be employed to imitate any black flies such as smuts, midges, gnats and hawthorn flies. A perusal of old angling books will reveal many different dressings, but the following may be recommended:

Black Spider (large).

- **Hook**: 20–14
- **Thread**: black tying silk (Pearsall's shade 9) waxed to appear glossy
- **Body**: black tying silk or floss silk. An optional thorax of peacock herl or black ostrich herl may be added
- **Hackle**: the reader may choose from the following: a black hen feather; a dark charcoal-grey feather from the bow of a coot's wing; a smoke-grey feather from a jackdaw's breast; a glossy dark starling breast feather with a green or purple tinge

When dressing small versions of the Black Spider there is no need to fiddle around trying to add a thorax; however, a peacock herl thorax is useful for midges and black gnats, while an ostrich herl thorax should be added when imitating the hawthorn fly. Black ostrich herl alone was used by Pritt in imitating the body of the black gnat and no hackle was added. While the Black Spider is an excellent general wet-fly throughout the season, it is also a very flexible fly. Add a little floatant (or 'flotant') and it makes a very good emerger dry-fly both for rivers and lakes and floats surprisingly well right in the surface film; not all dries require cock hackles to make them float. Trim the hackle down to a mere stub and you have a good midge pupa imitation. Of course, one of the most famous Black Spiders

Black Spider (small).

was the pattern developed by James Baillie and published via W.C. Stewart's *The Practical Angler* in 1857. The dressing details are given in Chapter 9. Among the many other dressings that may be termed 'Black Spider' it is worth picking out a fly that T.E. Pritt called the Little

Black. Hackled either with a black hen feather, or a starling neck feather, the fly is given a blended body of purple silk wrapped with magpie herl.

Dark Watchet

The Dark Watchet is really the classic north-country imitation of the iron-blue dun, although there were many variations on the theme; Pritt himself gives four different dressings. I like the following dressing from Pritt's list, which may not be better than other dressings from a trout's point of view, yet is the most attractive looking fly imaginable.

- **Hook**: 18–16
- **Thread**: purple tying silk (Pearsall's shade 8) and hot orange (shade 19); purple silk is used as the main tying silk
- **Body**: mole fur lightly spun on purple and hot orange tying silks twisted together and wound along the shank. A small purple tag is left at the tail. The mole fur must not obscure the colours of the tying silk
- **Hackle**: small dark and smoke-grey feather from a jackdaw's neck or a marginal covert feather from either a moorhen or coot

Some fly dressers preferred to twist crimson silk rather than orange with the purple tying silk. Skues used the fly and preferred crimson to orange. The silk should be left unwaxed so that it will darken considerably when immersed in water. Although I have specified the use of mole fur for the dubbing, Pritt's original dressing of the pattern given above calls for 'down from a water-rat' (vole?), although other Dark Watchet dressings he gave simply use mole fur. Writing of the iron-blue dun, Pritt informs us that 'The natural fly appears on the Yorkshire rivers about the same time as the swallows first come' and although some anglers would use the pattern from April to the end of May, Pritt used it throughout the season and particularly on cold days, declaring that 'The dark watchet is one of the daintiest morsels with which you can tempt a trout'. Sadly, hatches of iron-blue duns are not what they were, but then, the same could be said about most aquatic trout flies.

Like the word 'bloa', 'watchet' is one of the old dialect words that is never easy to pin down and it is subject to a variety of spellings, appearing frequently as 'watchett'. One suggestion has it that 'watchet' was a kind of pale blue cloth, but although we are talking about a fly that imitates the iron-blue dun, the shade of blue seems altogether wrong. Nor would that explanation help to explain why other flies are called Grey Watchet, Light Watchet or even Brown Watchet. Another theory is that 'watchet' is a corruption of 'watchman', as in 'night watchman', yet while the suggestion of darkness suits the Dark Watchet, it is completely inappropriate in the cases of pale flies such as the Grey Watchet. I give up – but it doesn't change the fact that this is a 'reet good fly'.

Dotterel Dun

Strictly speaking, there can no longer be a fly called a Dotterel Dun unless we are rather naughty in gathering our hackle feathers. Nevertheless, the name of the fly is retained even though a substitute hackle is required.

- **Hook**: 18–14
- **Thread**: pale yellow tying silk (Pearsall's shade 2)

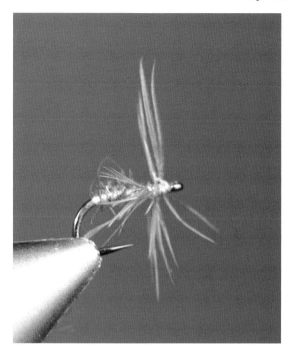

Dotterel Dun.

- **Body**: pale yellow tying silk dubbed sparingly with light hare's ear fur
- **Hackle**: light mottled starling feather with a brownish tinge to it which may be found on the underside of the wing; alternatively, a fawn feather from a jay's wing makes a good substitute, or even a golden plover marginal covert feather tinged fawn

Among those who frequently tied on a Dotterel Dun was G.E.M. Skues, who caught plenty of fish with it on the English–Welsh border streams – possibly the Teme and Onny. Skues thought that it was a good nymph pattern and provided an excellent imitation of the paler olives, while Pritt regarded it as a good standard fly throughout the season.

Hare's Lug and Plover

Like the Woodcock and Hare's Lug Spider, the Hare's Lug and Plover is not actually one of the old patterns. However, the Hare's Lug and Plover draws on the designs of a number of dressings and I claim little credit for its creation, even though it is a very effective fly.

- **Hook**: 18–14 for rivers; 16–12 for lakes and reservoirs
- **Thread**: lightly waxed primrose yellow tying silk (Pearsall's shade 3)
- **Body**: primrose silk with the lightest dubbing of hare's ear fur darkening at the thorax, which should be dubbed more fully. Pick out a few rough hairs at the thorax to merge with the hackle
- **Hackle**: well-marked golden plover feather from the marginal coverts or 'knuckle' of the wing; the correct feather is a buff-brown with golden yellow blotches around the edge; at a pinch, brownish starling feathers with pale tips, or even snipe feathers with pale tips, may be used, but the pale tips should be dyed yellow or coloured with a Pantone pen

The Hare's Lug and Plover, like the Dotterel Dun and Snipe Bloa, is a good fly to use when imitating either the nymphs of paler olives or the emerging adult flies. As a general emerger pattern it is hard to beat on rivers at any time during the season. Fished close to the surface, it has also proved its worth as a reservoir fly, even though it may seemingly bear little resemblance to any natural lake or reservoir trout flies.

Hare's Lug and Plover.

Greenwell Spider

How many fishermen have not heard of the Greenwell's Glory? It is such a good fly that it has gone through many transformations and has appeared as a dry-fly, as a winged wet-fly, as a hackled wet-fly, as a nymph and even, dressed on large hooks, as a loch and sea trout fly. Greenwell's Glories have undergone such changes that they no longer ought to bear that name, but it matters little and I am sure that when James Wright first tied the winged fly devised by Canon Greenwell neither man imagined the popularity it would have achieved. At the time, in May 1854, Canon William Greenwell was fishing the Tweed at Sprouston. Of course, the soft-hackled spider version of the Greenwell is not the original, though it was used commonly enough in this form by the time of Pritt. Even the Greenwell Spider is subject to variations, but the dressing I like is as follows:

- **Hook**: 18–14
- **Thread**: primrose tying silk (Pearsall's shade 3) waxed or greased so that it takes on an olive hue. The body should be ribbed either with unwaxed primrose tying silk or the finest gold wire obtainable
- **Body**: waxed primrose tying silk ribbed with the finest gold wire

- **Hackle**: two turns of greenwell hen feather, which is ginger with a black centre; alternatively, furnace or coch-y-bondhu hen hackle feathers may be used

Although the Greenwell Spider may suggest drowned or struggling insects, for me it is the ultimate nymphal spider pattern and, for this reason, I prefer the hackle to incline backwards when tying this fly. It is not an 'original' north-country spider, but it is a soft-hackled fly nevertheless and as a nymph pattern it is as good on stillwaters as it is on rivers. While it may be used to imitate dark and medium olives on rivers, it is also an excellent fly to have on the cast when pond olives (*Cloeon dipterum*) or lake olives (*Cloeon simile*) put in an appearance. The nymphs of pond and lake olives are classed as 'agile darters' and they are likely to be liveliest in and around weed beds. As a reservoir fly, I think it is at its most effective on the point, or middle dropper, from May onwards although it is worth using throughout the season on rivers. No fly box should be without Greenwell Spiders in a variety of sizes.

Miscellaneous Patterns

In selecting soft-hackled spider patterns I am open to the accusation that I have left out some very effective flies while including patterns that struggle to qualify under the category. For that I apologize, but then any selection of flies is bound to be subjective and it is not possible to please everyone. There are a few more flies that I would like to include, even though they may be regarded as 'imposters'.

The first 'imposter' is that famous Welsh pattern, the **Coch-y-Bondhu**, but in essence it is little different from the Black Snipe which is generally classed as a soft-hackled spider pattern. The Coch-y-Bondhu is dressed to represent a beetle common in hilly areas and is tied as follows:

- **Hook**: 16–12
- **Thread**: brown tying silk (Pearsall's shade 17)
- **Body**: about three strands of bronze peacock herl twisted with the tying thread into a 'rope' and wound along the shank. A gold tinsel 'tag' is often included

Coch-y-bondhu.

Red Tag.

- **Hackle**: natural coch-y-bondhu hen, which is dark red with a black centre and tips

I have also found that the fly is effective when hackled with a hen feather dyed claret and this makes a good general river and lake pattern. This was how Henry Wade dressed the fly and it appears in his book *Rod Fishing with Fly, Minnow and Worm* (1861). Although the Coch-y-Bondhu is of Welsh origin (and may loosely be translated as 'red with black trunk'), the beetle is common in most hilly regions and has gone under a variety of names including Bracken Clock, Marlow Buzz, Hazel Fly, Shorn Fly and Red Clock. Alfred Ronalds, writing in 1836, called it the Marlow Buzz and preferred a single strand of black ostrich herl wound into the peacock herl of the body; to Pritt it was the Red Clock. Trout gorge themselves on these beetles when they are blown onto the water, but it is worth having a Coch-y-Bondhu in the fly box for any occasion when the fishing is slow.

Close relatives of the Coch-y-Bondhu are the **Red Tag** and **Treacle Parkin**, both old patterns

Treacle Parkin.

that are as likely to be fished dry, and particularly for grayling, than as wet-flies. However, they do make good wet-flies and I have found the red and yellow tags of these flies to be particularly attractive to rainbow trout wherever they occur in running water. Both flies are dressed on a variety of sizes of hooks and with peacock herl bodies and dark ginger or red hen hackles (cock hackles for dry-flies). The Treacle Parkin is given a tag of bright yellow wool and the Red Tag of bright red wool and although they may be described as 'attractors' the Parkin also resembles a number of popular beetle patterns. Both flies are generally regarded as Yorkshire as Yorkshire pudding but, wait for it … the Red Tag was originally the Worcester Gem!

Finally, though I have alluded elsewhere to the west-country wet-flies dressed by H.C. Cutcliffe (*Trout Fishing on Rapid Streams*, 1863), I have tended to neglect the flies of that region. In order to make partial amends I now include the **Half Stone**, a Devon pattern not unlike the style of dressing used by Austin in tying the Tup's Indispensable (a fly much heralded by Skues). The Half Stone is dressed as follows:

Half Stone.

- **Hook**: 14–12
- **Thread**: primrose yellow tying silk (Pearsall's shade 3)
- **Body**: the rear half of primrose floss silk with a thorax of mole's fur
- **Hackle**: honey dun hen hackle
- **Tails**: optional tails of rusty-blue dun cock feather fibres

This is one of those patterns that works very well on rapid streams, though nobody can quite explain why. Perhaps it is just that the primrose yellow of the body attracts the fish's attention; it has not time to scrutinize the fly closely as it whips by and so it strikes immediately. 'Half Stone' may suggest a stonefly, but I have my doubts and, in any case, who would ever think of imitating only half a natural insect? It was more likely to have been developed as an imitation of the pale watery olives.

8 LITTLE WINGED WET-FLIES

Introduction

Winged wet-flies, not loch flies but imitations of natural insects, are really the lost generation of trout flies. Many of the soft-hackled spider patterns actually began life as winged patterns, although they gradually lost their wings during the last decades of the nineteenth century. Prior to that, most wet-flies were winged because anglers didn't realize that a hackle on a trout fly might represent both the wings and legs of a natural insect; each key attribute of a natural fly had to be imitated – body, tails, wings and legs (hackle). Certainly up to the time of Michael Theakston writing in 1853 (*British Angling Flies*) and John Jackson writing in 1854 (*The Practical Fly-Fisher*), the majority of wet-flies were dressed with wings generally made from slips of primary or secondary quill feathers. However, when Pritt published *Yorkshire Trout Flies* in 1885 he thought the winged wet-fly a thing of the past:

> It is a long stretch from the days of Theakston and Jackson to the present time, and in the interval there has grown up amongst observant anglers a decided preference for hackled flies, and wisely so, and this preference is by no means confined within the limits of our county.

Skues, too, pointed out that the hackles on spider patterns perfectly suggested both the wings and legs of a drowning or emerging fly, so the matter was proven and I concluded that spider patterns were far more effective than winged flies. I stopped tying winged wet-flies for river fishing. In any case, how many winged insects actually end up under the water? Very few, I presumed. Then I remembered that there are areas of Britain where winged wet-flies are still commonly in use, for example the winged wet-flies of the River Clyde, dressed with a tiny body, narrow almost upright wings, a wisp of hackle and so admirably described by John Reid in his book, *Clyde Style Flies*. Clyde-styled winged wet-flies are still used effectively, so the winged fly is perhaps not an anachronism.

Is it really true anyway that trout rarely encounter winged natural flies underwater? Plenty of emerging flies, both on rivers and lakes, fail to escape the water, even though their wings are fully formed, becoming drowned by the current or waves. On rapid-running rivers, a good proportion of the hatching flies will be swept away by the current and tumbled under the surface. There are also species of ephemeridae that lay their eggs underwater; the female imago swims under the surface to lay her eggs, is then exhausted and becomes a drowned winged fly. Other spinners too, that lay eggs on the surface, die and are then drowned by a rapid current. Then there are the multitudes of terrestrial flies which are blown onto rivers, lakes and reservoirs, struggle at the surface for a while and are drowned. Thus, trout do encounter plenty of drowned emerging and winged natural flies under the water. I came to the conclusion that winged wet-flies still perhaps had a role to play and thus started fishing them again from time to time. They are not my first choice of pattern however, simply because they take longer to tie than hackled flies!

The winged wet-flies of this chapter principally had their origins on rivers. They are slimly dressed imitative patterns seeking to copy specific aquatic and terrestrial insects, whereas loch flies are either generalized suggestions of food items or are purely attractors. It is an important distinction. Nevertheless, the small winged wet-flies developed for river fishing will take fish on lakes and reservoirs too; a Rough Olive or Greenwell's Glory, designed to imitate the dark olives or blue-winged olives of running water, will also tempt trout that are feeding on the pond olives and lake olives of stillwaters.

Although winged wet-flies tied today tend to be dressed with paired wings placed adjacent to one another and sloping backwards over the body of the fly, original patterns were slightly different in that the slender wings were usually split and often dressed vertically, or inclined only slightly backwards. As the hackle was intended to represent the legs only, it was usually a sparse beard hackle. In essence, it did not look a great deal different from the classic dry-flies of Halford's era. In earlier chapters I have sought to explain that in the days of horse-hair lines no distinction was drawn between 'dry-fly' and 'wet-fly' fishing, so that the fly would float when it alighted, then gradually sink as it drifted down the stream. A wet-fly dressed with split wings would initially float quite well and would not require several turns of cock hackle to float it. Even today, there is much to be said for tying split-winged flies that may be floated occasionally, or fished just under the surface to resemble an emerger or drowned fly, yet 'closed' wings, inclined backwards, enable a fly to sink more easily when it is specifically intended to be fished wet.

While the hackle of a spider pattern may represent both the wings and legs of an insect and may also provide a vague impression of the stage at which an adult fly emerges from the nymph, it is possible to argue that a winged wet-fly actually bears closer scrutiny from a trout's point of view, particularly in still or slowly flowing water. Although general appearance is important with respect to hackled spiders, it is the movement of the hackle that provides the salient attractor; in the case of winged wet-flies, movement is of less significance than appearance. The winged wet-fly must look, as far as possible, like the real thing. As I am not a trout, and thus cannot see how a trout sees, this is of course pure speculation, but it seems logical enough to me. I am still inclined to choose

hackled patterns whenever possible, for the simple reason that they are easier to tie, but winged wet-flies do have a part to play and may be more effective under certain circumstances.

Ultimately, how the wings are aligned on the fly is a matter of personal choice. Though they used few winged patterns, Edmonds and Lee followed the rules of nature so that ephemeridae were imitated with vertically winged wet-flies, while sedge imitations had wings inclining backwards. It is difficult to tell, but judging from the illustrations in *Brook and River Trouting* I should guess that vertical wings were tied slightly split. So the decision to be taken is whether wings should be tied on vertically, or inclined backwards, 'closed' or 'split'. Most of my patterns are dressed with the wings inclined backwards and the two slips of feather split ever so slightly apart, for I think that to split the wings too far apart runs the risk of creating a fly which swims badly underwater in quieter pools. Whether the wings are closed or split matters very little in rapid currents. Dressing a vertical wing to suggest ephemeridae may make sense, but the trout don't seem over-bothered if the wing slopes backwards. In any case, the wings of a drowned dun will be at the mercy of the current and are unlikely to remain in a neat vertical position. When at rest, many species of flies have their wings inclined backwards, or even flat over the body, and I also think that backward-inclining wings on an artificial best suggest the emergent wings of an insect metamorphosing from nymph to adult fly. In conclusion, I prefer to tie wet-flies with wing slips almost touching and inclined backwards, finding them suitable for both river and stillwater use.

The illustrations in many nineteenth-century books show hackle fibres tied in underneath the wing (a 'beard' hackle), rather than wound fully round the hook. This was for the simple reason that the hackle was intended to imitate only the legs of a natural fly. I doubt that trout are able to count the number of 'legs' on an artificial fly, therefore a fully wound hackle may just as well be dressed as a beard hackle. I am not a lover of beard hackles because aligning the fibres correctly is a troublesome business and it is all too easy to produce an unbalanced fly. Thus, I choose a fully wound hackle on winged wet-flies, although it must not be bushy; one turn of hackle about the hook is often enough, two turns ample.

I have spent time discussing the wings and hackles of winged wet-flies, yet have said nothing about bodies. It stands to reason that they should be slim, as slim as the bodies of the natural flies they imitate and no different to the bodies of the soft-hackled spider patterns treated in the previous chapter. A brief comment on the issue of tails is required. Whatever produced the changes that took place between Jackson, writing in 1854, and Pritt writing some thirty years later, it is clear that during the interim period wings gradually 'fell off' artificial flies. The same thing seems to have happened to tails. Most of the old winged wet-flies were given tails and fly dressers went to great lengths in order to select materials that matched the colour of a natural fly's tails, or 'whisks'. Cock hackle fibres were generally used for tails as they would stand out stiffly like those of a natural insect. Often, a fly dresser would only use two or three fibres in emulation of the number of tails possessed by the natural insect, though that seems particularly pedantic. In the dressing notes which follow I have included tails where standard dressings normally include them, but I doubt whether they are really necessary *in most cases*. There are, however, very important exceptions – adding tail fibres to artificial flies that we intend to fish close to the surface as emergers is a good idea because the 'tails' provide an impression of the nymphal case or pupal shuck from which the adult fly is emerging.

Materials for Winging Wet-Flies and Preparing Wings

The materials used for dressing soft-hackled spider patterns will equip us for the tying of most traditional winged wet-flies, but we may need some additional materials for winging. Some of the wings of birds that supplied soft hackles will also provide primary and secondary quills suitable for slips of feather from which wings may be constructed. Excellent primary and secondary feathers for winging may be obtained from the wings of woodcock, grouse (also centre tail feathers), snipe, partridge (also speckled tail

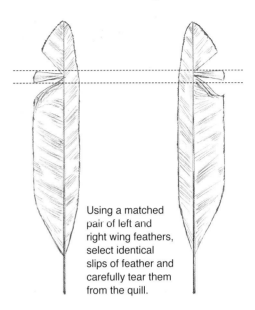

Using a matched pair of left and right wing feathers, select identical slips of feather and carefully tear them from the quill.

Selecting matching wing slips.

feathers), French partridge, moorhen, coot and starling, although to this list I would also add hen blackbird and hen feathers dyed in various colours. This selection of feathers will cater for most winged wet-flies and will also supply substitute winging materials for some of the more obscure feathers specified in old dressings. If it is possible to visit a good fly-dressing material supplier, the easiest way to acquire the necessary winging materials is to select whatever feathers are available in the key colours – pale grey, mid-grey, dark grey/black, pale brown, a rich plain brown, mottled fawn and brown, dark freckled brown and white.

Selecting and preparing slips of feather to form the wing is perhaps the most critical stage in dressing a winged wet-fly. Imagine that we are going to form a wing out of primary wing quills; the first essential will be a *pair* of wings, for it is not possible to produce perfectly matched slips from a single wing. Select two identical feathers, one from a 'left-hand' wing and one from a 'right-hand' wing, ensuring that each feather forms a smooth plane and has even fibres that knit perfectly into each other. If fibres are split apart, they can be stroked back together, but any primary quill with several splits in it is likely to have a weakness that will impair the production of neat wings. Once you are happy that the quills match perfectly and are of the correct colour and quality, select matching slip sections from each quill and carefully separate them from the fibres at each side of the chosen slips. Remove the slips by carefully tearing the soft fibres attached to the quill; the tear should be made towards the base of the quill and the slips should come away fairly easily. Do not cut slips from a quill with a pair of scissors, as this will result in a weakening of the bond between the fibres, which then separate from one another all too easily. When slips are torn from the quill it is possible that a few fibres split apart, but they can be remarried by stroking gently so that the edges of the fibres interlock again. When the slips have been removed from the 'left-hand' and 'right-hand' quills, lay them side by side to ensure they match and have exactly the same number of fibres. Place the slips over the top of the hook that is going to be used to tie the fly and if they appear a little too large, one or two fibres may be carefully removed from each slip. It is very important that the wing should be in proportion to the rest of the fly.

Finally, carefully place the slips together, generally with the underside of the feather inwards and the top side of the feather on the outside, and stroke them to make sure that there is a perfect match from tip to base. The inner face (or underside) of the feather slip is usually slightly concave and the outer face (or top side) convex, so that when the slips are placed together there is a nice shape to them and they are not completely 'flat'. There should also be a nice even curve and tapering from the base to the tip of the prepared wing. It is a matter of personal choice as to whether the fly dresser prepares each wing as individual flies are being dressed, or saves time by preparing several wings at once; a series of prepared wings may be kept in something like a bulldog clip.

Tying a Winged Wet-Fly – The Rough Olive

By means of illustration, we will dress a version of the Rough Olive, which provides a good imitation of drowning or emerging dark olives. Rough Olives appear in a variety of colours and

shades and it is not unusual to see examples dressed with olive-green bodies and olive-green hen hackles. However, I generally prefer a version dressed with a brown-olive body. Several traditional dressings of this pattern called for bodies of heron herl dyed a brown-olive shade, but heron herl is not always readily available, as well as being fragile and easily shredded. A fine dubbing of seal's fur or Partridge SLF is to be preferred for a more modern dressing.

- **Hook**: 14
- **Thread**: lightly waxed brown tying silk (Pearsall's shade 17)
- **Body**: a slim body of brown-olive seal's fur or 'Partridge SLF' (shade 11)
- **Rib**: fine gold wire
- **Wing**: slips of feather from a darkish starling primary quill
- **Hackle**: couple of turns of hen hackle feather dyed brown-olive
- **Tails**: an optional tail from a few fibres of dark olive-brown cock hackle

Tying the Rough Olive – Step 1.

Having prepared wing slips the Rough Olive is then dressed as follows:

Step 1
Fix the brown tying silk behind the eye of the hook and run it in touching turns halfway down the shank where the cock hackle fibres, intended as tails, are caught in. Snip off any excess fibre butts. Continue winding the silk to the end of the body so that the tails protrude beyond the bend of the hook. The fibres of the tail should be slightly splayed.

Step 2
Tie in a length of fine gold wire at the bend, being careful not to disturb the tail fibres, then spin a small amount of brown-olive seal's fur or SLF onto the waxed tying silk.

Step 3
Wind the dubbing to a point behind the eye that will leave just enough space for fixing in the wing and winding the hackle. The body of the fly must

remain slim. Remove any excess dubbing fur from the tying silk.

Step 4
Wind the gold wire in open turns from bend to eye in a contrary direction to the winding of the dubbing (that is, one should be clockwise and the other anti-clockwise). Fix in the ribbing wire and snip off any excess.

Step 5
Now I apply the hackle, although some fly dressers prefer to hackle the fly after winging, which is necessary if the wings are to be split. Strip the fluffy fibres from the base of a small brown-olive hen hackle and fix it onto the hook behind the eye. Snip off any excess stalk. Wind two turns of hackle round the hook, carefully wind the tying thread through the fibres towards the eye and then wind two or three turns of thread close to the base of the hackle so that the fibres incline slightly backwards.

Step 2.

Step 3.

Step 6

Grip the prepared wing slips firmly but gently between the thumb and forefinger of the left hand (if you are right-handed) and present them on top of the hook so that the base of the wing will be directly in front of the hackle. Hold the wing and body of the fly between the finger and thumb, ensuring that the wing is perfectly straight and that the tip of the wing reaches to a point slightly beyond the bend of the hook.

Step 7

The next process is critical and unless it is done correctly the wing will twist. Take a loop of tying thread over the wing slips so that it too will be within the thumb and forefinger, which will hold both the wing and loop of thread in a vertical plane. Keeping pressure on both the wing slips and the loop, draw the tying silk down firmly but slowly, so that the feather fibres come down one on top of the other and do not twist. Providing

that the first turn of silk kept the wing straight, take two more turns over the wing, which should now be fixed in and sloping backwards over the body. (Refer to the line drawing opposite showing this procedure.)

Step 8

If the wing slips are to be closely abutted, simply snip off any excess feather and the wing is completed. (If a split-winged fly is preferred, the wing slips should be parted carefully using a dubbing needle. Then a figure-of-eight winding of tying silk should be taken between the wing slips, in order to keep them apart, followed by another turn of silk just in front of the wings before any excess feather is snipped off. A split wing should be constructed before hackling.)

Step 9

Finish off the head and apply a drop of varnish, ensuring that there is no 'bulk' from remaining wing fibres.

Step 4.

Step 5.

Step 6.

Step 7.

Step 1

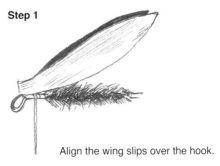

Align the wing slips over the hook.

Step 2

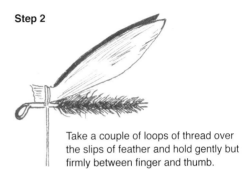

Take a couple of loops of thread over the slips of feather and hold gently but firmly between finger and thumb.

Step 3

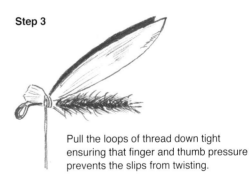

Pull the loops of thread down tight ensuring that finger and thumb pressure prevents the slips from twisting.

Step 4

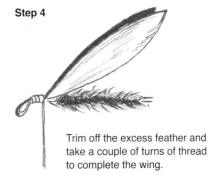

Trim off the excess feather and take a couple of turns of thread to complete the wing.

Tying a wing.

Step 8.

Step 9.

A Selection of Traditional Winged Wet-Flies

Space precludes an exhaustive list of winged wet-flies. Many of the soft-hackled spider patterns in the previous chapter may be given the addition of wings and indeed were often winged patterns before they became spiders. The reader may wish to experiment accordingly, for example by adding starling wings to a Snipe and Purple.

Alder

I have never had much success when trying to imitate natural alder flies and have rarely experienced trout showing a great deal of interest in them. However, I have had a great deal of success when using the artificial Alder, which I regard principally as a general pattern.

- **Hook**: 14–10
- **Thread**: mulberry tying silk (Pearsall's shade 15)
- **Body**: bronze peacock herl which should be twisted around the mulberry tying silk when wound along the hook shank
- **Wings**: dark brown speckled hen feather
- **Hackle**: black hen hackle feather, which is normally tied in front of the wings

This is a brilliant general river and reservoir fly, particularly early in the season, and I dress it on hooks no larger than size 14, which is somewhat smaller than a natural Alder. The Alder fly (*Sialis*) has appeared under various names; it is the Maure Fly of Dame Juliana's *Treatyse* (1496) and the Orl Fly in many other old books. Alders generally appear in May and June and are like very dark brown and heavily built sedge flies. They have similar roof-shaped wings with distinct black veins on them and they *ought* to be a juicy morsel for a trout because they are big flies. It is possible for alders to be as long as an inch (2.5cm) in length, although most specimens I have seen recently have been smaller. Although the nymph of the alder is aquatic, it crawls onto dry land and pupates for a week or so before the adult fly emerges. Adult flies often fly low over the surface of the water and are blown onto it. Recently I heard of a small lake where trout go mad for alders, although I have not experienced this at first hand. The Alder pattern given above is similar to a wet-fly designed by the novelist, Charles Kingsley, and much heralded by G.E.M. Skues, who apparently caught many trout on it when natural alders were in evidence.

Black Gnat.

Black Gnat

With the addition of pale starling wings, any of the Black Spider designs will produce a passable imitation of the black gnat and there have been many Black Gnat dressings over the centuries. The following dressing was a favourite of E.M. Tod, who published *Wet-Fly Fishing* in 1903:

- **Hook**: 16–14
- **Thread**: black tying silk (Pearsall's shade 9)
- **Body**: waxed black tying silk
- **Wings**: slips taken from a pale starling primary feather
- **Hackle**: small black hen hackle feather

Tod dressed his original fly with two strands of black hen hackle for a tail, but this hardly seems necessary as the natural fly does not possess tails. More often than not, imitations of the black gnat (*Bibio johannis*) are fished dry, yet a small wet-fly fished close to the surface will often do better than a floating-fly. There is no doubt that trout can become preoccupied with black gnats when swarms suddenly appear over the water and a breeze results in casualties which the trout mop up avidly. At such times, a dry-fly may be ignored because it is competing with so many natural flies on the surface, yet a wet-fly, appearing as if it is a drowned gnat, is selected and taken. T.E. Pritt, Roger Woolley and G.E.M. Skues were among the notable anglers who preferred to fish a wet-fly during black gnat feeding frenzies.

Black Quill

The Black Quill may also be used to imitate black gnats, but it is much better as an imitation of emerging midges and adult midges that fail to escape the surface of the water once their wings have emerged. It is worth adding tails to this dressing in order to suggest the empty shuck from which the adult fly is emerging.

- **Hook**: 16–14
- **Thread**: either black tying silk (Pearsall's shade 9) or brown (Pearsall's shade 17)
- **Body**: natural stripped peacock herl
- **Wings**: slips from a pale starling primary feather
- **Hackle**: small black hen hackle feather wound sparsely
- **Tails**: white, cream or blue dun cock hackle fibres

Black Quill.

The stripped peacock herl body provides a superb segmented effect, but the material is fragile and easily broken. One solution is to varnish the completed body, although a similar segmented effect can be achieved by winding double strands of flexi-floss along the shank; use either brown and white flexi-floss, or black and white. By varying the colour of the hackle and by using dyed stripped peacock herl in matching colours (or appropriate colours of flexi-floss) a series of flies may be dressed to imitate various colours of midges: Red Quills and Olive Quills are particularly useful.

Blae and Black

Continuing the theme of black midges, or 'duck flies', we now have that famous Irish pattern (though it may well have originated in Scotland!), the Blae and Black:

- **Hook**: 16–12
- **Thread**: black tying silk (Pearsall's shade 9)
- **Body**: black wool or seal's fur ribbed with fine oval silver tinsel
- **Wings**: slips from a medium grey starling feather
- **Hackle**: black hen hackle feather

It may be argued that the Blae and Black should have been included in Chapter 10 (loch flies) rather than in the present chapter, yet it fits the description of a small winged wet-fly intended to imitate a specific insect, so I decided to include it here. Whether of Irish or Scottish origin, it is clear that the dialect word 'blae', referring to the wing colour of the pattern, is closely related to 'bloa'. The Blae and Black is still a popular fly and is used effectively on many loughs, lochs, lakes and reservoirs as an imitation of black chironmids, or simply as a general pattern. The Blae and Black has been subject to a number of variations including the addition of various tail materials such as red ibis. A tail of red ibis, or any white feather dyed pillar-box red, or even fluorescent red floss, has become a fairly standard addition to the Blae and Black and I must agree that it makes a very effective fly. Perhaps the red tail provides a 'target' attractor, but it may also be that red acts as a trigger for trout because it exaggerates the red haemo-globin present in many species of midges. As the pupal shuck splits open and the adult fly begins to emerge, even black midges possess a distinct red glow and this may be something that trout lock on to. The Blae and Black, usually fished on

Blae and Black.

the point or middle dropper, accounts for many stillwater trout and certainly deserves its continuing popularity.

Bluebottle

Trout eat bluebottles whenever these flies are blown onto the water and I once fished a lake close to a piggery (not a pleasant place to fish!) where bluebottles became the trout's staple diet on warm and windy days. The artificial Bluebottle will take trout at any time during summer and it is a good fly to have in the box when other patterns fail. The following dressing is based on a tying given by Alfred Ronalds:

- **Hook**: 14–12
- **Thread**: black tying silk (Pearsall's shade 9)
- **Body**: bright blue floss silk
- **Wings**: slips from a pale grey starling feather
- **Hackle**: black hen hackle feather semi-palmered to suggest the 'buzz' of a struggling insect

As tinsels are now available in an 'electric blue' colour it is a good idea to rib the floss body with bright blue tinsel in order to enhance the attractive properties of the fly. On windy days, the Bluebottle is best fished close to the surface,

either on lakes and reservoirs, or the quieter reaches of rivers; a few twitches imparted to the fly will suggest a struggling insect.

Blue Dun

There is no such thing as *the* Blue Dun, since it is such an old pattern that it has appeared in many different dressings over the centuries. It has also been dressed as a soft-hackled spider, winged wet-fly, hackled dry-fly and split-winged dry-fly, although it is in its guise as a winged wet-fly that it has become most neglected. The following dressing may be recommended as an imitation of emerging or drowning olives (dark or medium), pale wateries and other ephemeridae:

- **Hook**: 16–12
- **Thread**: waxed primrose tying silk (Pearsall's shade 3)
- **Body**: a light dubbing of mole fur over primrose tying silk
- **Wings**: slips from medium to dark grey starling feathers or hen blackbird
- **Hackle**: pale blue dun hen hackle feather either from a natural or dyed cape
- **Tails**: a few fibres of blue dun cock hackle feather

Blue Dun dressings go back at least to the days of Charles Cotton and while the Blue Dun was regarded as essentially a dry-fly in the days of Halford, it was as a wet-fly that it originally gained its reputation. I have found the Blue Dun to be an excellent river pattern, but disappointing as a lake and reservoir fly even when pond or lake olives have been in evidence. The Waterhen Bloa, described in Chapter 7, was a variation on the Blue Dun theme and the winged wet-fly may also be hackled with a waterhen (moorhen) feather rather than a hen feather. Alternatively, a 'bloa' coloured feather from the underside of either a starling or young grouse wing also makes an appropriate hackle. An almost identical pattern to the dressing given above was included by Skues in *Minor Tactics of the Chalk Stream* (1910), although he dressed the wings with slips taken from snipe primary feathers. *Minor Tactics* is an important book because Skues counters the accusation that wet-fly fishing was simply 'raking the water', by pointing out that casting wet-flies upstream was every bit as sophisticated and effective as the dry-fly. While Skues used a similar Blue Dun to the one given above, Blue Duns in other parts of the country were often rather different. For example, in Derbyshire there was a popular old pattern dressed with a body of stripped peacock herl, known as the Blue Dun Hackle, while stripped peacock herl was also favoured in a number of west-country dressings.

Broughton's Point (or Dark Bloa)

The dressing of the Broughton's Point is usually given as follows:

- **Hook**: 16–14
- **Thread**: either claret tying silk (Pearsall's shade 14) or mulberry (Pearsall's shade 15)
- **Body**: either plain claret/mulberry tying silk or floss silk of the same colour
- **Wings**: slips of medium 'blae', or grey, starling feather
- **Hackle**: black hen hackle feather

Tails are not generally included in the dressing of the Broughton's Point, even though it may have been originally developed to imitate a member of the ephemeridae. As with many

Broughton's Point.

traditional flies, the Broughton's Point has been subject to a number of variations including the use of a double hackle of red-brown and black hen. The fly was reputedly invented around 1830 by a Mr Broughton, a Penrith shoemaker, who fished on Ullswater.

While the Broughton's Point seemingly originated in the Lake District, it also became a popular fly on the rivers of Yorkshire, where it was known as the Dark Bloa. Pritt gives a dressing of the Dark Bloa with a body of dark claret silk, wings from a starling feather and a black hen hackle, which is clearly the same as the Broughton's Point dressing given above. Pritt comments: 'Jackson dresses this fly somewhat similarly, and adds a tail as in the real insect. It is identical with one well-known and valued in the north as Broughton's Point.'

John Jackson, who published *The Practical Fly-Fisher* in 1854, actually dressed the fly a little differently. He dressed it with a body of red-brown silk, wing slips taken from dark feathers from the inside of a waterhen's wing and both hackle and tails of black cock. Writing of Jackson, Pritt says that he 'adds a tail as in the real insect', but what was the real insect that the fly sought to imitate? I am inclined to believe that as the fly originated on Ullswater, it was intended to be an imitation of the claret dun (*Leptophlebia vespertina*).

The claret dun may be in evidence on lakes and reservoirs throughout the season, although the maximum period of emergence tends to be May and June. It is a strangely neglected fly, perhaps because it is not as common in the south as it is in the hillier lakes of the Pennines, Lake District, Wales and Scotland. The nymphs of claret duns are 'laboured swimmers', but do become active prior to emergence and at such times the Broughton's Point will work well fished at a variety of depths. When duns are emerging and trout are rising to them, the Broughton's point should be fished just under the surface. In appearance, the wings of an emerged dun are dark grey and while the body may superficially appear umber in colour, it does have a claret tinge on close inspection. More widely distributed across the country is another lake fly, the sepia dun (*Leptophlebia marginata*), which is very similar in appearance to the claret dun; the body of this fly is a very obvious sepia brown in colour and the Broughton's Point may also be used to imitate it.

Cinnamon Sedge

There are quite a few wet-flies suggesting the sedges, but the following dressing offers a good general pattern:

- **Hook**: 14–10
- **Thread**: brown tying silk (Pearsall's shade 17)
- **Body**: either a single strand from a cinnamon turkey tail feather, fibres from pheasant tail centre feathers, brown seal's fur or Partridge SLF (shade 35 or 37)
- **Wings**: the wings were originally fashioned from corncrake feathers, but slips from a light brown hen feather will do nicely
- **Hackle**: ginger or light brown hen hackle feather

The above artificial, though a good general sedge pattern, was intended to imitate the natural cinnamon sedge (*Limnephilus lunatus*), which has a body varying from rich brown to a greenish-brown and possesses roof-shaped

Cinnamon Sedge.

cinnamon wings. It is a widely distributed species, normally appearing from June onwards, and although it is sometimes seen during the day it is more likely to appear at dusk. There is also the large cinnamon sedge (*Potamophylax latipennis*), which is fairly common and a number of other sedges that are aptly imitated by the pattern given above. Imitating sedges is usually thought to be the province of the buoyant dry-fly, yet wet-flies are equally successful.

From May onwards, both on rivers and lakes, sedges flutter across the surface or zigzag along it, causing quite a disturbance, and an erratically retrieved wet-fly stands a good chance of success. Evening fishing when sedges are in evidence may mean breaking the accepted 'rule' of avoiding drag. I have found that when using wet-flies such as the Cinnamon Sedge, generally towards dusk when trout are less cautious, a fly that drags across the stream may well result in an aggressive take because it emulates a skittering sedge fly. As light thickens, it becomes possible to cast downstream and across, so that the flies skate across the stream and the result may be quite explosive takes.

Coachman (and the 'Something and Nothing')

The Coachman is a very effective general wet-fly and is also regarded as a fair sedge imitation:

- **Hook**: 16–12
- **Thread**: brown tying silk (Pearsall's shade 17)
- **Body**: green or bronze peacock herl
- **Wings**: slips of white swan or hen feather or from the underside of a duck's wing
- **Hackle**: red-brown hen hackle feather

As is the case with old flies, there are many variations on the Coachman theme, including some fancy American patterns, but the original is good enough. Having said that, it is difficult to judge what the original dressing might have been, for though the Coachman is invariably now dressed with a white wing, it has been dressed in the past with wings of corncrake and starling. The Coachman is an excellent general wet-fly pattern for rivers and lakes alike. It has certainly stood the test of time, yet its origins are a little obscure and there are several claimants to its invention. Some say that it was invented by a coachman named Tom Bosworth, others favour a coachman by the name of John Hughes, while there was also an identical fly known as the Harding Fly and, for all I know, Mr Harding too may have been a coachman. Whatever the case, the fly seems to have emerged around 200 years ago.

The Coachman is an excellent fly for summer evenings when sedges are around, though it doesn't resemble any particular species, but it is also a good general pattern and I have done well with it on an early season reservoir cast. A small Coachman was among the few patterns that I possessed when I started fly fishing and in those days a fly was kept in commission until it was completely worn out. It was a ragged Coachman that led to my discovery of a nymph to beat all other nymphs; a pattern so seemingly unprepossessing that it earned itself the title of 'Something and Nothing' or simply 'S & N'. It is not a traditional wet-fly *per se*, but it is a pattern worth the giving. It has caught wild brownies and big rainbows, trout from tiny brooks to large reservoirs, from tumbling rivers to the hallowed Test, and while it may be fished on its own as a nymph, weighted or unweighted, it is also a useful point-fly on a three-fly cast. The S & N began life as a Coachman, but it has been modified a little since then; I will give you the dressing here:

Coachman.

Something and Nothing.

- **Hook**: 16–10 (a leaded version on long shanked hooks may also be dressed to represent caddis larvae)
- **Thread**: brown tying silk (Pearsall's shade 17)
- **Body**: an underbody of fine dark copper wire (or lead wire if it is to be fished deep) wrapped over with three or four strands of bronze peacock herl
- **Wings**: white hen feather or wool trimmed to a mere stub or tuft
- **Hackle**: various shades of hen feather from ginger to coch-y-bondhu; wind two turns of feather around the hook and then trim down the fibres with scissors so that the hackle is no more than a 'ruff' with a few longer fibres sticking out

Cowdung Fly

The natural cowdung fly is a nasty little critter with an unpleasant bite and unseemly dining habits, but the artificial wet-fly is actually rather pleasing. I rarely experience the need to imitate natural cowdung flies, yet the artificial makes a pretty good sedge pattern!

- **Hook**: 14
- **Thread**: brown tying silk (Pearsall's shade 17)
- **Body**: a mixed dubbing of yellow, amber, olive and brown seal's fur or wool
- **Wings**: slips from a fawny-brown hen feather
- **Hackle**: dark ginger hen hackle feather

The dressing given above is a modified version of a dressing given by Ronalds in 1836. He originally dressed the pattern with a body dubbed from mixed yellow mohair and brown fur, a landrail wing and a ginger hen hackle. While cowdung flies are still common enough and are blown onto the water from time to time, I tend to think of the artificial as a good sedge pattern and a useful reservoir fly for the summer months. In that role, it is best fished on the top dropper so that it may be tripped through the waves on a warmish breezy day and it can be improved by winding the hackle along the shank in palmer style.

Fog Black

The Fog Black, another old pattern from the north of England, was greatly valued as an imitation of black gnats. Although there are variations in the dressing, the following is pretty standard:

- **Hook**: 16–14
- **Thread**: well-waxed purple tying silk (Pearsall's shade 8)
- **Body**: purple silk dubbed sparingly with heron herl or more sparingly with black ostrich herl
- **Wings**: slips taken from a dark grey starling feather
- **Hackle**: dark feather from a cock starling's neck which should have a glossy purple or green sheen to it

Pritt gave a dressing of the Fog Black that called for slips of feather from a bullfinch's wing. Just try obtaining that material! Pritt thought the Fog Black 'suitable for cold days, from June to the end of the season', but it is a good fly to use whenever trout are feeding on something small and black. On close inspection, the bodies of many black insects glow with iridescent purples and greens and this is imitated by the choice of materials used for the body of the Fog Black.

Gold Ribbed Hare's Ear

The Gold Ribbed Hare's Ear, or 'GRHE' as it is often called today, is still a very popular pattern, although modern dressings often bear little real resemblance to the wet-flies of old. It is impossible to tell when the fly was first

Fog Black.

Gold Ribbed Hare's Ear.

developed, who invented it and what it initially looked like, but the following dressing provides a superb emerger pattern aided by the addition of tails to suggest an empty nymphal shuck:

- **Hook**: 16–12
- **Thread**: waxed primrose tying silk (Pearsall's shade 3)
- **Body**: a mix of different shades of hare's ear fur spun on primrose silk (different mixes may be used to produce light, medium and dark versions of the fly). The body is ribbed with very fine embossed oval gold tinsel.
- **Wings**: slips of pale starling primary feathers
- **Hackle**: spikey guard hairs picked out with a dubbing needle
- **Tails**: optional tails of white or cream hare's ear hairs

Modern versions of the dressing are often far too bulky. The body must be quite slim, although a little more dubbing should be added at the thorax where fibres are picked out to splay under and around the wing. The Gold Ribbed Hare's Ear, in its various shades, is an excellent wet-fly to use when any of the ephemeridae hatch; the lightest version will suggest the palest of pale olives, while the darkest version will imitate the darkest of dark olives. It is a very versatile fly and while it is used as a nymph, or even dry-fly, it is in the role of emerger that it excels best and should be used on rivers or lakes whenever trout are bulging to ascending nymphs and hatching flies.

It is interesting that even F.M. Halford appreciated the Gold Ribbed Hare's Ear as an emerger pattern. In his *Dry Fly Man's Handbook* (1913) he wrote of the GRHE:'It has always been my theory that it is a fair representation of a dun in the act of disentangling itself from the nymphal shuck.'

That was certainly borne out a few years ago on the Derbyshire Wye when trout were feeding avidly on emerging dark olives and wouldn't look at a dry-fly or conventional nymph. Wet-flies too that sank even an inch or two stood little chance of success. I discovered, however, that when I cast a GRHE upstream, I started to get takes almost as soon as it landed and I caught a few trout in that manner. Once the fly drifted a little downstream and began to sink, the trout ignored it. It was when the fly was actually *in* the surface film that it was successful. Eventually, I worked out that a little grease applied to the picked-out hairs of the hackle would keep that part of the fly in the film, with the body of the fly tilted at an angle underwater. As soon as the fly was fished in that manner it became deadly and I took trout after trout.

Grannom or 'Greentail'

The Grannom is a good general sedge pattern, but it was first dressed to imitate a specific early season fly that rivals the mayfly's importance on some rivers. The winged wet-fly is dressed as follows:

- **Hook**: 14
- **Thread**: green tying silk (Pearsall's shade 18)
- **Body**: a darkish tan mix of hare's ear fur
- **Tag**: bright green floss silk or Partridge SLF (shades 1 or 2)
- **Wings**: slips of feather from a hen pheasant or partridge wing quill
- **Hackle**: pale ginger hen hackle feather

The grannom (*Brachycentrus subnubilis*) still makes an appearance on many rivers and the above pattern provides a good imitation. It should be fished close to the surface, a method which may be used also when imitating other sedges with this fly. The natural grannom appears as early as April, when the weather is

Grannom.

mild or there has been a particularly mild winter, and it can emerge in numbers up to the end of May. Unlike many sedges, the grannom is a daytime emerger, with noon being the likeliest time of emergence, and while trout may gorge themselves on the fly, hatches are often short-lived. It is a small sedge with fawn-grey wings and body and it is the distinctive green egg sac of the female that the tag of the artificial seeks to imitate. Grannom mate very soon after emergence so it is possible to have emerging adults and egg-laying females on the water at the same time. While the grannom only occurs on rivers, the artificial fly may also be used on lakes and reservoirs as a general sedge pattern.

Finally, it has often been noted that the artificial may be fished equally well as a floating- or sinking-fly during a grannom hatch. Referring to the dressing given above, the Reverend E. Powell (rector of a small Shropshire parish, Munslow, who fished the Welsh border streams around the late nineteenth century/early twentieth century) commented, 'The queer thing about this pattern is that the fish will take it wet or dry', and I imagine that the wet-fly may be taken for a mature ascending pupa, emerging adult or egg-laying female.

Greenwell's Glory

The Greenwell's Glory hardly requires any further introduction, save to say that the winged wet-fly version is by no means as popular as the spider version or hackled or winged dry-fly. That is a pity because it remains a very good fly and, dressed as follows, was the all-round favourite of that great exponent of the wet-fly, E.M. Tod:

- **Hook**: 18–14
- **Thread**: well-waxed primrose tying silk (Pearsall's shade 3), or primrose silk impregnated with line grease so that it turns a nice light olive shade
- **Body**: well-waxcd primrose tying silk ribbed with the finest grade of gold wire
- **Wings**: slips of feather taken from the inside (or underside) of a hen blackbird's wing
- **Hackle**: greenwell hen hackle feather (ginger with black centre)
- **Tails**: greenwell cock hackle fibres (optional)

Greenwell's Glory.

The winged Greenwell is a good general pattern to suggest emerging flies and drowned duns and it is as effective on lakes and reservoirs as it is on rivers. I can highly recommend an 'all-Greenwell' cast combining dry-fly, winged wet-fly and soft-hackled spider and think that it is an ideal set-up both for larger rivers and stillwaters. Before leaving the Greenwell, it is worth mentioning that a large version, dressed on hooks up to size 8, makes an excellent loch and sea trout pattern, as does a variant dressed with a body of flat gold tinsel.

Hawthorn Fly

Hawthorn flies are often imitated by dry-flies, yet the wet-fly perhaps offers a more effective approach, particularly because these clumsy flies are easily drowned in a wave or moderately fast current. There have been many wet-fly imitations of the hawthorn fly (*Bibio marci*) stretching as far back as the *Treatyse* of 1496, but the following dressing is as good as any:

- **Hook**: 14–12
- **Thread**: black tying silk (Pearsall's shade 9)
- **Body**: black floss silk with a pronounced thorax of black ostrich herl
- **Wings**: slips from pale starling or any other light grey feather
- **Hackle**: black hen hackle feather

Hawthorn flies have long gangly hind legs which may be imitated either by tying in two knotted strands of black ostrich herl sloping backwards, or by using a long-fibred hackle which seems to work just as well. The natural hawthorn fly may appear as early as mid-April, though it is more common in May. When it does appear, it is one of those terrestrials that is often blown onto the water in great numbers because it is a very poor flier and it may become the trout's staple diet on rivers or lakes for at least a couple of weeks. The hawthorn is quite a large black fly with a distinctive bulbous thorax, followed by a slimmer black abdomen, and of course those long black and hairy hind legs. For such a bulky kind of fly it is blessed with a fairly small pair of wings, resulting in erratic and clumsy flight patterns. It is no wonder that it ends up on the water in great numbers under windy conditions and I have certainly had some success with a dry-fly, although a wet-fly, retrieved slowly in little erratic pulls, is likely to increase the number of takes.

Hawthorn Fly.

Hen Blackie

The Hen Blackie is rather like a darker version of the Greenwell's Glory:

- **Hook**: 16–14
- **Thread**: well-waxed yellow tying silk (Pearsall's shade 5)
- **Body**: plain waxed yellow tying silk
- **Wings**: slips from a dark hen blackbird primary or secondary feather
- **Hackle**: black hen hackle

The Hen Blackie may be fished as a general pattern or as a dark olive imitation and is a particularly good early season fly. Tom Stewart (*Fifty Popular Flies*, Volume 4, 1973) thought it was a good fly throughout the season and he caught many fine trout from the Clyde on the pattern tied on a size 14 hook. He used it too on lochs and suggests that an optional small gold tag may be added for lake or loch fishing. The Hen Blackie may be sparsely dressed in the Clyde-style with a short body and slim wings which are split and tied in an almost upright position.

March Brown

Although the following wet-fly may well provide a passing imitation of the natural march brown (*Rhithrogena haarupi*), and has done so for centuries, I regard it more as a 'sedgey' looking general fly which is at its best when fished on lakes and reservoirs. It is a good early season fly yet, in spite of its name, it is a very effective summer fly too. I can guarantee that most commercially dressed March Brown wet-flies sold today are fished as loch flies, rather than an imitative river patterns. Dressed on larger hooks, the March Brown is also a popular sea trout fly on some rivers. The March Brown has been subject to many variations, but I favour the following:

- **Hook**: 14–10
- **Thread**: pale orange tying silk (Pearsall's shade 6a)
- **Body**: a dark mix of hare's ear fur spun on orange silk. Pick out some of the 'spikey' hairs with a dubbing needle and rib the body with fine embossed oval gold tinsel
- **Wings**: slips from a speckled partridge tail feather or mottled hen pheasant tail
- **Hackle**: brown speckled partridge back feather
- **Tails**: a few fibres as per hackle

March Brown.

As a general lake and reservoir pattern there is also a fairly standard dressing with a body of purple seal's fur, ribbed with fine oval gold tinsel, and this is a very attractive and effective 'fancy' fly that works throughout the season. Given that I find the March Brown a good sedge pattern, the Purple March Brown gave me the idea of using other colours of body dubbing when dressing the fly and it is also effective therefore when the body is dubbed with yellow, amber, orange or olive-green seal's fur.

Olive Duns

Various olive duns are among the commonest and most numerate river ephemeridae and there are many wet-flies capable of representing them. As olives may appear from the beginning to the end of the season it is worth reminding ourselves of the range of natural flies that form this 'group'. There is the large dark olive (*Baetis rhodani*), the medium olives (*Baetis vernus*, *B. Tenax* and *B. Buceratus*), the small dark olive (*Baetis scambus*), the ubiquitous blue-winged olive (*Ephemerella ignita*), the olive upright (*Rhithrogena semicolorata*) and other species which, though less common, are very similar in appearance. We must not forget also that on

Olive Quill.

lakes and reservoirs we are likely to encounter the pond olives (*Cloeon dipterum*) and lake olives (*Cloeon simile*). It is clear that olive-bodied ephemeridae are extremely important to the angler.

Winged wet-flies are capable of imitating emerging duns, drowning duns and those species whose females swim under the surface to lay their eggs, and even when there is a good rise in progress wet-flies will often score as well as dries. It then becomes a matter of personal preference as to which method we employ. If the choice is a wet-fly, then Pritt's Olive Bloa is worthy of consideration:

- **Hook**: 16–12
- **Thread**: primrose yellow tying silk (Pearsall's shade 3)
- **Body**: primrose tying silk waxed to a yellow-olive shade
- **Wings**: slips of feather from a starling primary or secondary quill
- **Hackle**: olive hen hackle feather (Pritt recommended a 'white hackle from a Hen's neck, stained to olive in onions')
- **Tails:** a few strands of feather as per hackle

Pritt believed that the Olive Bloa 'will kill well on cold, windy days, particularly about midday in March and April' and these are classic times for the large dark olive to appear during the early part of the season. The appearance of the dark olives may be a real comfort to the angler for, after a fruitless and cold morning when the river seemed completely empty, the first trickles of flies drifting down the river signal a few rises here and there. Then, suddenly, there are flies emerging everywhere and a river that seemed devoid of trout is now clearly full of them.

The Olive Quill is also an effective fly when trout are feeding on olives:

- **Hook**: 16–12
- **Thread**: olive tying silk (Pearsall's shade 16)
- **Body**: stripped peacock herl dyed olive-green
- **Wings**: slips from a mid-grey starling wing feather
- **Hackle**: medium olive-green hen hackle feather
- **Tails**: A few strands of feather as per hackle

Rough Olive.

The delicate body of stripped peacock herl may be varnished to protect it or, as in earlier dressings, it is worth experimenting with different colours of flexi-floss.

Finally, when considering imitations of the olives, we must not forget the Rough Olive that we dressed towards the beginning of the present chapter as an example of the winged wet-fly:

- **Hook**: 16–12
- **Thread**: brown tying silk (Pearsall's shade 17)
- **Body**: olive-brown seal's fur or Partridge SLF (shade 11). Rib the body with fine gold wire
- **Wing**: slips from a dark starling primary quill or hen blackbird
- **Hackle**: olive-brown hen hackle feather
- **Tails**: olive-brown hen or cock hackle fibres

As with the Olive Quill, the Rough Olive may also be dressed in a lighter version using a dubbing of various shades of olive-green (SLF shades 5, 6 or 7), a lighter starling wing and an olive-green hen hackle.

Pale Watery Dun

Like Pritt before them, Edmonds and Lee had a preference for hackled patterns over winged wet-flies, but they did include a few favoured winged patterns in their list including the Pale Watery Olive.

- **Hook**: 18–14
- **Thread**: yellow tying silk (Pearsall's shade 5)
- **Body**: yellow silk dubbed with the palest buff fur from the flank of an opossum (any pale buff fur or wool will suffice and SLF shade 39 is close enough)
- **Wings**: from a young starling's light primary quill feather, the inner side of the feather as the underside of the wing (These are very precise instructions but the reader may rest assured that any pale grey winging material will be appropriate)
- **Hackle**: light blue dun hen hackle feather
- **Tails**: a few strands of pale ginger cock hackle (Actually, the authors specify only 'two strands' for the tail but I think this over-estimates the trout's powers of observation)

This is a good fly to use for the pale wateries and spurwings, though we must not forget that we also have soft-hackled spider patterns such as the Snipe Bloa and Poult Bloa in our fly box. It is not worth distinguishing between different

Pale Watery Dun.

Yellow Legged Bloa.

species, but it is worth remembering that pale ephemeridae are quite common on rivers and are represented by the pale watery dun (*Baetis bioculatus*), the small spurwing (*Centroptilum luteolum*), the large spurwing (*Centroptilum pennulatum*) and the pale evening dun (*Procloeon pseudorufulum*). I used to worry a great deal about insect identification and even carried handbooks from the Royal Entomological Society of London in my fishing bag. It was interesting but it took time away from fishing and it strikes me that if we are able to imitate the basics of a natural insect – size, profile, colour and movement (if any) – and that results in a fish in the net, then that is all the entomology we need. If I look closely at a specimen, then I can just make out the tiny spur on the hindwing of a spurwing, but this is not something that concerns a hungry trout. In any case, insect

identification is not always that straightforward, as all the olives vary so much in colour. Some very pale dark olives may even be the same colour as dark pale wateries. Some females of the latter species can actually have quite dark bodies.

Yellow Legged Bloa

This is another one of the winged wet-flies included in the list given by Edmonds and Lee and probably the best wet-fly to use when we wish to imitate yellow stoneflies or ephemeridae.

- **Hook**: 16–14
- **Thread**: primrose yellow tying silk (Pearsall's shade 3)
- **Body**: primrose yellow tying silk
- **Wings**: slips from a young starling's primary quill feather (the outer side of the feather as the underside of the wing)
- **Hackle**: primrose yellow hen hackle feather
- **Tails**: two strands from a very pale ginger cock hackle feather

Pritt also gives this pattern but uses a ginger hackle rather than the primrose yellow feather specified by Edmonds and Lee. Edmonds and Lee recommend the Yellow Legged Bloa as a fly to use from the end of May until the end of June, but Pritt is somewhat vague as to its season. At a pinch, I am sure that a large version of a Yellow Legged Bloa could be used when the mayfly makes its appearance, although it was originally tied to imitate the smaller yellow ephemeridae such as the yellow may dun (*Heptagenia sulphurea*) and the yellow evening dun (*Ephemerella notata*). Yellow may duns are quite widespread throughout Britain and actually emerge in both rivers and lakes, though hatches may be sparse. The adult dun is a very distinctive fly, having a yellow body, yellow legs, pale yellow wings and startling bright blue eye, yet there are many who believe that trout do not have much of a liking for the naturals.

9 PALMERS

Introduction

Palmers are quite simply artificial flies that have a hackle wound the length of the body, or part-way along the body in the case of Stewart's spiders. It may be considered that palmer-dressed flies are essentially dry-flies and are therefore out of place in a book about wet-fly fishing; far from it. Palmers do make exception-ally good dry-flies – they float well when there is either a good wave on a lake or a rapid current in a river – but they are also useful as top dropper flies employed to keep two wet-flies close to the surface. In that role, they will attract trout to the wet-flies, act as a strike indicator and take a few fish in their own right. On the other hand, palmers can also be fished wet or 'damp' as top dropper flies, so that they sink below the surface during the retrieve and are then dibbled at the surface as the cast is fished out.

On the surface the palmer hackle suggests a buzz of movement, while even underwater there is that extra sense of 'kick' and struggle. Palmers may be dressed with cock or hen hackles, or even a combination of the two, depending on the way in which they are to be used. Good quality cock hackles will provide a very buoyant dry-fly, whereas hen hackles may be preferred for a palmer that is mainly intended to be fished as a sunk-fly. It is also possible to construct a good top dropper fly for loch fishing with a hen body hackle and a front cock hackle. However, I prefer to dress all my palmers with cock hackles even if they are intended to be fished under the water for part of the time. Cock hackles, being stiffer than hen hackles, provide a better impression of a kicking and struggling insect and this is particularly useful in rough water or a strong current. Palmers on the top dropper are particularly good when adult sedges are skittering across the surface and the more commotion the palmer creates, the better; this will attract the trout's attention and even if it does not take the palmer itself, it is likely to take one of the accompanying wet-flies.

Palmer-dressed flies are ancient patterns and probably existed at the time of the *Treatyse* in 1496. The name 'palmer' is somewhat obscure, so I will offer only a suggestion as to its origins. Palm Sunday is the Sunday before Easter and celebrates the time when Jesus rode into Jerusalem on a donkey and the crowds waved palm branches, age-old symbols of victory. In Britain, the palm not being an indigenous tree (although it is said that crusaders brought palm leaves back from the Holy Land as emblems of victory), branches of pussy willow were used as substitutes in ritual enactments of the event and I even recall waving such branches around at Sunday school in the 1950s. The pussy willow is replete with furry and silvery-yellow catkins, which bear a distinct resemblance to the woolly caterpillars which palmer-dressed flies were first intended to imitate and thus the style of dressing became known as a 'palmer'. In more recent times furry caterpillars have been given names such as 'woolly bears', but they may have been called 'palmers' in the past. Even as late as the nineteenth century many of the illustrations of palmer dressings look more like caterpillars than anything else and they are more densely hackled than we would dress our palmers today. (Alfred Ronalds, writing in 1836, was of this school, as is illustrated by Plate XIX of The *Fly-Fisher's Entomology*, which shows three woolly cater-pillars and their palmer imitations. Of the Black and Red Palmer dressing he says, 'this is the caterpillar of *Arctia caja*, or the Garden Tiger Moth, full-grown'.) Some angling writers assumed that 'palmer' was synonymous with 'caterpillar', yet this was not a universal idea and certainly not the way Charles Cotton viewed palmer dressings as early as 1676. It seems, therefore, that there were two approaches to palmer-dressed flies: on the one hand, those who thought that palmers simply imitated caterpillars; and, on the other hand, the more enlightened anglers who realized that this style of dressing had a much more flexible role to play.

Enlightened anglers, who believed that palmers were more than simply imitations of caterpillars, often referred to flies fashioned in this way as being 'dressed buzz' and that is a useful description. In *The Way of a Trout with a Fly* (1921), G.E.M. Skues has the following to say about palmers:

> Many of the sedges flutter upon the surface; and may not the saying that they are dressed 'buzz' be wiser than it looks? The effect of fluttering and the effect of a bush of hackles may not look dissimilar to the trout. Palmers, I have no doubt, are as often taken for struggling sedge flies as for the woolly bears and other caterpillars they are fancifully supposed to represent.

Skues assumes that palmers imitate fluttering sedges, and they do, but they will also imitate other insects and other stages in insect life cycles. For example, a Black Palmer creates a fair impression of a struggling hawthorn fly, while a Bibio is a good imitation of emerging black chironomid midges. Although I will offer a few specific palmer dressings in the current chapter, it is worth making it clear that many other patterns may be dressed palmer-style and this is particularly true of the soft-hackled spiders given in Chapter 7. For example, palmer dressings of the Woodcock and Hare's Lug Spider, Poult Bloa, Snipe Bloa, Olive Bloa, Waterhen Bloa and Hare's Lug and Plover make excellent emergers, while a palmer-dressed Black Snipe or Black Spider provides a useful pattern when any beetles or black terrestrials are struggling to avoid drowning.

The success of palmers has a great deal to do with the sense of movement that they provide and this is a constant feature of this dressing style whether the fly is floating or sunk, fished statically or retrieved. The 'buzz' of a palmer is appropriate when we wish to suggest insects struggling to emerge, struggling to avoid drowning, or even struggling to lay their eggs either at the surface, or under it. This was certainly something understood by Thomas Barker, who published *The Art of Angling* in 1651, for he dressed many of his flies in the palmer style and particularly when imitating struggling terrestrials such as the 'Hauthorn Flie'. Here is how he describes the method of dressing a palmer:

> Wee will begin to make the Palmer Flie: You must arm your line on the inside of the hook; take your Scisers and cut so much of the brown of the Mallards feather, as in your own reason shall make the wings, then lay the outmost part of the feather next the hook, and the point of the feather towards the shank of the hook, then whip it three or four times about the hook with the same silk you armed the hook; then make your silk fast; then you must take the hackle of the neck of a Cock or Capon, or a Plovers top, which is the best; take off the one side of the feather; then you must take the hackle silk, or cruell, gold, or silver thred; make all these fast at the bent of the hook, then you must begin with cruell, and silver, or gold, and work it up to the wings, every bout shifting your fingers and making a stop, then the gold will fall right, then make fast; then work up the hackle to the same place, then make the hackle fast; then you must take the hook betwixt your finger and thumb, in the left hand, with a neeld or pin, part the wings in two; then with the arming silk, as you have fastened all hitherto, whip about as it falleth crosse betwixt the wings, then with your thumb you must turn the point of the feather towards the bent of the hook; then work three or four times about the shank; so fasten; then view the proportion.

Barker was tying a winged palmer, and without a vice at that, but it is rare for many palmer dressings to be given wings today other than some dry-fly imitations of sedges. Barker's instructions are difficult to follow yet one thing is quite clear, unlike the heavily hackled palmers dressed to imitate caterpillars, Barker used only a few turns of hackle to suggest the buzz of a variety of natural insects.

Some twenty-five years after Barker, Charles Cotton also favoured the palmer-dressed fly when imitating a variety of insects including the mayfly (*Ephemera danica* or *E. vulgata*), which he tied as follows: 'Next, a Great Hackle, or Palmer-Fly, with a yellow body, ribbed with gold twist, and large wings of mallard's feather dyed yellow, with a red Capon's hackle over all.'

Cotton's Great Hackle, either fished on the surface or just beneath it, would aptly suggest a mayfly struggling to break free of the stream. Among several other palmers used by Cotton is a Black-Fly, or Black Palmer, which is still a useful top dropper fly and no mean performer when hawthorn flies are in evidence. Cotton's dressing used black ostrich herl, which is still a common ingredient of hawthorn dressings today: 'The next May-fly is the Black-Fly; made with a black body, of the whirl of an ostrich feather, ribbed with silver twist, and the black hackle of a cock over all, and is a killing fly ...'

The above pattern would make an excellent reservoir dry-fly and a useful top dropper pattern, but it may also be dressed with a black hen feather and used as a wet-fly. After Charles Cotton, a number of angling authors also chose palmer dressings to imitate hawthorns, as this style of fly best suggests the desperate struggles of this ungainly insect when it falls onto the water. It is interesting that the father and son combination of Richard and Charles Bowlker, who published *The Art of Angling* in 1747, refer to a palmered hawthorn imitation as a Black Caterpillar, thus illustrating the fact that palmered dressings probably originated as caterpillar imitations before their real values were comprehended.

Whether termed 'palmers' or 'caterpillars', flies dressed with hackles wound the length of the body have a long history and there were many local variations and parochial terms for them. In Derbyshire, for example, palmer-dressed flies were called 'bumbles', which suggests that the style of dressing may once have been used to imitate bumble bees, or it may simply be that the hackle added a buzz of movement to the fly. Even Halford fished Bumbles as dry-flies! Derbyshire Bumbles were quite fancy flies and were dressed by such famous characters as George Eaton of Matlock, David Foster of Ashbourne and Roger Woolley of Hatton. James Ogden too came from Derbyshire, before he moved to Cheltenham, and it is possible that the palmered hackle of the Invicta had its origins in the Derbyshire Dales. David Foster established a famous tackle shop, Fosters of Ashbourne, which sadly closed down only a few years ago. Foster's favourite grayling fly was a Honey Dun Bumble while Roger Woolley used a Steel-Blue Bumble as a wet-fly when pursuing brown trout. In 1896, Roger Woolley became employed as a coachman in Ireland and it is just possible that he took the 'Bumbles' over to the Emerald Isle, where Mr Justice Kingsmill Moore finally converted them into flies for 'white trout', or sea trout. David Foster's Honey Dun Bumble grayling fly was a fancy pattern dressed with a pink floss silk body ribbed with a strand of peacock's sword feather and a palmered honey dun cock hackle. Similarly, Roger Woolley's Steel-Blue Bumble was also a fancy fly, being dressed with a body of light orange, dark orange and dark red floss silk twisted together and ribbed with peacock herl; the palmered hackle was, of course, steel-blue in colour. Foster and Woolley produced palmers with blended bodies but when Bumbles reached Ireland it was blended hackles that became the main innovation.

T.C. Kingsmill Moore published *A Man May Fish* in 1960 and introduced a new series of Bumbles, which combined the Derbyshire design of fly with the Irish flair for blending colours. Although he fished them principally for sea trout, his design of fly is no less effective as a stillwater trout pattern and they seem to be gaining popularity as modern reservoir dry-flies. Kingsmill Moore sought two principal attributes in a good artificial fly – a suggestion of life and an impression of translucency. Not being concerned with exact imitation, the palmer hackling of a fly provided all that he required in terms of the suggestion of an insect struggling in the surface film, while for translucency Kingsmill Moore blended different colours of cock hackles to produce 'gleam' without dazzle. The blending of different colours of hackle is an excellent innovation and the reader may wish to experiment with this idea.

My final introductory observation on palmer dressings is to suggest that there are occasions when a densely hackled palmer, without any body dubbing, is worth trying. It may take a couple of cock hackles to completely cover the shank of a light wire hook and a contrasted front hackle (generally lighter in colour) may also be added, but this will produce a very buoyant and light dry-fly. While this design of palmer may generally be associated with dapping, it is also a buoyant design of fly suited to the roughest of days on reservoirs and to the turbulence of upland streams, where it will act as a good strike indicator for the wet-flies on the cast.

A Note on Materials for Palmers

Most of the materials assembled for the tying of soft-hackled flies and winged wet-flies will equip us for tying palmers. We should already have different colours of tying silk, seal's fur (or SLF), other furs, tinsels and a variety of hackle feathers. However, buoyant palmers require good quality cock hackles, which may be purchased on 'necks' or 'capes', or in selected packets of natural or dyed feathers. Good quality capes don't come cheap, but it is really the only way to guarantee steely feathers that will repel water, rather than absorb it, and to provide a supply of feathers small enough for the dressing of small palmers on hooks ranging from 16 to 14. Good capes will have long narrow feathers capable of producing two or three flies; packets of feathers may only hold a small percentage of usable feathers, so that there will be inevitable wastage. With the exception of the Bumbles listed, the cock hackle colours required to dress my selection of palmers are: red-brown; black; ginger; white; badger (cream with white centre); and golden-olive (dyed hackles).

Most of the palmers are dressed with bodies of seal's fur in colours we should already possess, although wool, antron or SLF may also be used (Antron is a synthetic seal's fur substitute, although I prefer to use Partridge SLF for this purpose). Wherever applicable, I have listed the shade of SLF suited to an individual pattern. When dubbing the body of a palmer it is often a good idea to pick out fibres with a dubbing needle so that they will blend with the body hackle and thus suggest that impression of translucency sought by Kingsmill Moore. In any case, roughly dressed flies are often more effective than the neatest of creations!

Although palmers work perfectly well without a wing, it is sometimes nice to add a wing and particularly when imitating sedge flies. Choosing a winging material such as deer hair, coastal deer hair, or elk hair and tying it in to slope backwards in imitation of the roof-shaped sedge wing, not only creates a good imitative pattern but also adds further to the fly's buoyancy. I rarely bother with a wing when using a palmer as a top dropper fly, but it is a good addition when the palmer is cast as a single dry-fly.

Tying a 'Standard' Palmer –
The Red Palmer

The Red Palmer, or Soldier Palmer, is a brilliant pattern for both river and reservoir fishing. It may not be an imitative pattern in the strictest sense, but it has accounted for some very discriminating and finicky trout that seemed to find the red body completely irresistible. In the following dressing instructions I am going to use two hackle feathers to dress the Red Palmer, but it is worth pointing out that the smallest sizes of palmers may be dressed with a single feather tapered from head to butt. When applying the body hackle to a palmer, unless it is a densely hackled pattern without body dubbing, the hackle should be wound in open turns so that the body colour shines through the hackle fibres. Open turns of hackle also provide an enhanced sense of movement and translucence.

We are now ready to dress a Red Palmer and the materials required are simple enough. Of course, we will require a hook and it should be pretty light in the wire if the fly is intended to float or remain close to the surface. The required tying silk is either scarlet (Pearsall's shade 11a) or crimson (shade 13). The body of the Red Palmer may be dubbed with red wool, red seal's fur or Partridge SLF (shade 17), and is ribbed with fine oval gold embossed tinsel. The hackling may be carried out with ginger, red-brown or even furnace cock hackles, depending on whether a light or dark version of the fly is required. Now for the tying:

Step 1
Having fixed the hook in the vice, attach the scarlet or crimson tying silk behind the eye. The tying silk may be very lightly waxed so that the spun dubbing adheres to it.

Step 2
Wind the tying silk along the shank in touching turns to the point where the bend of the hook begins.

Step 3
At the bend of the hook, fix the gold ribbing tinsel in and snip off any excess. Then fix in the body hackle by the tip of the feather and snip off any excess feather. The feather should be fixed in so that the outer side faces the eye of the hook. The body hackle, which may be a

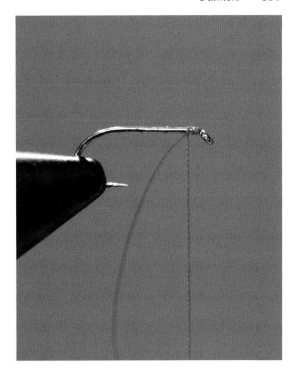

Tying the Red Palmer – Step 1.

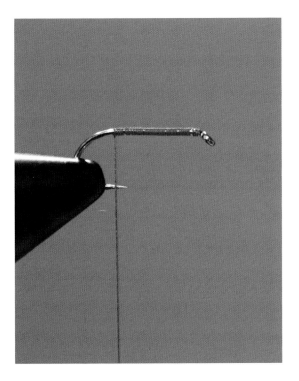

Step 2.

Step 3.

Step 4.

ginger, red-brown or furnace cock feather, should be a little smaller than the feather used for the front hackle.

Step 4
Spin the red dubbing lightly onto the tying thread. Remember that too thick a dubbing will make the fly too heavy.

Step 5
Wind the fur dubbing along the shank and tie off at a point a little behind the eye of the hook; leave just enough room for the front hackle and head. Once any excess dubbing has been scraped off the tying silk I like to pick out some fibres of the body with a dubbing needle; these fibres will blend nicely with the body hackle. The tying thread will now be hanging behind the eye of the hook.

Step 6
Using hackle pliers to grip the stalk, wind the body hackle in turns that are close but not actually touching, to the point behind the eye where the

Step 5.

Step 6.

body was completed and fix in with a couple of turns of thread. Snip off any excess feather.

Step 7
Now comes the tricky bit. The fine oval tinsel has to be wound and worked in open turns through the feather fibres and it should be wound in the opposite manner to the winding of the hackle (that is, if the hackle was wound clockwise, then the tinsel should be wound anti-clockwise). This will now ensure that the body hackle is firmly in place and once the ribbing reaches the front of the hackle it is fixed with three turns of tying silk and any excess ribbing cut off. When winding the ribbing, great care must be taken to avoid trapping the feather fibres. If the odd fibre is trapped, it may be freed carefully with a dubbing needle.

Step 8
Now is the time to apply the front hackle; choose a feather that is a little longer in the fibre than the body hackle. In general, the same colour of hackle should be chosen as the body hackle, from ginger to furnace depending on whether a

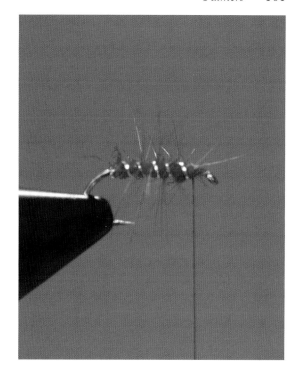
Step 7.

Step 8.

Step 9.

light or dark fly is to be tied. The front hackle is tied in, wound two or three times about the hook, then the tying thread carefully worked through the fibres to hold them in place. As with the body hackle, the outer side should face the eye of the hook. I like to tie a couple of turns of thread close up to the front of the hackle so that the front hackle fibres incline slightly backwards.

Step 9

Finish the head of the fly with a couple of half-hitches, or a neat whip finish, then apply a drop of varnish to complete the fly.

A Selection of Palmers

Bibio

The Bibio is a little Irish palmer and is a very handy fly to use when trout are feeding on black gnats (*Bibio johannis*), hawthorns (*Bibio marci*) or emerging black midges. The Bibio is dressed as follows:

- **Hook**: 16–12
- **Thread**: black tying silk (Pearsall's shade 9)
- **Body**: black seal's fur, wool or SLF, with a band of claret or crimson in the middle (SLF comes in three shades of claret: dark claret [12], fiery claret [13] and light claret [14])
- **Rib**: black tying thread or the finest available silver wire
- **Body hackle**: black hen hackle feather
- **Front hackle**: as body hackle

On the smallest versions a single hackle will suffice, while larger versions require separate front and body hackles. The pattern was developed by William Hewetson, who fished on Lough Mask, and the central band of the body dubbing was originally claret, although a crimson band may be thought effective when fishing for trout feeding on emerging black chironomid midges. The brighter crimson band not only provides a more obvious target, but also suggests the haemoglobin present in many species of emerging midges. The central band of the body is often dubbed in other colours, fluorescent orange or pink being very popular today. The name 'Bibio' suggests that the fly was developed to imitate black gnats or hawthorn flies, but I think it is at its best when used as a midge pattern and fished either as a single fly or on the top dropper of a three-fly cast. The Bibio is generally regarded as a small fly and should therefore be dressed on hooks in the 16 to 14 range.

Bi-Visibles

I am not going to provide dressing notes *per se* for the Bi-Visibles, as they essentially represent a modification to a range of dark palmers. Whenever the light is poor, or for those who struggle to see a fly at any time, the addition of a white cock hackle in front can be a real boon. The idea was developed a little over a century ago by E.R. Hewitt, a famous American angler.

A Bi-Visible also makes an attractive fly from a trout's point of view, because the contrasted white hackle on a dark palmer acts as a 'target' for the trout to home in on. Adding a white cock hackle to patterns such as the Black Palmer, Fiery Brown Palmer, or even Bibio and Zulu, makes them much easier to see when the light begins to fall, but there is a downside. Good quality white cock hackles are extremely difficult to obtain and most commercial Bi-Visibles tend to absorb water and sink easily, as they are dressed with poor cock hackles, or even white hen hackle feathers.

Black Palmer

The Black Palmer is an extremely old design of fly and the forerunner of modified designs such as the Bibio or Zulu. Charles Cotton's Black-Fly, dressed with a body of black ostrich herl ribbed with silver twist and palmered with a black cock hackle, is clearly a Black Palmer, yet the fly had already been in use for many years before Cotton. The following standard modern dressing is to be recommended:

- **Hook**: 14–10
- **Thread**: black tying silk (Pearsall's shade 9)
- **Body**: black seal's fur or Partridge SLF (shade 41)
- **Rib**: fine oval embossed silver tinsel
- **Body hackle**: black cock hackle feather
- **Front hackle**: as body hackle

Charles Cotton's fly was tied to imitate the hawthorn fly but the Black Palmer may be dressed on different sizes of hooks to imitate any black insects and it also makes a good general top dropper pattern, especially on overcast days. Even when trout are feeding on small black gnats a large Black Palmer may do better than a small imitation because it offers a contrast and stands out from the crowd. On the water, black gnats also have the habit of ending up in little knots or clumps which may be suggested by the Black Palmer.

The addition of a wing of dyed black deer hair produces a very attractive and buoyant pattern, which will not only keep the wet-flies close to the surface in rough water but will also create a good disturbance as a 'wake' fly when retrieved through the waves. Trout sometimes hit this pattern very hard so that a strong leader is called for. The addition of a deer hair wing also converts the Black Palmer into an excellent imitation of the black sedges, such as the black silverhorns, yet trout seem to respond differently to these flies on different waters. I have seen trout feeding avidly on black sedges on one local reservoir while completely ignoring them on another.

The Black Palmer is a very good top dropper pattern at the beginning of the season and on those days when it is windy, dull and cold. At such times, trout can be quite dour and it is often necessary to provide an extra stimulus in order to stir them into taking the fly; a tail of fluorescent lime-green floss added to a Black Palmer may just tip the balance in the angler's favour.

Bumbles

Although Bumbles originated in Derbyshire, they were further developed by T.C. Kingsmill Moore and made famous in his book *A Man May Fish* (1960). Kingsmill Moore dressed palmers with blended hackles to create a sense of sparkle, translucency and liveliness and the recent republication of his excellent and evocative book has led to the Bumble series of flies gaining renewed popularity among loch and reservoir fishers. Kingsmill Moore provides the dressings of seven palmered Bumbles, but you must read his book for all of them. I have selected just three typical Bumbles which may be used to good effect when there is a fair wave on the lake, reservoir or loch.

Golden-olive Bumble

- **Hook**: 14–10
- **Thread**: amber tying silk (Pearsall's shade 6)
- **Body**: golden-olive seal's fur or SLF shade 10
- **Rib**: fine oval gold tinsel
- **Body hackles**: golden-olive cock hackle mixed with medium red natural cock hackle feather
- **Shoulder hackle**: barred blue jay feather
- **Tail**: golden pheasant topping

Palmers are rarely given tails, yet Kingsmill Moore obviously believed that the addition of a golden yellow tail to his palmer enhanced its attraction. Similarly, the addition of a blue jay feather may suggest that the pattern is purely an 'attractor', yet it is the very same feather which helps to make James Ogden's Invicta such a good imitator of emerging sedge flies. Kingsmill Moore admitted that the colour of the Golden-olive Bumble was based on the Invicta.

Claret Bumble

- **Hook**: 14–10
- **Thread**: mulberry tying silk (Pearsall's shade 15)

Claret Bumble.

- **Body**: claret seal's fur or SLF shades 12, 13 or 14
- **Rib**: fine oval gold tinsel
- **Body hackles**: medium claret cock hackle mixed with natural black cock hackle feather
- **Shoulder hackle**: barred blue jay feather
- **Tails**: golden pheasant topping

Kingsmill Moore says that he caught over 800 sea trout on the Claret Bumble, but he also considered it equally good as a brown trout fly.

Fiery Brown Bumble

- **Hook**: 14–10
- **Thread**: brown tying silk (Pearsall's shade 17)
- **Body**: fiery brown seal's fur, or SLF shade 35, with an optional tag of brown floss silk
- **Rib**: fine oval gold tinsel
- **Body hackles**: fiery brown and blood-red cock hackle feathers
- **Shoulder hackle**: dark mottled grouse feather
- **Tails**: indian crow or golden pheasant topping

The author suggests that the Fiery Brown Bumble is a good fly to use in coloured water, yet I have found it to be an effective pattern on warm summer evenings when the water is clear.

Fiery Brown Bumble.

- **Hook**: 16–12
- **Thread**: ash grey tying silk (Pearsall's shade 10)
- **Body**: a mixed dubbing of hare's ear fur and either light rabbit fur, mole fur or grey seal's fur (SLF shade 28)
- **Rib**: plain grey tying silk
- **Body hackle**: badger or cree cock hackle feather (I now prefer cree)
- **Front hackle**: as body hackle; in small sizes the fly may be dressed with a single feather

The Duster Palmer is a good dry-fly for use on rapid streams because it is quite buoyant, but it is also a good top dropper fly on rivers or lakes and is useful in conditions of low light because it is a highly visible fly. I prefer it dressed in small sizes accompanying soft-hackled wet-flies on a three-fly cast and find that it accounts for more trout in its own right than some of the larger palmers which tend only to attract trout to the wet-flies.

Duster Palmer

As a general river and reservoir dry-fly it is hard to beat the Grey Duster and the present fly is simply a palmered version of this great pattern. The Duster Palmer may be fished as a small top dropper dry-fly, or in the surface film as an emerger pattern. The dressing is as follows:

Fiery Brown Palmer

Duster Palmer.

The Fiery Brown Palmer is a simpler pattern than Kingsmill Moore's Fiery Brown Bumble, but it is no less effective. It is a good sedge pattern for summer evenings, particularly as light falls, when the addition of a white front hackle will make it more visible if it is fished at the surface (it then becomes a Bi-Visible). It is dressed as follows:

- **Hook**: 14–10
- **Thread**: brown tying silk (Pearsall's shade 17)
- **Body**: fiery brown seal's fur or SLF shade 35
- **Rib**: fine oval gold tinsel
- **Body hackle**: red-brown cock hackle feather
- **Front hackle**: as body hackle, or white cock hackle feather

Fished either as a dry-fly, or as a fly just beneath the surface, the Fiery Brown Palmer is a good summer top dropper pattern, especially on lakes and reservoirs. A small version is sometimes successful during the day in rougher reaches of rivers, or in the evening on quieter pools, but I have found the fly much more effective on reservoirs. Fished as a 'damp' top dropper fly, just under the surface, the Fiery Brown imitates emerging adult sedges and may be fished on a dead drift, or with an erratic retrieve. As an imitation of sedges, emerging from the pupal state, it is also worth dressing a few additional patterns with amber, orange and olive seal's fur bodies. As a very buoyant dry-fly, the Fiery Brown Palmer may be given the addition of deer or elk hair wings, which enhance its appearance as an imitation of adult sedge flies and make it more visible to the angler.

Hare's Ear Palmer

Like the Fiery Brown Palmer, the Hare's Ear Palmer is also a good sedge dry-fly and top dropper pattern, particularly when elk hair wings are included. Along with my wet-flies, if I were limited to only a couple of dries, then I think I would choose a Grey Duster, or Cree Duster, and a Hare's Ear Palmer. The Hare's Ear Palmer, apart from its 'sedgey' appearance, is an excellent general dry-fly for lakes and reservoirs and it has also taken its fair share of river trout, particularly from rapid runs. The qualities that make it a good dry-fly also make it a good stillwater top dropper pattern too, whether it is fished statically or retrieved. It is not a fly to fish sunk, or 'damp', but a fly that will remain on the surface without sinking; in that respect it is a very handy fly to use when the wet-flies on the point or top dropper need to stay close to the surface. It is dressed in the following way:

- **Hook**: 14–10
- **Thread**: brown tying silk (Pearsall's shade 17)
- **Body**: a rough mix of hare's ear fur, a medium shade and not too dark. Pick out a few fibres with a dubbing needle so that they merge with the body hackle
- **Rib**: fine oval gold tinsel
- **Body hackle**: ginger cock hackle feather
- **Front hackle**: dark ginger or red cock hackle feather
- **Wings**: pale elk hair

The Hare's Ear Palmer is not a fly I would generally use when the reservoir surface is glassy calm, or on the still pools of rivers, but it is a fly that comes into its own on rougher water. On reservoirs it has a habit of bringing fish up from the deeps on breezy days when there are no evident rises. On rivers, the Hare's Ear Palmer is buoyant enough to provide control over the wet-flies in rapid runs and it will act as an effective strike indicator.

Mayfly

A palmered Mayfly, you may ask – but why not? There have been so many imitations of the mayfly (*Ephemera danica*, *E. vulgata* and the rarer *E. linneata*) over the centuries that it is difficult to know which one to choose, but as far as I am concerned a single pattern is sufficient, either fished as a wet or a dry, and it is based on the dressing given by Charles Cotton more than 300 years ago. Cotton's Great Hackle was winged with mallard's feather, dyed yellow, but I have taken a liberty and dispensed with the wing:

- **Hook**: size 12 long shank but fine in the wire
- Thread: primrose yellow tying silk (Pearsall's shade 3)
- **Body**: a mix of creamy white seal's fur (or SLF shade 48) with a pinch of yellow seal's fur (SLF shade 20)
- **Rib**: either fine brown floss silk or a thicker grade of brown tying silk (Pearsall's Naples silk) ribbed in open turns along the body. Leave a brown tag at the tail (Floss silk is tricky to wind through the body hackle fibres without damaging them, so that the reader may prefer to use a thicker grade of brown tying silk)
- **Body hackle**: pale ginger cock hackle feather
- **Front hackle**: golden-olive cock hackle feather
- **Tails**: three strands of brown pheasant tail fibres

Like Cotton, I believe that a mayfly struggling to emerge, trying to free itself from the water, or even drowning in the current, is best copied by the buzz of a palmer hackle and the above dressing is equally effective as a dry-fly, as a 'damp' fly fished in the surface film, or fished as a wet-fly. 'Duffer's Fortnight' often turns out to be anything but the easy pickings it is thought to be and the dry-fly is sometimes ignored as trout slash everywhere at naturals. At such times the palmered Mayfly, fished as a single wet-fly, will often do better than a dry-fly. It represents an easy morsel for a trout because a fish does not need to expend energy chasing other flies that are about to leave the stream. Some of the largest and wisest trout would prefer to mop up drowned duns rather than rise at quickly escaping adults. Mayfly duns are also an easy target when they are in the very act of emergence, so that the palmered Mayfly may also be fished damp in the surface film, yet it does not 'stand out from the crowd' like the wet-fly representing a drowned natural. An ideal 'hedging-your-bets' method is to cast a damp artificial upstream so that it floats a little before sinking as it drifts downstream; this is how flies

Mayfly.

were fished in the days of loop rods and horse-hair lines and it is still very effective.

Mayflies are not as abundant as they once were and have disappeared altogether from some rivers and lakes where clouds of them once filled the air. Hatches also vary from year to year and if a hatch of mayfly is poor, then fewer eggs will have been laid by female spinners to furnish the next generation. Mayflies traditionally appear in late May or early June, but their actual time of emergence may be difficult to predict and it is always worth having a few patterns handy just in case. Even if the main hatch has been missed, a trickle of emerging mayflies may keep the trout interested unless they are satiated.

Mayfly nymphs are 'silt burrowers' and only tend to become active just prior to emergence, when they may be taken by trout. However, it tends to be the emerging duns that provoke greatest interest. The emergent dun, usually known as the 'greendrake', is a large and distinctive fly with grey-yellow wings and a creamy-white body marked with brown blotches; I think the above pattern bears a good enough resemblance to the natural fly. Of the three species, *Ephemera danica* is the most common, although *E. vulgata* is quite common in the north of England. *Ephemera linneata*, a slightly smaller and darker species, is much less common, although I have seen some good hatches of this fly on lakes. On stillwaters, as with rivers, the wet-fly will often catch more fish than the dry-fly when mayflies emerge in fair numbers.

Muddler Palmer

I was undecided as to whether this pattern, or patterns, should be termed 'Palmered Muddler' or 'Muddler Palmer'. Whatever! I eventually settled on the latter. Over the last decade, something strange has happened with respect to Muddlers on *all* my local reservoirs. At one time, trout would take Muddlers with great confidence. They would chase a Muddler retrieved through the waves and take it with a bang, and they would also rise and take a static Muddler as if it were a small dry-fly. Then things changed dramatically. A fish might occasionally inspect a static Muddler, but it wouldn't take it. It would still chase a retrieved fly, occasionally take it, but more often than not would swirl, turn and take a wet-fly if the Muddler was the top dropper on a three-fly cast. As things now stand, Muddlers are rarely taken in their own right, but they do provoke follows and takes to the wet-flies during a good ripple. Sometimes, however, Muddlers simply seem to scare the fish.

Nevertheless, Muddlers are just about as buoyant as you can get, so they are ideal top dropper flies for use in rough conditions when other top droppers may be swamped or difficult to see. Currently, my solution has been to combine a Muddler with a Fiery Brown Palmer, or palmers dressed with amber, orange and olive seal's fur bodies. This is the 'Muddler Palmer' – a palmer with a deer-hair head – and dressed in small sizes (14 to 10) they seem effective enough *at the moment*. They float well, produce just enough surface disturbance to attract a trout's attention when retrieved and don't seem to scare the fish unduly. Time will tell whether or not this continues to be the case.

Olive Palmer

My Olive Palmer was developed specifically as a river fly to suggest emerging ephemeridae, mainly dark olives, and it is intended to be fished damp in the surface film, or just under it. The Olive Palmer is what the American angler, Vernon Hidy, would have called a 'flymph', and it is akin to Stewart's famous trio of spiders. Here is the dressing:

- **Hook**: 16–12
- **Thread**: olive tying silk (Pearsall's shade 16)
- **Body**: stripped peacock herl (or strands of cream and brown flexi-floss wound together)

Muddler Palmer.

Olive Palmer.

- **Rib**: fine gold wire
- **Body hackle**: ginger hen hackle feather
- **Front hackle**: a small dirty grey-olive marginal covert feather from a French partridge wound very sparsely
- **Tails**: blue dun cock hackle fibres

This is a good fly to use on the top dropper of a river cast when dark olives are emerging and it can be combined with soft-hackled wet-flies such as the Olive Bloa, Waterhen Bloa or Greenwell Spider given in Chapter 7. The blue dun cock 'tail' is intended to represent the shuck from which the adult fly is in the process of emerging.

Red Palmer (or Soldier Palmer)

I have always known this pattern as a 'Red Palmer', although it was often called the 'Soldier Palmer' as if it wore the attire of a redcoat army. It has also been suggested that this palmer was called the Soldier Palmer because it originated as an imitation of the soldier beetle; I am doubtful of that, although Skues did use a similar pattern to imitate soldier beetles when fishing on the Nadder. I believe that the fly was called the Soldier Palmer to distinguish it from a quite different dressing known as the Red Palmer, which Pritt gives as number 17 on his list of flies (this fly had a red cock hackle wound over a body of peacock herl). Pritt's pattern is rarely used today, so I will stick to Red Palmer for the present fly. It has always been one of my

favourite flies and that is why I chose it to illustrate how palmers are dressed earlier in the present chapter. I will give the dressing again:

- **Hook**: 14–10
- **Thread**: scarlet tying silk (Pearsall's shade 11a) or crimson (shade 13)
- **Body**: red wool, seal's fur or Partridge SLF shade 17
- **Rib**: fine oval gold tinsel or gold wire
- **Body hackle**: ginger cock hackle feather
- **Front hackle**: ginger, red-brown or furnace cock hackle feathers depending on whether a 'light' or 'dark' version is preferred

Dressed in small sizes the Red Palmer makes a good dry-fly for rapid streams and a good evening sedge pattern. I have had some big trout from rivers on the Red Palmer, but it is also a good top dropper fly on reservoirs. On reservoirs it is always worth trying as a single dry-fly. Either as a single dry-fly, or top dropper on a three-fly cast, the Red Palmer does seem to bring better than average trout to the surface even when they are lying quite deep down and I am sure that the red body has a great deal to do with that. In clear deep water I have watched trout ascend vertically to grab the Red Palmer confidently and when they rise in that manner it is rare for them to reject the fly. Finally, as with many palmer flies, the Red Palmer will certainly take fish *under* the water, fished as a conventional wet-fly, and this minor tactic is worth trying on reservoirs during those dour days when everything you knot onto the cast fails to produce a fish. I have been saved from a number of blank days by fishing a Red Palmer as a wet-fly.

Stewart's Spiders

The spider patterns made famous by W.C. Stewart were cited in Chapter 7, but it is worth looking at them again because Stewart does not supply all the dressing details, so that a little reconstruction work is required. As far as we can gather, Stewart's trio of spiders, made famous by his publication of *The Practical Angler* (1857), were actually invented by a James Baillie. As Stewart is a little vague about the dressings I have taken the liberty of offering modernized dressing prescriptions:

Stewart's Black Spider.

Stewart's Red Spider.

Black Spider
- **Hook**: 16–14
- **Thread**: brown tying silk (Pearsall's shade 17)
- **Body**: well-waxed tying silk assuming a dark shade
- **Hackle**: small glossy purple-black or green-black cock starling feather wound halfway down the body

Red Spider
- **Hook**: 16–14
- **Thread**: yellow tying silk (Pearsall's shade 5)
- **Body**: lightly waxed yellow tying silk
- **Hackle**: small red-brown hen hackle feather wound halfway down the body

Dun Spider
- **Hook**: 16–14
- **Thread**: primrose tying silk (Pearsall's shade 3)
- **Body**: primrose tying silk waxed so that it assumes an olive shade
- **Hackle**: snipe marginal covert feather dyed pale brown (the original called for a dotterel feather)

Stewart's Dun Spider.

Stewart's spiders are essentially river patterns, although the Black Spider may be used on reservoirs when small black midges are emerging. Stewart would fish the whole season with only his trio of flies and still presumably end up with prodigious baskets of trout. I have had success with the Black Spider, although I must confess that I haven't given the Red and Dun Spiders much of a wetting. Palmering the hackle part-way down the body of the fly has much to be said in its favour. It provides that buzz of movement suggestive of a struggling insect, which means that these spider patterns are good emergers and very similar to Vernon Hidy's 'flymphs' – that key stage between mature nymph and fully emerged adult fly. Of course, most of the patterns given in Chapter 7 may be dressed in this style.

White Palmer

I regard the White Palmer as a fly for one situation only – at dusk on a summer's evening when there is hardly any light left in the sky and it is extremely difficult to see the top dropper. Actually, it could be used during any conditions of very poor light. A white fly is about as visible as a fly can be, so that the angler has some idea where the flies are fishing and does not need to rely solely on touch to know that a trout has taken. Here is the dressing:

- **Hook**: 12–8
- **Thread**: white tying silk (Pearsall's shade 1)
- **Body**: a strand of brilliant white wool (the kind of wool used on that once popular lure, the Baby Doll)
- **Rib**: fine oval silver tinsel
- **Body hackle**: dirty white cock hackle feather

- **Front hackle**: as body hackle, or badger cock if good quality white cock hackles are not available
- **Tails**: several tips of white cock hackle feathers (optional)

It is an unlikely looking fly but it works as a sight indicator and it actually catches fish too! The White Palmer should always be fished as a floating top dropper on a three-fly cast that is simply allowed to drift. No matter how startling this 'fly' may appear to be, there are a number of natural creatures that it may even imitate at dusk on a warm summer evening – the ermine moth, for example.

Wickham's Palmer

The Wickham's Fancy is a palmered fly once popular as a sedge imitation and fished both as a wet-fly and dry-fly. By removing the wing from the original dressing, a good 'attractor' palmer is created and it is a top dropper fly par excellence when sunshine plays on a good ripple. At such times, the gold body of this fly definitely attracts the trout's attention. We may now call the wingless Wickham's Fancy simply the Wickham's Palmer! I dress the fly as follows:

- **Hook**: 14–10
- **Thread**: brown tying silk (Pearsall's shade 17)
- **Body**: flat gold tinsel or Mylar
- **Rib**: fine gold wire
- **Body hackle**: dark ginger cock hackle feather
- **Front hackle**: as body hackle
- **Tails**: fibres of ginger cock hackle

The original dressing, attributed either to a Dr Wickham or a Captain Wickham, had a starling primary quill wing, but this can be dispensed with to no ill effect. It was developed just over a century ago and was heralded as an excellent chalk stream dry-fly when imitating sedges. In small sizes it is a good grayling fly and a useful fly to try when the river has a tinge of colour in it. On lakes and reservoirs, a larger Wickham's Palmer is a good top dropper fly (and a good single dry-fly for that matter) for use when sedges are in evidence. It is best tripped along a ripple on a sunny evening, so that the glint of gold will attract the trout's attention.

Zulu

My final palmer is the famous Zulu, which is little more than a Black Palmer with a red tag added. The Zulu is probably older than its name might imply, its name deriving from the Zulu uprising of the 1880s when British rifles struggled against Zulu spears at places such as Rorke's Drift. Here is the usual dressing:

- **Hook**: 14–12
- **Thread**: black tying silk (Pearsall's shade 9)
- **Body**: black wool, seal's fur or SLF shade 41
- **Rib**: fine oval silver tinsel
- **Body hackle**: black cock or hen hackle
- **Front hackle**: as body hackle
- **Tag or tail**: bright red wool or floss silk. I like to use fluorescent red floss

Unlike other palmers, usually fished as floating top droppers, the Zulu is often dressed with hen hackle feathers and fished wet, even when it is placed on the top dropper. Whether dressed with hen or cock hackles, it remains a good 'bob-fly' to trip through the waves, and as an attractor for trout it seems to work better in smaller sizes. There are a number of variations on the Zulu theme which have enjoyed popularity as loch and sea trout flies. The Blue Zulu is given a front hackle of bright blue or turquoise hen or cock feather, although a barred blue jay feather has also been used, and this is a stunning looking fly. There is also a Gold Zulu but it is a completely different fly, having a peacock herl body, ribbed with gold tinsel and hackled with coch-y-bondhu hen or cock feathers. Another Gold Zulu is more like the standard dressing with a body of flat gold tinsel replacing the original black body. Zulus may be regarded as traditional attractor loch flies, but they have caught many fish in the past and that is a good enough reason for not neglecting them.

Blue Zulu.

10 LOCH, OR LAKE FLIES

Introduction

What are generally known as 'loch', or 'lake', flies are a heterogeneous bunch and therefore less easy to categorize than the styles of fly we have thus far encountered. It may be argued that even though they may differ in appearance, their commonality lies in the supposed fact that they are all flashy 'attractors'. However, as we shall see, this is not accurate, as a good number of loch and lake patterns owe their effectiveness to the fact that they at least provide a good impression of natural insects. I think the word 'impression' is apt, for I would not choose to argue that they are intended to offer exact imitations, whatever that might be.

The flies in this chapter were mainly designed for use on stillwaters and while they may have lost some of their popularity, they work as well today as ever they did. Of course, there is an overlap between river and stillwater wet-fly patterns so that a number of flies cited in previous chapters might well have found their way into the present chapter, for example the Coch-y-bondhu (Chapter 7), most of the palmers (Chapter 9), or the Broughton's Point and Blae and Black (Chapter 8). Indeed, many of the soft-hackled spider patterns discussed in Chapter 7 will do good work on lakes and reservoirs under the right conditions.

The notion that loch flies are all fancy attractor patterns undoubtedly led to the belief that using them is merely 'chuck-and-chance-it' fishing. This is an unfortunate and misguided view. Some flies are essentially attractors, but since they are effective in that respect I see no ethical argument against using them. When we think of attractors, then patterns such as the Alexandra, Peter Ross, Teal, Blue and Silver, or Butcher spring readily to mind; they may attract fish throughout the season, yet we must not neglect the fact that they are also excellent fry imitations when trout are chasing tiny fish during the latter part of the season. Is there a better perch fry imitation than the Alexandra, or a better roach fry imitation than the Teal, Blue and Silver? Further, it has been noted that small versions of the Peter Ross or Butcher will often do well when trout are feeding on midge pupae ('duck-flies' or 'buzzers') and while they may not look anything like the natural creatures from the point of view of human perception, who knows how a trout views an artificial? It may just be that the red, black and silver materials used in these patterns provide some exaggerated trigger points that suggest emerging midge pupae. While the majority of pupae are black, there is also a silvery sheen in evidence as the pupal case splits and several species display a red colouring produced by the haemoglobin.

Nevertheless, we cannot always logically account for the reasons why a fish takes a specific fly – suffice it that it does. Other loch flies, such as the Mallard series or Woodcock series, dressed with different colours of seal's fur bodies, or the famous Invicta (one of the few loch flies to retain popularity), clearly provide excellent sedge imitations regardless of what their original purpose was when they were first developed. The Mallard and Claret, dressed in an appropriate size, offers one of the best imitations of the claret dun (*Leptophlebia vespertina*), as well as being a pretty good general fly. I could cite many other examples. You may, if you choose, continue to regard loch flies as merely fancy patterns, but that would be to neglect some of the most effective lake and reservoir wet-flies ever invented.

Loch patterns are generally fished as a cast of three flies, although, when fishery rules dictate that only a single fly may be used, I have often had satisfying sport with a single fly. However, loch flies certainly increase their effectiveness when used as a team of three. At one time, four or more flies were employed on a loch cast, but this seems a little unnecessary and only increases the risk of tangles, particularly during windy conditions. Even a three-fly cast is difficult enough to handle when there is a good blow on the water. Obviously, at the simplest level, the use of three flies would appear to increase the angler's chances three-fold as the trout are provided with alternatives; if a fancy attractor fails, then a more sombre pattern may do the trick. It may also be argued that the use of three flies allows the angler to fish simultaneously at different depths, but this argument should not be given too much weight as traditional wet-fly fishing is mainly top-of-the-water fishing. There will not be a great difference in depth between the top dropper and the point-fly; fished on a floating line, the point-fly is likely to be only a few feet down when the top dropper is at the surface. You may fish all three flies much deeper on a sinking line, but there will still be little difference in depth between them. Nevertheless, there are times when even a few feet can make all the difference. If trout are feeding very close to the surface they may largely ignore the point-fly which lies a little deeper, so that the droppers are the only flies that stand a chance of taking a fish. However, variation in depth is not the prime reason for employing a three-fly cast and it must be noted that during a retrieve all three flies are likely to fish more or less in the same plane.

The key reason, I think, for employing three flies is concerned with the impression created by them working alongside each other. I believe that whatever attraction an individual fly may provide, three flies working together provide an extra stimulus for a trout to strike. For example, when the flies are retrieved, however slowly, it may appear as if natural creatures are chasing one another. This stimulates a trout into joining the chase. There is a further point to be noted concerning the three-fly cast and it is by no

means of minor importance. Without the top dropper, or 'bob-fly', stillwater wet-fly fishing would lose one of its most effective attributes. Apart from what the top dropper may achieve as an individual fly, the point and middle dropper flies would also be less effective without it. Towards the end of the retrieve, the top dropper fly is held at the surface, particularly effective in a wave, and it is this action that will attract a trout's attention through the commotion it produces. A long rod will ensure that the top dropper plays at the surface for as long as possible before we recast. Once a trout's attention has been grabbed, it comes to investigate and if it believes the top dropper to be an escaping insect then it will take confidently. Quite often, however, a trout will swirl at the bob-fly without taking it, but it is still a mistake to lift the flies off the water too quickly because the fish may come again at the top dropper, or more likely take one of the other flies on the cast.

The top dropper fly, or 'bob-fly' for those who prefer that term, provides other possibilities as well. We may, for instance, fish a dry-fly on the top dropper in order to ensure that it remains permanently at the surface. Thus, throughout the time the flies are on the water it may be worked along the surface or simply be allowed to drift. Individually, it will operate as any dry-fly, but it will also attract attention to the other two flies while ensuring that they fish close to the surface. If the trout are feeding in the upper layer then this is an obvious advantage. A dry-fly fished in this way also signals a take to the wet-flies and seems to me preferable to some fluorescent orange strike indicator. A top dropper dry-fly needs to be buoyant, but large dry-flies should only be used in rougher conditions; they will cause too much disturbance and scare fish when it is calm. In calmer conditions, or when fishing calm lanes on breezy days, I prefer small wet-flies on the point and middle, and a smaller dry-fly on the top dropper.

Many anglers believe that the largest fly of a three-fly cast should be placed on the point so that the point will sink deepest, thus ensuring that all three flies fish at different depths. This may seem logical but it is not my preference. For one thing, a large fly requires a strong tippet, whereas the point is the finest length of a tapered leader. If you do choose to sink the leader point a little deeper then it is better to use a small weighted pattern. Large hooks require a little more force to pull home, so that stronger leader material is inevitable. Normally, the point will be the finest part of the leader, the middle dropper will be a little thicker in diameter and stronger, while the top dropper will be thickest and strongest. This means that the flies will follow suit so that you will probably fish a size 14 on the point, size 12 on the middle and size 10 on the top dropper. As a result, the point and middle dropper flies usually fish in a level plane, the middle dropper may even hang a little lower than the point, but this does not seem to matter and does not mar the effectiveness of the three-fly cast. On some occasions, when, for example, trout are feeding on small chironomids, it may be necessary to employ three small flies on the cast, which becomes problematic with the standard tapered leader. There is an obvious solution. Construct a tapered leader whereby the sections of different thicknesses are joined by little silver leader rings, as outlined in Chapter 4. A leader constructed in this manner allows the angler to attach dropper lengths to the rings as fine as the point of the leader so that all three small flies fish in a natural manner.

There is a psychology involved in fishing any flies; you have to believe in them. It is no less true of loch flies, for you have to have faith in them in order to fish them effectively. Concentration too is required, for not all takes will be signalled by a strong pull and fish will rarely hook themselves. If you have not previously tried a team of loch flies, choose your initial session on a day when most types of fly might do well, for example when trout are showing at the surface and clearly feeding in earnest. Once you begin to catch fish on loch flies, you will have confidence in them. Having faith in loch flies also necessitates having loch flies that merit the faith you put in them. Overdressed specimens will not fish effectively and, all too often, commercially dressed patterns are overdressed, possess heavily wound hackles and wings that are far too large. As it is with wings and hackles, so too the bodies of flies must remain slim in order to at least give an impression of a natural insect. However, they do not have to be neat, for

a rough seal's fur body, with the fibres picked out, provides a greater sense of mobility, while the fibres also trap a little air which creates an enticing silvery sheen.

Considerations of colour in a fly may arise according to the level at which the trout are lying in the water and the depth at which the flies are fishing. If, for example, it is a bright day and the trout are lying below the level at which the flies are generally fishing, then colour loses some of its significance, since all flies lying above the fish are likely to appear only as silhouettes. On the other hand, any fly with a silver or gold body will undoubtedly glint from time to time as the sun's rays catch it. If your flies swim at the depth at which the trout are lying, colour becomes more significant. If trout are feeding close to the surface and your flies are fishing in the same plane, colour can become very important indeed and it is sometimes the case that only a single colour of fly will take fish. There are times when trout 'turn on' to a colour, for whatever reason, and it is not always possible to offer a logical explanation. It is true that trout sometimes prefer green because they are currently feeding on green-bodied sedge pupae, but this kind of logical situation is by no means the norm. Today only the Teal and Yellow will produce takes, tomorrow it may be the Teal and Red. While most colours have their 'on' and 'off' days, I think, however, that some colours are more consistent than others in attracting trout. Black, red and silver, when combined, seem particularly attractive and this surely accounts for the consistent effectiveness of flies such as the Zulu, Peter Ross or Butcher.

A Note on Materials for Tying Loch Flies

In essence, the materials gathered together for tying soft-hackled spiders, palmers and winged wet-flies will provide the basis of the materials required for dressing loch flies, although larger and stronger hooks will be needed for flies placed on the middle and top droppers. We will already have a good supply of tying silks and floss silks in a variety of colours and probably enough silver and gold flat tinsels (or Mylar tubing) and fine embossed tinsels. We will also have hen hackles in a variety of colours and seal's fur too. If seal's fur is not readily available there are a number of good dubbing substitutes including the excellent Partridge SLF ('synthetic living fibre') dubbing, which is available in forty-eight colours. Although loch flies are often dressed with the same colour of body and hackle, I prefer a little contrast, or blending of colours, so that the Teal and Red, for example, will be given a red seal's fur body but a hackle of ginger hen. I think this makes the fly in some way appear more 'natural' and less garish. However, as a simple checklist, it is useful to have hen hackle feathers available in the following colours: black; ginger (light and dark); brown; coch-y-bondhu or furnace; hot orange; claret; purple; olive; and sky blue. Seal's fur (or a preferred substitute) in the following colours will definitely be required: black; fiery brown; claret; green (light, dark and olive); hot orange; purple; yellow (a deep shade rather than pale); amber and red (various shades).

Many loch flies are winged with feathers that should already be in our collection, such as grouse and woodcock, but individual flies will call for new winging materials as indicated in the text. Above all, teal and bronze mallard feathers will be required for dressing a good number of the most popular patterns. Teal, or widgeon feathers, which may be used as a substitute, are soft white feathers distinctly barred with flecks of black. When inspecting the feathers, select those that are as white as possible and have distinct black markings; if the markings are pale grey, or there is a brownish tinge to the background of the feather, reject them. Good quality bronze mallard feathers are not particularly cheap and there is no escaping the fact that we have to purchase small packets of preselected feathers.

Tails are often a very distinctive feature of traditional loch flies and it is certainly necessary to acquire golden pheasant topping and tippet feathers; the purchase of a whole head, or even an entire body skin, will be a good investment. Many loch flies have tails formed from orange and black pheasant tippet fibres, or the golden yellow topping crests and they certainly add a little something to the attractive properties of a fly. Some flies are given tails of red ibis (dyed hen

or swan feather is now used as a substitute) and this undoubtedly adds effectiveness to flies such as the Blae and Black.

Loch flies also call for a number of other materials unique to individual patterns – the mallard blue feather of a Butcher wing, the cinnamon hen feather wing of the Cinnamon and Gold, or blue jay feathers incorporated into the dressings of both the Connemara Black and Invicta – but rather than list them at this stage, these materials will be given as part of the individual dressings. The reader may therefore choose to dip into the listed dressings and begin by selecting those patterns for which materials are already available.

Dressing loch flies does not differ a great deal from tying traditional winged wet-flies and the winging procedure is identical when slips of feather from primary and secondary wing quills are used (the reader may wish to consult the advice on winging given in Chapter 8). However, loch flies are often tied with softer-fibred and more mobile wings of teal, bronze mallard and even peacock herl in the case of the Alexandra, and softer fibres actually make the winging procedure easier. There was once a fashion for using hair for winging rather than traditional feathers (grey squirrel was often employed), but I don't care for hair-winged loch flies and find them top-heavy. Soft-fibred feathers such as teal or bronze mallard may be tied in using the same technique as we used when tying traditional winged wet-flies. Tear off slips of feather of the same size from two identical feathers and place them together so that the outer faces of the slips become the outside of the fly's wing. Moistening the fingers and running them gently along the wing helps the fibres to adhere together so that the wing holds its shape when tied in. As in tying a wing when using slips taken from primary or secondary wing quills, it is most important that the wing is perfectly in line with the shank of the hook so that the fly will swim in a balanced manner.

An alternative method when winging with soft-fibred feathers is to form a wing from a single feather. This is only viable for flies dressed in larger sizes. In order to form a wing from a single feather, carefully strip the fibres from each side of the stalk and place them on top of one another. Then, moistening the fingers, roll the fibres into a 'tube' and stroke them towards the tip of the fibres so that a shaped wing is formed. It can then be tied in using the normal winging method. It is very important that no slivers of stalk are still attached to any of the fibres when constructing a wing in this manner, as this will cause the resulting wing to twist during rolling. When a wing is rolled, it is sometimes necessary to realign some of the fibres carefully so that the tips reach the same point and are not staggered.

Tying a Loch Fly – The Teal and Red

In order to tie a Teal and Red, the following materials will be required:

- **Hook**: 14–10
- **Thread**: crimson silk (Pearsall's shade 13)
- **Body**: red seal's fur (I prefer a rather faded red to a bright red) or Partridge SLF shade 17
- **Rib**: fine oval gold tinsel
- **Wings**: well-marked teal flank feather
- **Hackle**: medium ginger or ginger-brown hen feather
- **Tails**: golden pheasant tippet fibres

The Teal and Red is then dressed as follows:

Step 1
Fix the tying silk to the hook behind the eye and wind it in touching turns halfway down the shank where about six golden pheasant tippet fibres are tied in. They should protrude beyond the bend of the hook for a little over half the body length of the fly.

Step 2
Continue to wind the silk towards the bend of the hook, ensuring that the tail fibres remain in alignment with the hook shank but are slightly fanned out beyond the hook rather than stuck firmly together.

Step 3
Fix in the fine oval gold tinsel near the bend of the hook and carefully snip off any excess. Then dub red seal's fur onto the tying thread. It is best to moisten the fingers and then to spread the fur

Tying the Teal and Red – Step 1.

Step 2.

Step 3.

Step 4.

Step 5.

Step 6.

thinly along the thread before spinning it. The resulting dubbing 'rope' should not be too tight and dense. The ribbing will ensure that it adheres to the shank and a little roughness in the completed body is to be preferred.

Step 4

Wind the dubbing along the shank and tie off behind the eye after scraping any excess dubbing from the tying thread. Leave enough room behind the eye for the addition of wing and hackle. The completed body should remain slim, but should also have a slight taper from the eye of the hook to the tail of the fly.

Step 5

Wind the ribbing along the body in open turns and tie off behind the eye of the hook. In order to ensure that the dubbing remains firmly in place, wind the ribbing along the hook in the opposite manner in which the dubbing was wound (that is, if the dubbing was wound in a clockwise manner around the shank, the ribbing should be wound anti-clockwise).

Step 6

Strip the fluffy base fibres from a ginger hen hackle and tie onto the hook behind the eye. Ensure that the outer face of the feather (convex) faces forwards towards the eye. When the feather is tightly attached to the hook, snip off any excess stalk.

Step 7

Wind the hackle two or three times around the hook and carefully weave the thread forward through the fibres to fix the hackle in place. Finish off the hackle by inclining the fibres slightly backwards and take a couple of turns of thread around the hook in front of the hackle. This will ensure that the wound hackle inclines backwards.

Step 8

Prepare a teal or widgeon wing as previously described and place it on top of the hook, just behind the eye and slightly forward of the completed hackle. Making sure that the wing is perfectly in line with the hook shank, take a couple of loose loops of thread over the

Step 7.   *Step 8.*

Step 9.

wing. Hold thumb and finger over the thread and wing and close them tightly together before tightening the loops of thread. The wing should now be in place and aligned correctly. Take a few further turns of thread over the base of the wing and snip off any excess fibres.

Step 9
Tie off a neat head and varnish.

A Selection of Loch Flies

Alexandra
- **Hook**: 14–10
- **Thread**: black tying silk (Pearsall's shade 9)
- **Body**: flat silver tinsel or Mylar
- **Rib**: fine oval silver tinsel
- **Wing**: strands of green peacock herl (taken from the eye feather) with 'cheeks' of red ibis substitute feather (hen or swan feather strips dyed pillar-box red) on either side
- **Hackle**: black hen hackle feather
- **Tail**: red ibis substitute

The Alexandra has always been regarded as a fancy fly and although it was once reputedly banned on many waters, being considered too killing a fly, it seems to be little used today. It enjoyed something of a revival after appearing in T.C. Ivens' *Still Water Fly-Fishing* (1952), but there was always disagreement as to what trout took it for – if anything. Personally, I must admit that my results with the Alexandra have been a little patchy except towards the end of the season when trout are bashing shoals of fry. The downside of the Alexandra during the September fry bonanza is that the wing is quite fragile and as takes can be aggressive the wing soon becomes ragged. Nevertheless, I have continued to catch trout when only a couple of strands of peacock herl were left in place. Unfortunately, I have also caught plenty of perch. If the Alexandra is a good imitation of perch fry, then it is also a cracking fly to use if you intend to catch perch rather than trout!

The Alexandra probably originated around the middle of the nineteenth century and was once known as the 'Lady of the Lake'. It was rechristened 'Alexandra' in honour of H.R.H. Princess Alexandra, who was married to Edward VII, and this partly accounts for

Alexandra.

the popularity it once enjoyed. The Alexandra has been variously attributed to W.G. Turle of Newton Stacey, to a certain Dr John Brunton and to a number of other esteemed anglers.

Black Pennell

- **Hook**: 16–10
- **Thread**: black silk (Pearsall's shade 9)
- **Body**: black floss silk, seal's fur (if seal's fur is used it should remain a very slim body) or SLF shade 41
- **Rib**: fine oval gold tinsel (although silver tinsel may be used if preferred)
- **Hackle**: black hen hackle feather
- **Tails**: golden pheasant tippets

This fly is named after its creator, H. Cholmondeley Pennell, a prolific angling writer who penned, among other books, *The Modern Practical Angler* (1870). Cholmondeley Pennell was very much an all-round angler and wrote about most branches of the sport. A popular worming hook rig is also named after him. The Black Pennell, a variation on the old Black Spider theme, provides an excellent imitation of a host of black insects such as gnats, midges ('duck flies'), hawthorn flies and so on. I have found that a shorter hackled version, dressed on smaller sizes of hooks, provides an excellent fly to use when trout are preoccupied with black chironomid midges. A three-fly cast with a Black Pennell in every position will do just as well as

Purple Pennell.

any team of pupal imitations and the Black Pennell may be taken for pupa, emerger or even adult fly. The golden pheasant tippet tail used in the dressing provides a good suggestion of the pupal shuck of an emerging fly. In contrast, a Black Pennell dressed with a long-fibred black hen hackle makes an excellent top dropper, or bob-fly, for tripping through the waves and it was once popular in this style for sea trout fishing on lochs. There are a number of useful variants including the Purple Pennell (with a body of purple floss silk and either a black or purple hen hackle) and Pennells dressed with silver or gold bodies. The silver-bodied variant is an excellent early season fly, particularly on dull days, and I have had a good deal of success with it on rivers too when tied on smaller hooks.

Black and Orange
- **Hook**: 14–10
- **Thread**: hot orange silk (Pearsall's shade 19)
- **Body**: orange floss silk (optional gold rib)
- **Wing**: slips of dark feather from either a coot or a blackbird
- **Hackle**: black hen hackle feather
- **Tails**: golden pheasant tippets

I cannot really pretend that the Black and Orange has ever really been a popular wet-fly and yet it is a very distinctive fly and has given

Black and Orange.

Black and Peacock Spider.

good account of itself when used – that tends to be when other flies have failed. I was given a copy of the fly many years ago when fishing on Loch Awe, although I am led to believe that it may actually be of Irish origin. Some anglers have had considerable success with the Black and Orange when pursuing sea trout and I am sure that it is also worthy of trying on any British reservoir, even if what it may have been tied to represent is far from clear.

Black and Peacock Spider

- **Hook**: 14–10
- **Thread**: black silk (Pearsall's shade 9)
- **Body**: four to six strands of peacock herl (depending on the size of fly) twisted together and wound tightly along the shank
- **Hackle**: black hen hackle feather, quite long in the fibre

When constructing the body of this fly it is best to moisten the herls thoroughly before twisting them around the thread. The resulting 'rope' of herl and thread makes for a stronger body than a body constructed solely of peacock herl, which is a fragile material. Although some dressing notes have suggested that the B & P should be tied with bronze peacock herl (green herl dyed in magenta dye), the usual green variety is certainly good enough. An underbody of lead wire, or lead

foil, may be added to this pattern when you require a fly to fish deep in the water.

While the Black and Peacock Spider probably gained its popularity as a result of T.C. Ivens' *Still Water Fly-Fishing* (1952), it has a much older heritage and is little different from the Black Snipe listed in Chapter 7. Over the years, along with the Peter Ross, the Black and Peacock Spider has accounted for the greatest number of reservoir trout I have caught on any individual pattern, and some of the largest fish too. There was a time when a Black and Peacock Spider was automatically knotted onto the top dropper and I wondered what other two flies to select. I may experiment a little more these days, but I am sure that I would hardly miss out if I decided to stick with the B & P as my top dropper fly.

On cold, or really dull and overcast days, or at any time when sport is slow, the addition of a fluorescent floss silk tag to the B & P will work wonders. The most successful colours seem to be lime green or scarlet. This variant does seem to attract trout to the other two flies on the cast and I have known plenty of times when the fluorescent-tailed version has brought trout up from the deeps to take one of the other flies near to the surface. In clear water, trout lying quite deep down can see a large surface area and will be prepared to make an ascent if the prize is worth having. Of course, a weighted version will sink to the feeding depth of the trout and this may be necessary when there is some colour in the water.

Although I believe that the Black and Peacock Spider suggests a variety of food items, it is usually said to imitate beetles and snails. It will certainly do well fished on a greased leader when trout are feeding on beetles or snails in the upper layers of the water. There are times when snails seem to migrate to the surface and float around in the surface film. If you encounter such a phenomenon, don't hesitate to knot a couple of Black and Peacock Spiders onto your cast. However, I do not believe that this is a pattern simply restricted to the imitation of beetles and snails, for it is a fly that positively cries out 'food'; it looks like a natural creature and a hungry trout finds it hard to resist. I have even known the Black and Peacock Spider to be taken as a 'floater' on a surprising number of occasions and this too has happened with other loch flies. For this reason, I no longer soak the flies before making my initial cast and allow them to sink naturally in their own time; you never know, a trout may just take the flies before they sink.

Butcher

- **Hook**: 14–10
- **Thread**: black silk (Pearsall's shade 9)
- **Body**: flat silver tinsel or Mylar
- **Rib**: fine oval silver tinsel
- **Wing**: slips of blue-black feathers from a mallard drake's wing (generally known as 'Butcher blues'). At a pinch, feathers from crow, rook or magpie may be used as substitutes
- **Hackle**: black hen hackle feather
- **Tails**: red ibis substitute (white hen or swan feather dyed pillar-box red)

The Butcher is one of those patterns, like the Peter Ross or Black and Peacock Spider, that may be used throughout the season and during a variety of contrasted conditions. The Butcher is also an excellent fry-imitating pattern for use towards the end of the season. In the past, a number of writers have suggested that the Butcher is best placed either on the middle or top dropper of the cast and although I

Butcher.

sometimes place it on the middle, with a Peter Ross on the point, my experience suggests that the Butcher is more effective on the point and dressed in small sizes at that. I have even taken good catches on a small Butcher when trout are feeding on chironomid midges. Chironomid pupae often possess a silvery sheen, represented by the body of the Butcher, and the red tail may provide a trigger point that suggests the haemoglobin present in many species. On dour days, the silver body and red tail undoubtedly provide the kind of stimulus that induces a torpid trout into action. I have also found wingless Butchers, or 'Butcher Spiders', to be effective patterns; versions tied with fluorescent floss tails in red, orange and lime green are worth experimenting with. I suppose such patterns cease to be Butchers, but they are fairly close relatives nevertheless.

Like many old patterns, there is a certain lack of clarity concerning the Butcher's origins. It is sometimes said that the fly was originally known as the 'Moon Fly' and was developed by a Mr Moon, who was a butcher from Tunbridge Wells in Kent. It would then seem natural for anglers to rechristen the fly 'the Butcher', both with reference to the inventor's occupation and perhaps as a testimony to the fly's trout-killing properties. There is also a claim that the fly was invented by another butcher by the name

Butcher Spider.

Bloody Butcher.

of Andrew Hamilton who hailed from Pollok-shields in Scotland, but it is more likely that he developed one of its variants. I believe that Mr Hamilton was fishing in the latter years of the nineteenth century and the fly is almost certainly somewhat older than that.

The two most popular variants of the Butcher are the Bloody Butcher and the Kingfisher Butcher. The Bloody Butcher only differs from the original in that it is dressed with a blood-red

Kingfisher Butcher.

hen hackle in place of the original black. The Kingfisher Butcher, however, is given a blue tail (originally from a kingfisher's wing), a body of flat gold tinsel ribbed with fine oval gold, a bright orange hen hackle and the standard Butcher wing. Although the Bloody Butcher has yielded me a few fish, the very fancy Kingfisher Butcher hasn't produced a single trout. Finally, as the feathers for winging the Butcher are few in number on a mallard's wing, the fly may also be tied with a teal wing and this makes a very good midge pattern.

Cinnamon and Gold

- **Hook**: 14–10
- **Thread**: brown silk (Pearsall's shade 17)
- **Body**: flat gold tinsel or Mylar
- **Rib**: fine oval gold tinsel
- **Wing**: slips of white hen feather dyed cinnamon brown (originally either brown owl or corncrake feather was used)
- **Hackle**: light ginger or cinnamon-dyed hen hackle feather
- **Tails**: golden pheasant tippets or topping

This is a beautiful-looking fly that graces any fly box. I have caught fish on it during warm summer evenings and while I have not had great sport with it, there are other anglers who have fared rather better. It does have a certain

Cinnamon and Gold.

Colonel Downman.

'sedgey' appearance and although its origins are obscure, it might well have been developed to imitate natural cinnamon sedges (*Potamophylax latipennis*; *Limnephilus lunatus*), which could suggest its success as a summer evening fly. The late Tom Stewart suggested that it was a useful fly to put on the mid-point of the cast when uncertain as to what fly to use; he claimed that it did well when trout were rising but refused to take dry-flies. At such times, I have often found small flies dressed with gold bodies will do reasonably well and it is perhaps the case that the flash of gold distracts the trout from the natural flies that they are seemingly preoccupied with. 'A thing of beauty is a joy forever', as John Keats would have it. I am sure he would have liked the Cinnamon and Gold.

Colonel Downman
- **Hook**: 14–12
- **Thread**: black silk (Pearsall's shade 9)
- **Body**: black floss silk, seal's fur or SLF shade 41
- **Rib**: fine oval silver tinsel
- **Wings**: slips of 'blae' feather from a jay or starling with small pieces of jungle cock eye feathers on each side of the wings as 'cheeks'
- **Hackle**: either black hen hackle feather or coch-y-bondhu
- **Tails**: (optional) golden pheasant tippets

Who was Colonel Downman? I really have no idea. However, his eponymous fly is one of the lost legions of patterns that once enjoyed considerable popularity. It is a good fly which still works and this probably has a great deal to do with the attractive properties of the jungle cock cheeks. Jungle cock eye feathers can still be obtained today, although they are expensive. There are a number of plastic substitute imitations on sale, but I do not like them for they are inert and tend to render the fly lifeless. In reality, the Colonel Downman is a version of the Blae and Black and, like that fly, it is a good pattern to use when trout are feeding on emerging chironomids. It is certainly a fly worth trying.

Connemara Black
- **Hook**: 14–10
- **Thread**: black silk (Pearsall's shade 9)
- **Body**: black seal's fur, wool or SLF shade 41
- **Rib**: fine oval silver tinsel (although some anglers prefer gold and it seems to matter little)
- **Wings**: slips of feather from the bronze shoulder feathers of a mallard duck
- **Hackle**: black hen hackle feather with the addition of a turn of barred blue jay feather. Some fly dressers add the blue jay only as a beard hackle
- **Tails**: a small golden pheasant crest or topping feather

Unlike many loch flies, the Connemara Black is still relatively popular and is an excellent reservoir and sea trout pattern. It obviously originates from Connemara, a mystic land of trouty streams and lakes that I have sadly never visited. I have a feeling that my maternal great-grandmother came from Connemara, so I really ought to wet a line there and, if I do, then the Connemara Black will be the first fly I knot onto my cast.

In small sizes the Connemara Black makes a good chironomid midge pattern, but its real Irish magic lies in the blended hackle of black hen and blue jay. Irish fly dressers often have a penchant for blending materials and we have much that we can learn from them. I have found that the Connemara Black will do well enough at any time of the season, though I do tend to regard it mainly as an early season fly and at any position on the cast, although I favour either a small version on the point, or a large version on the top dropper. As a top dropper fly it works best when the cast is well sunk, for it is not one of those flies designed for dibbling at the surface. Having said that, there is no reason why a good dibbling version cannot be created by adding a palmered body hackle. As a top dropper fly it could perhaps be used to imitate any of the darker sedge flies.

There are those who regard the Connemara Black as essentially a fancy fly, but I prefer to consider it as a fly that provides a generalized impression of food items. It particularly suggests to me an emerging insect and the addition of the blue jay feather provides that impression of 'messiness' which the process of metamorphosis from nymph, or pupa, to adult fly creates. In this respect, it is similar to the Invicta and employs the same blue jay feather in its dressing. The golden topping feather, used for the tail of the Connemara Black, may also provide an impression of a pupal shuck. When tying the Connemara Black it is important to remember that the fly should be slim and not bulky if it is to remain effective. A bulky fly provides no sense of translucence and provides little impression of movement. Commercially dressed flies are often too bulky and will simply become lifeless in the water.

Dunkeld

- **Hook**: 16–12
- **Thread**: brown silk (Pearsall's shade 17) or hot orange silk (shade 19)
- **Body**: flat gold tinsel or Mylar
- **Rib**: fine gold wire (which is also used to hold the body hackle in place)
- **Wing**: strips of brown speckled mallard feather with the addition of jungle cock eye feather 'cheeks' optional

Connemara Black.

Dunkeld.

- **Hackle**: dyed hot orange hen hackle feather palmered down the body in open turns and held in place with the gold wire ribbing
- **Tails**: golden pheasant topping

This scaled-down Scottish salmon fly is unashamedly a pure attractor and I have done well with it as a deeply sunk fly on hot summer days when the surface is mirror calm and there is a tendency to think that a snooze is preferable to casting the flies repeatedly with little reward. Conversely, I have also found it useful when fished at the surface, as we shall see at a later stage. Recently, I have seen plenty of Dunkelds on sale in tackle shops, although they tend to be much larger than those I choose to use, so I can only conclude that it is gaining in popularity once more. Although I tend to regard the Dunkeld as something of a last-resort fly, it will take trout throughout the season and at any position on the cast, although I have a preference for using it on the point.

I regard the Dunkeld as a fly to use during the hot dog days of July and August, a time when I have found that hot orange will often stir a fish or two. [Orange does seem to be a colour for hot days. That old T.C. Ivens favourite, the Jersey Herd, also does well at such times and as it is a leaded pattern it is useful when trout are lying deep. The Jersey Herd is dressed on long shanked hooks and has a copper tinsel body, hot orange hackle and a head, back and tail constructed of copper-coloured peacock herl. Although Ivens dressed the fly as a lure, I prefer to fish it as a size 14 nymph on the point, combined with a couple of loch flies on the middle and top dropper.]

I have been informed that a large Dunkeld makes a good sea trout fly, but for summer trout, and particularly when it is calm, I certainly prefer a small pattern. As with the Cinnamon and Gold, the Dunkeld is also a good fly to try when there is a good evening rise on but the dry-fly is proving pretty useless. A size 16 Dunkeld is not too small but it takes a bit of tying, for this is a fairly complex pattern for a small hook. Either cast the small Dunkeld out and leave it stationary for a while, or retrieve it very slowly so that it remains just below the surface film.

Green Peter

- **Hook**: 14–12
- **Thread**: olive silk (Pearsall's shade 16)
- **Body**: green seal's fur (a mix of pea green and dark olive in equal quantities makes an attractive dubbing), or a mix of SLF shades 3 and 6
- **Rib**: fine oval gold tinsel
- **Wing**: slips of speckled grey pheasant
- **Hackle**: ginger hen hackle feather dressed fairly bushy
- **Tails**: the fly is usually dressed without tails, but golden pheasant tippets may be added

The Green Peter, in a number of variations, is a famous and popular Irish lough pattern widely used on Conn, Mask and Corrib. It is an excellent top dropper, or bob-fly, when you wish to imitate a variety of sedge flies and it is particularly effective on rough and windy days when it may also be used as a dry-fly dressed with a bushy ginger cock hackle. Dressed in this manner, the Green Peter will bounce around seductively in the waves, ensuring that the other flies on the cast remain close to the surface if trout are feeding in the upper layers. At such times it may be retrieved in little darts to attract the trout's attention and although they may take it confidently, they will often swirl at it before taking one of the other flies on the cast.

The Grouse Series of Flies

There are four principal series of flies – Grouse, Mallard, Woodcock and Teal – distinguished from one another by the choice of winging material. The Grouse series of flies is undoubtedly centuries old and originates from Scotland where grouse were common and provided a ready source of fly-dressing materials. When tying the Grouse series many dressers tend to use the same body and hackle colour but my preference is for natural hackle colours, so that I dress the Grouse and Green with a dark ginger hen feather which provides a nice blend and avoids the garishness of a dyed green hackle. Given that the Grouse flies have been around for a long time, there are a considerable number of dressing variations, so that the tails are sometimes of cock feather fibres, brown speckled partridge back feather, golden pheasant topping or golden pheasant tippets. The latter is now generally regarded as the standard. However, there has been little variation in the winging material – slips of grouse centre tail feathers, which are a very dark chocolate brown flecked with distinct markings of orange-brown; some speckled hen primary quill feathers have a similar marking.

The Grouse series may be tied with bodies of black, brown, claret, gold, green, orange, purple, red and yellow. Dressed with brown, green and yellow bodies, the Grouse flies provide fair imitations of sedge flies, particularly emerging flies, but this is also true of the Mallard and Teal series. It would seem unnecessary to provide dressings of all the Grouse flies and I propose only to offer a selection of those that I generally favour:

Grouse and Brown (or Fiery Brown Grouse)
- **Hook**: 14–10
- **Thread**: brown silk (Pearsall's shade 17)
- **Body**: fiery brown seal's fur or SLF shade 35
- **Rib**: fine oval gold tinsel
- **Wing**: mottled brown-orange feather slips from a grouse's tail
- **Hackle**: ginger-brown hen hackle feather
- **Tail**: golden pheasant tippets

This is a good imitation of various brown sedge flies and is a good fly to have on the top dropper

Grouse and Brown.

at almost any time, but particularly on a summer's evening. Coincidentally, one of the smaller natural sedge flies (*Mysticides longicornis*) is commonly known as the 'grouse wing'. It is a very common fly on stillwaters and can appear in numbers between June and September.

Grouse and Orange

- **Hook**: 14–10
- **Thread**: hot orange silk (Pearsall's shade 19)
- **Body**: hot orange seal's fur or SLF shade 15
- **Rib**: either fine oval gold or silver tinsel

- **Wing**: mottled brown-orange feather slips from a grouse's tail
- **Hackle**: ginger hen hackle feather
- **Tails**: golden pheasant tippets

The Grouse and Orange probably falls into the 'fancy fly' category and when trout are 'on' orange, as they often are, this fly will take its quota of fish. However, the blend of hot orange body and ginger hen hackle does seem to render the pattern effective when sedge flies are emerging.

Grouse and Purple
- **Hook**: 14–12
- **Thread**: purple silk (Pearsall's shade 8)
- **Body**: purple seal's fur or SLF shade 26
- **Rib**: fine oval gold tinsel
- **Wing**: mottled brown-orange feather slips from a grouse's tail
- **Hackle**: black or dark purple hen hackle feather
- **Tails**: golden pheasant tippets

The Grouse and Purple is a good general purpose fly for early season fishing. It is best dressed in small sizes and should be fished on the point or middle dropper.

Hardy's Favourite
- **Hook**: 14–10
- **Thread**: crimson silk (Pearsall's shade 13)
- **Body**: bronze peacock herl (that is, green herl dyed in magenta dye)
- **Rib**: fine crimson floss silk
- **Wing**: slips of dark brown turkey feather or well-marked woodcock primary wing quill
- **Hackle**: a well-marked and darkish brown-speckled partridge back feather
- **Tails**: originally fibres of bronze mallard but golden pheasant tippet feathers are also used

The Hardy's Favourite is a fancy fly (though it may be reminiscent of some alder imitations) and was developed by J.J. Hardy of the famous fishing tackle company. While it does not represent any natural creature, there is something distinctly 'buggy' about it when wet; how true that is of so many flies dressed with peacock herl bodies. Traditionally, the Hardy's

Grouse and Purple.

Favourite has been regarded as a good early summer lake fly, fished on the point of the cast, but it will do well enough throughout the season. It was regarded as a very reliable pattern on Loch Awe when the water was rough and I have also found it a good point-fly for rough conditions. Indeed, I once fished a reservoir which was fed by a very turbulent stream and the Hardy's Favourite, drifted out into the reservoir along that rough current, would take fish after

Hardy's Favourite.

fish. Eventually, having run out of the standard dark brown turkey feathers for the wings, I experimented with other materials and, for whatever reason, tried a couple of cree cock hackle tips. This made an attractive-looking fly, caught plenty of fish and is now my favoured tying, although rather different from the original.

Heckham Peckham

- **Hook**: 14–10
- **Thread**: scarlet silk (Pearsall's shade 11a)
- **Body**: red seal's fur or SLF shade 17
- **Rib**: fine oval silver tinsel
- **Wings**: slips of white-tipped mallard drake feather with a greenish tinge to it
- **Hackle**: red-brown hen hackle feather
- **Tails**: golden pheasant tippets

This is not a fly that I have used much, but how could I omit a fly with such a fascinating name? Indeed, its name alone has probably rendered it one of the best known yet least used loch flies. I have given the usual red-bodied dressing, but there is also a version tied with a green body. The now standard tying of the Heckham Peckham renders it little more than a variant of flies such as the Grouse and Red, Teal and Red, Woodcock and Red and so on, but that is perhaps a little unfair to its originator. The original Heckham Peckham was the invention of Mr William Murdoch of Aberdeen and he

actually dressed the fly with a body of hare's ear fur. The original hare's ear dressing was once a popular fly in Canada and the United States and was presumably exported by expatriates from Scotland. It has also enjoyed a reputation in the past as a sea trout fly.

Invicta
- **Hook**: 14–10
- **Thread**: yellow silk (Pearsall's shade 5)
- **Body**: a deep yellow or amber seal's fur or SLF shade 33
- **Rib**: fine oval gold tinsel
- **Wing**: slips of hen pheasant tail feather
- **Body hackle**: red-brown cock or hen hackle (a smallish feather) palmered along the body
- **Front hackle**: red-brown cock or hen hackle with a couple of additional turns of barred blue jay feather
- **Tails**: golden pheasant topping or crest feather (optional)

There are probably few fly fishers who have not heard of the Invicta and doubtless there aren't many reservoir anglers who don't have an Invicta, or one of its modern variants, somewhere in their fly boxes. I prefer to use the Invicta as a top dropper fly and, depending on whether it is intended to sink or float, I dress it

Invicta.

with hen or cock hackles. In my opinion, it works best when fished in, or just under the surface, in which role it provides one of the best impressions of emerging sedge flies. The Invicta, initially called the 'Victor', was developed by the great Cheltenham fly dresser, James Ogden. Ogden lived in Derbyshire before moving to Gloucestershire and may have originally developed the fly for the rivers of the Dales rather than for lakes. It works well enough on rivers, but its reputation today is very much as a lake and reservoir fly; it has the typical colour and 'messiness' about it that we see when a sedge fly emerges from the pupal case. Courtney Williams considered the Invicta a deadly fly during the spring, but I view it more as a summer fly, the time when sedges appear in greatest numbers, though it will take fish throughout the season. On warm and breezy summer evenings it performs well when tripped through the waves as a 'wake-fly' and is quite deadly at times. While I tend to use the Invicta as a top dropper pattern, it is by no means ineffective when dressed in smaller sizes and fished on the middle dropper or point.

When using the Invicta as a wake-fly, to skip across the surface rather than to sink just below it, it is necessary to dress it with good quality cock hackles, which will also provide it with a real sense of buzz and movement. As usual, care must be taken when winding the fine gold tinsel through the fibres of the body hackle so that they are not trapped and flattened. A small feather should be used for the body hackle, while the front hackle benefits from being quite bushy in order to add buoyancy to the fly. A tip worth noting when adding the blue jay feather is that it is much easier to wind round the hook if one side of the feather is stripped from the stalk before hackling. Of course, the blue jay feather may be applied as a 'beard' hackle, although a wound hackle is probably more effective.

There are many variations on the Invicta theme. For example, it is sometimes dressed with a flat gold or silver tinsel body and the addition of a red ibis substitute tail is quite common (white hen feather dyed pillar-box red). There are other variations too, but they merely tweak what was already an excellent and effective fly.

The Mallard Series of Flies

Like the Grouse series of flies, flies dressed with bronze mallard shoulder feathers form a whole series of flies by simply changing the body colour. Bronze mallard shoulder feathers share with teal feathers the properties of softness and mobility and they are among the very best feathers for winging loch flies. The correct mallard feathers have a beautiful bronze-brown sheen over them and a darker brown flecked patterning not unlike teal feathers. There is no real substitute for the bronze mallard feather; packets of selected shoulder feathers are readily available but are quite expensive; on the other hand, bulk-buy packets rarely contain many usable feathers, most of them being fairly grey with hardly any bronze in them. It is certainly worth paying a little extra for packets of selected feathers. Given the relative scarcity of good feathers, I tend to wing this series with a slip from a single feather (as described earlier in the present chapter), rather than from two matching feathers. The Mallard series of flies can be dressed in just about any colour of body, but we will restrict our selection to the most famous and effective patterns.

Mallard and Claret

- **Hook**: 16–10
- **Thread**: claret silk (Pearsall's shade 14)
- **Body**: dark claret seal's fur, wool or SLF shade 14
- **Rib**: fine oval gold tinsel
- **Wings**: dark bronze-brown mallard shoulder feather
- **Hackle**: dark claret or even black hen hackle feather
- **Tails**: golden pheasant tippets

Most commercially dressed flies are much too bright, being dressed with a fiery or bright claret seal's fur body and bright claret hen hackle; the real Mallard and Claret should err towards drabness. I actually prefer to dress this pattern with a black, rather than claret, hen hackle. The Mallard and Claret is probably a variant of the Grouse and Claret and its invention has been attributed to William Murdoch, the originator of the Heckham Peckham. The Mallard and Claret is one of the best all-round lake and loch flies and will take fish throughout the season at any

Mallard and Claret.

Mallard and Yellow.

position on the cast. It is one of those flies that anglers have often reached into their boxes for when unsure what flies to use, particularly when visiting a water for the first time. I prefer to fish the fly either on the point or first dropper and have found small sizes more effective than large patterns. The Mallard and Claret works surprisingly well when trout are feeding on chironomid midge pupae and it is certainly a good wet-fly imitation of the claret dun (*Leptophlebia vespertina*), but it also succeeds on waters where this upwinged fly is rarely in evidence. Wild brown trout, rainbow trout and even sea trout will take the Mallard and Claret with real confidence and, ultimately, it doesn't really worry me what they take it for!

Mallard and Yellow

- **Hook**: 14–10
- **Thread**: yellow silk (Pearsall's shade 5)
- **Body**: dullish yellow seal's fur with a touch of olive mixed in (SLF shades 20 and 8)
- **Rib**: fine oval gold tinsel
- **Wings**: bronze-brown mallard shoulder feather
- **Hackle**: darkish ginger hen hackle feather
- **Tails**: golden pheasant tippets

I regard this pattern as a darker version of the Teal and Yellow and it is a particularly good pattern for any water that has a slight peaty tinge

to it. Like the Grouse and Yellow and Woodcock and Yellow it is a good fly to use as an imitation of emerging sedges, although it does well throughout the season and especially in spring. Trout sometimes seem to be really 'on' to flies dressed with yellow bodies and sometimes not. While the Mallard and Yellow may be used at any point on the cast I have a preference for a fairly small fly fished on the middle dropper. As with the Mallard and Claret, the Mallard and Yellow benefits from a toning down of colours; commercial dressings do veer towards the garish. For this reason I blend a little olive seal's fur with the yellow when forming a dubbing and much prefer a ginger hen hackle to one dyed bright yellow. A brightly coloured Mallard and Yellow becomes a pure attractor fly and fails to suggest the colours or hues of nature.

Mallard and Green

- **Hook**: 14–10
- **Thread**: green silk (Pearsall's shade 18)
- **Body**: dark green seal's fur or SLF shade 4
- **Rib**: either gold or silver fine oval tinsel
- **Wings**: bronze-brown mallard shoulder feather
- **Hackle**: red-brown hen hackle feather
- **Tails**: golden pheasant tippets

As with the Mallard and Yellow, the Mallard and Green benefits from a blending of body and

Mallard and Green.

Mallard and Gold.

hackle colours and an avoidance of too much brightness. It also provides a good impression of emerging sedge flies and it is always a good idea to combine the yellow and green versions on the same cast. On some days it will be the yellow that takes all the trout and on other days the green. In general, it is to be preferred to the Grouse and Green, which was probably its forerunner.

Mallard and Gold
- **Hook**: 14–8
- **Thread**: hot orange silk (Pearsall's shade 19)
- **Body**: flat gold tinsel or Mylar
- **Rib**: fine gold wire
- **Wings**: bronze-brown mallard shoulder feather
- **Hackle**: hot orange hen hackle feather
- **Tails**: golden pheasant tippets

Having argued that the colour of other Mallard patterns should be toned down in order to emulate the hues of nature, the Mallard and Gold is the product of a completely different approach. It is unashamedly a fancy attractor pattern and does not seek to imitate any natural creature – but it is still a very good fly and has rescued many a potential blank day! It is the kind of fly that stocked rainbows find difficult to resist, although it has taken its quota of brown trout too. I have caught trout on the Mallard and Gold when other wet-flies, as well as an array of

nymphs and dries, have proved utterly useless. It has accounted for trout during the cold and raw days of spring and also during the dog days of July and August when trout can be very dour. Like other gold-bodied patterns, a small Mallard and Gold, fished close to the surface, will often take trout during an evening rise when dry-flies fail to attract. A small version is suitable for the point or middle dropper, but a larger fly, tied on a size 10 or even 8 hook, may be used on the top dropper. In passing, while we are considering a gold-bodied fly, another useful pattern is a large gold-bodied version of the Greenwell's Glory wet-fly, which is particularly attractive to reservoir trout.

McCleod's Olive
- **Hook**: 16–12
- **Thread**: primrose silk (Pearsall's shade 3)
- **Body**: primrose silk lightly dubbed with darkish olive wool, seal's fur or SLF shade 6
- **Tag**: flat gold tinsel or Mylar
- **Wings**: slips of starling secondary quill feather
- **Hackle**: medium olive-green hen hackle feather
- **Tails**: fibres of medium olive cock hackle

It is thought that this pattern originates from the early years of the twentieth century. I have absolutely no idea who Mr McCleod was, though it seems a reasonable assumption that he probably fished on Scottish rivers and lochs. I like the blended body of tying silk and wool, a technique which has much in common with the construction of many soft-hackled spider patterns. The fly is an excellent imitation of the stillwater olives, the pond olive (*Cloeon dipterum*) and the lake olive (*Cloeon simile*), while that little gold tag adds an extra point of sparkle and attraction for trout. Clearly, the above pattern was intended by its inventor to imitate natural insects, probably in the emerging or drowned state, and it certainly catches fish when they are feeding on olives, but it also catches fish when they are not feeding on the olives. It is best fished either on the point or middle dropper. The McCleod's Olive might also be taken for some of the olive-coloured chironomid midges that are common enough on many lakes and reservoirs. The McCleod's Olive was once a very popular fly on Loch Leven.

McCleod's Olive.

Peter Ross

- **Hook**: 16–10
- **Thread**: black silk (Pearsall's shade 9)
- **Body**: flat silver tinsel or Mylar for the rear two-thirds of the body with a thorax of crimson seal's fur, wool or SLF shade 17

- **Rib**: either fine silver wire or fine oval silver tinsel depending on the size of fly. The ribbing is often taken the full length of the body, although the reader may prefer to leave the thorax without a rib
- **Wings**: well-marked teal flank or breast feather; widgeon provides a good substitute
- **Tails**: golden pheasant tippets

The Peter Ross, in essence, is really a modified Teal and Red, although this modification does make it a much more effective fly. I have sung the praises of this pattern elsewhere in the current book and I am amazed that some anglers claim to have had little success with it. The Peter Ross has accounted for some of my largest reservoir rainbows and browns and even some of my largest river trout when there has been a tinge of colour in the water after heavy rain. Although the Peter Ross will catch fish wherever it is placed on the cast, I much prefer it as a point-fly and dressed on smaller sizes of hooks. I even dress the fly on size 16 hooks, either for very calm reservoir conditions or for fishing on rivers. There are copies of this pattern in every one of my fly boxes and I would argue that there is nowhere that it will fail to catch fish. There have been many attempts to rationalize the effectiveness of the Peter Ross, some of them extremely fanciful (one writer even suggested it resembled a shrimp!), yet it is possibly just the combination of colours and flash that makes it such a good fly.

However, I have to say that the fly does unusually well in small sizes when trout are preoccupied with chironomid pupae ('duck-flies' or 'buzzers'), which, at first glance, it would not seem to resemble in the slightest. Nevertheless, there are exaggerated points of resemblance. Ascending pupae do possess a silvery sheen, while the red thorax may suggest the haemoglobin present in many species. The emerging wings and legs of the natural insect are represented by the wings and hackle of the artificial, while the pheasant tippet tail is as good a suggestion of a pupal shuck as you will ever need. I cannot prove any of this but it hardly seems to matter when the fly works so well at 'buzzer time'. In complete contrast, a large Peter Ross provides a good fry imitator and is one of the best attractor patterns throughout the season. I have fished the Peter Ross for the best part of fifty years and what strikes me most is its consistency; while some patterns do well for a spell and then seem to lose their magic, the Peter Ross continues to catch trout without them 'wising up' to it.

As is the case with many commercial examples, too often the Peter Ross is heavily dressed, which certainly impairs its effectiveness. Both the body and wing should remain slim and a couple of turns of hackle is all that is required. Incidentally, while this pattern is often given a beard hackle, a fully wound hackle is much better and helps the fly to 'swim' in a balanced manner. A slimly dressed Peter Ross is particularly effective when fished in little darts with pauses in between and it does look uncommonly like a small bait fish when worked in this manner. On the other hand, even when fished with a dead-drift technique, the Peter Ross remains a very reliable fly. I invariably fish it either as a point-fly, or as a single fly when circumstances dictate.

It may come as little surprise to the reader that this archetypal loch fly was invented in Scotland by a man called – Peter Ross. He lived from 1873 to 1923 and kept a small general store in Killin, Perthshire. He did not tie his own flies, so suggested this modification of the standard Teal and Red to a professional fly dresser. Little did he realize that this suggestion would immortalize his name, for there are few anglers who have not heard of the Peter Ross. Ironically, there are probably few who currently use it and that is a great pity.

I have also had success with a Peter Ross 'nymph', which is actually a superb midge pupa imitation. I do not know who originated this idea, but I came across some examples on sale in a tackle shop in the mid-1970s, bought a couple and found them extremely effective when fished statically just under the surface. The 'nymph' is dressed as follows:

- **Hook**: 16–14
- **Thread**: black silk (Pearsall's shade 9)
- **Body**: as per the standard Peter Ross
- **Rib**: fine silver wire ribbed only over the flat tinsel

Peter Ross.

- **Wing cases**: a strip of teal feather pulled over the red thorax
- **Hackle**: the smallest available black hen feather, two turns at the most
- **Tails**: golden pheasant tippets

Professor
- **Hook**: 14–10
- **Thread**: primrose silk (Pearsall's shade 3)
- **Body**: originally tied with yellow floss silk, although seal's fur may also be used (or SLF shade 20)
- **Rib**: flat but narrow gold tinsel or Mylar
- **Wing**: mottled grey mallard feather, or a pale teal feather with greyish markings
- **Hackle**: ginger hen hackle feather
- **Tails**: red ibis substitute

This is a little like a fancy variant of the Teal and Yellow and is very much one of those 'what-shall-I-try-next?' kind of patterns. It is an old pattern named after a John Wilson (no, not him, he's not that ancient!), who became Professor of Philosophy at Edinburgh University in 1820. He wrote under the pseudonym 'Christopher North', although the pattern first appeared in *The Rod and Gun* (1840), written by his brother, James. James Wilson was also a professor at the same university. The original pattern did not

Professor.

Sam Slick.

have a ginger hen hackle. Indeed, we are advised by James Wilson not to include a hackle at all, but if we do to use either a red or black hen feather. I first came across the fly in an American book and naturally assumed that it was a flashy fly from the other side of the pond; however, although the Professor was indeed once popular in the States, it was definitely invented in Scotland.

Sam Slick

- **Hook**: 14–12
- **Thread**: brown silk (Pearsall's shade 17)
- **Body**: rear half of yellow floss silk, with the half nearest the eye of brown seal's fur or SLF shade 37
- **Rib**: fine oval gold tinsel
- **Wings**: slips of feather from a speckled partridge tail
- **Hackle**: speckled brown partridge back feather
- **Tails**: golden pheasant tippets

This slimly dressed fly is unusual but very effective. It is a little like a March Brown variant (and March Browns dressed on large hooks do make good loch flies) and the body can also be dubbed from hare's ear, or even purple seal's fur, rather than the prescribed brown seal's fur. The

origins of the pattern are obscure, but it always had a reputation in Scotland as a great 'killer' on dull and cool days when conditions might best be described as dour. It is also said to be a good pattern for peaty water and no mean sea trout fly. I must admit that I have only used it a few times, on each occasion netting a few small brownies, but they were difficult days and the Sam Slick probably deserves a few more outings.

Sooty Olive

- **Hook**: 14–10
- **Thread**: brown silk (Pearsall's shade 17)
- **Body**: dull brownish-olive seal's fur (or SLF shade 11) picked out with a dubbing needle
- **Rib**: fine oval gold tinsel or Mylar
- **Wings**: bronze-brown speckled mallard shoulder feather
- **Hackle**: black hen hackle feather
- **Tails**: either golden pheasant tippets or topping

The Sooty Olive is a very popular Irish lough fly often used in late spring and early summer. On waters such as Conn and Mask it is often employed as a top dropper fly, but I feel that it is just as good a midge pattern as it is an imitation of the natural pond and lake olives. The name 'Sooty Olive' derives from the black hackle and dark olive-brown body, but it may also refer to the darker olives present on some waters. The Sooty Olive is also a good general pattern and while flashy flies often attract trout but only result in plucks, duller flies such as the Sooty Olive have a more natural appearance to them, which results in solid takes. For whatever reason, while the Sooty Olive has earned a great reputation in Ireland, it seems to be little used on English lakes and reservoirs where it is just as effective.

The Teal Series of Flies
Like the Grouse, Mallard and Woodcock series a whole range of flies can be created with teal wings and different body colours. If I were to be restricted to only two of the four series I would choose flies winged with mallard and teal feathers. Mallard and teal feathers are soft, mobile and beautifully marked and they produce nicely contrasted dark-winged and light-winged patterns. Flies dressed with teal wings were among the earliest loch flies I used and I have a special affection for them because they resulted in the magic of actually catching fish which seemed like something of a miracle to a small boy. The Teal and Red was of course the forerunner of the Peter Ross and it is the latter fly that I tend to use. Other Teal flies that I favour are the Teal and Black, Teal and Green, Teal and Yellow and the Teal, Blue and Silver (which is just about the best imitation of roach fry). The

correct teal feathers for winging should be as white as possible with the blackest of markings on them yet commercially dressed flies often possess wings with pale grey markings from second-rate feathers. Any bulk-buy packets of teal feathers, or widgeon, should be sifted carefully and the best feathers stored separately. Strangely, I have often found that bulk-buy packets of widgeon feathers provide more usable feathers than packets of teal. Having previously given the dressing of the Teal and Red I will now offer the dressings of my other favourite Teal flies:

Teal and Black

- **Hook**: 14–10 (and preferably 14)
- **Thread**: black silk (Pearsall's shade 9)
- **Body**: black seal's fur or SLF shade 41. The body should be slim but fibres of the dubbing may be picked out to create a rough appearance
- **Rib**: fine oval silver tinsel
- **Wings**: well-marked teal flank feather, or widgeon if preferred
- **Hackle**: black hen hackle feather
- **Tails**: golden pheasant tippets

The Teal and Black is a traditional pattern probably originating centuries ago. While it is often regarded as a general early season fly it succeeds throughout the season, particularly on dull days, and in small sizes is an excellent imitator of small black chironomid midges. The golden pheasant tippet tails provide an impression of the pupal shuck from which the adult fly is emerging and, at such times, a cast comprising entirely of this pattern is hardly a waste of time. However, I prefer to use the Teal and Black either as a point-fly, or on the middle dropper with other Teal patterns in the other positions on the cast. Incidentally, a Teal and Black with the wing trimmed down to a mere stub makes an excellent midge pupa imitation.

Teal and Green

- **Hook**: 14–10
- **Thread**: green silk (Pearsall's shade 16)
- **Body**: darkish green seal's fur or SLF shade 4
- **Rib**: fine oval gold or silver tinsel
- **Wings**: well-marked teal flank feather
- **Hackle**: dark ginger or red-brown hen hackle feather
- **Tails**: golden pheasant tippets

Like the Grouse and Green, Mallard and Green and Woodcock and Green, the Teal and Green may be used to represent any of the green-bodied sedge flies. However, with its lighter coloured wing and dressed in small sizes, the Teal and Green is a good fly to tie onto the leader when any of the green chironomid midges are emerging. The Teal and Green is also a good

general pattern and there are times when trout lock somewhat unaccountably onto green as a colour. It is often a useful ploy to employ three Teal flies, each having a different body colour, when it is difficult to know what flies to use. The Teal and Green seems to work best either on the middle or top droppers. As with most of the patterns in the Teal series it becomes an excellent pupal or nymphal imitator when the wing is worn down to a mere stub and it is not a bad idea to dress a few examples intentionally in this style. Commercial dressings of the Teal and Green often give it a bright green body and green hen hackle, but a duller green body and contrasted hackle of ginger or red-brown produces a better and more natural looking fly. While the Teal and Green is as good a fly as any in open water, it is also an extremely effective fly to fish close to weed beds.

Teal and Yellow

- **Hook**: 14–10
- **Thread**: yellow silk (Pearsall's shade 5)
- **Body**: yellow seal's fur which should not be too bright. I like to dull down a mid-yellow dubbing with a little ginger seal's fur. As a substitute dubbing, use a mix of SLF shades 20 and 40
- **Rib**: fine oval gold tinsel
- **Wings**: well-marked teal flank feather
- **Hackle**: ginger or light brown hen hackle feather
- **Tails**: golden pheasant tippets

The Teal and Yellow is an excellent catcher of trout if it is not dressed too bright and garishly. The colours really do need to be toned down. Dressed with a bright yellow seal's fur body and yellow hackle it definitely ceases to be anywhere near as effective. As with other flies in this series, the blend of contrasted body and hackle colours adds much to the trout-attracting properties of the fly. The Teal and Yellow is among my most reliable and favoured patterns and I have used it since my early teens. It was in those far-off days that I discovered how effective it is when fished close to weed beds and in open pockets of water between weeds, although the reason for this is not so easy to discern. In such locations it ought to be fished as a single fly on the point, for using

Teal and Yellow.

Teal, Blue and Silver.

droppers close to weeds is simply asking for trouble. It may suggest a sedge fly, even perhaps a shrimp, but rather than spend time guessing what it may be taken for it seems enough to know that it is a good general pattern throughout the season. It is particularly useful as a middle dropper pattern in spring, or on summer evenings when the action is rather slow. On hot and still days a tiny Teal and Yellow fished on the point is capable of saving the day. It should be fished with the slowest of slow retrieves.

Teal, Blue and Silver

- **Hook**: 14–8
- **Thread**: white silk (Pearsall's shade 1)
- **Body**: flat silver tinsel or Mylar
- **Rib**: fine oval silver tinsel or wire
- **Wings**: well-marked teal flank feather
- **Hackle**: sky blue hen hackle feather
- **Tails**: golden pheasant tippets or red ibis substitute (white hen feather dyed pillar-box red)

The rather flashy Teal, Blue and Silver is not a consistent trout fly, but when it is good it is very good and it is perhaps a more consistent sea trout fly. The Medicine sea trout fly made famous by Hugh Falkus was little more than a Teal, Blue and Silver. I also believe that it would

succeed consistently as a saltwater pattern. While it remains very much in the attractor category, the Teal, Blue and Silver is an excellent fry pattern and suggests roach fry. In this role the addition of a red ibis substitute tail, in place of the standard tail of golden pheasant tippets, greatly improves the fly. Roach fry are more common in lowland reservoirs rather than highland lochs, but there are still times when this pattern will take fish on waters that have never seen roach. As a fry pattern, it should be worked through the water in little darts and it certainly seems to suggest a small fish.

Watson's Fancy

- **Hook**: 14–10
- **Thread**: black silk (Pearsall's shade 9)
- **Body**: rear half of dark red seal's fur (SLF shades 17), front half of black seal's fur (SLF shade 41)
- **Rib**: fine oval silver tinsel
- **Wings**: dark crow quill slips with 'cheeks' of jungle cock eye feathers at each side
- **Hackle**: black hen hackle feather
- **Tails**: golden pheasant topping

Fancy by name and fancy by nature – the fly, of course, and not Mr Watson! This pattern was invented by Donald Watson of Inverness and

Watson's Fancy.

Woodcock and Red.

clearly makes no real pretence at imitating any natural insect. Nevertheless, it is a brilliant attractor pattern and has enjoyed a high reputation for catching trout, sea trout and even salmon. The jungle cock cheeks certainly add to the effectiveness of the fly and it is nowhere near as good without them. I imagine that it is still used by a number of anglers today as I often see it on sale in tackle shops. For reservoir fly fishing the Watson's Fancy works best when tied on small hooks and when fished on the point. It is particularly effective towards the start of the season when it can be cold, dark and windy. In the roughest of conditions the Watson's Fancy is a good fly to have on the leader. Some anglers even swear by the Watson's Fancy, dressed on small hooks, when midges or buzzers are emerging.

The Woodcock Series of Flies

As traditional as the Grouse, Mallard and Teal series of flies, the Woodcock series has a long history and it is impossible to guess when these flies were first used. They have always had an excellent reputation as consistent fish takers, although I must admit that my preference remains for flies dressed with mallard or teal wings. The Woodcock flies are usually dressed

with the underside of the primary wing quill slip facing outwards and this does provide a fair impression of the wings of a number of sedge flies. The correct feather to select is darkish brown with paler buff-orange blotches at the edges. When slips of feather are tied on to form a wing, they will have distinctive paler patches towards the tip of the wing.

The Woodcock series originates from Scotland and has been subjected to many variations in addition to the different colours employed for dubbing bodies. It is difficult, therefore, to say what the 'standard' dressing ought to be. The Woodcock-winged fly is rarely dressed with a black body, but the red, green and yellow versions are common and, in terms of fishing them, what has been said of similar Grouse and Mallard flies still holds good.

Woodcock and Red
- **Hook**: 14–10
- **Thread**: crimson silk (Pearsall's shade 13)
- **Body**: dark crimson seal's fur or SLF shade 17
- **Rib**: fine oval silver tinsel
- **Wings**: inside slips of woodcock primary wing quill feathers
- **Hackle**: natural red-brown hen hackle feather
- **Tails**: golden pheasant tippets

Woodcock and Green

- **Hook**: 14–10
- **Thread**: green silk (Pearsall's shade 18)
- **Body**: darkish green seal's fur or SLF shade 4
- **Rib**: fine oval silver tinsel
- **Wings**: inside slips of woodcock primary wing quill feathers
- **Hackle**: dark ginger or brown hen hackle feather
- **Tails**: golden pheasant tippets

Woodcock and Yellow

- **Hook**: 14–10
- **Thread**: yellow silk (Pearsall's shade 5)
- **Body**: yellow seal's fur or SLF shade 20
- **Rib**: fine oval silver or gold tinsel
- **Wings**: inside slips of woodcock primary wing quill feathers
- **Hackle**: ginger hen hackle feather
- **Tails**: golden pheasant tippets

Woodcock and Green.

For whatever reason, I have found the above Woodcock flies to be more effective when dressed on the smaller sizes of hooks and particularly the Woodcock and Yellow fished as a point-fly. In larger sizes the woodcock wings soon become tatty and, unlike some other winging materials, tend to render the fly less effective. Two other Woodcock flies are certainly worthy of consideration, the Woodcock and Mixed and the Woodcock and Harelug:

Woodcock and Mixed

- **Hook**: 14–10
- **Thread**: yellow silk (Pearsall's shade 5)
- **Body**: rear half of bright yellow seal's fur (SLF shade 19), front half of red seal's fur (SLF shade 17)
- **Rib**: fine oval silver tinsel
- **Wings**: inside slips of woodcock primary wing quill feathers
- **Hackle**: ginger or red-brown hen hackle feather
- **Tails**: golden pheasant tippets

The Woodcock and Mixed was once a very popular loch pattern, particularly on Loch Leven where it was usually fished on either the point or middle dropper. Though effective throughout the season, it was held in highest regard when sedges appeared in numbers during late spring or early summer. The mixed body does resemble a number of more recent sedge pupa imitations and it is worth experimenting with other colour combinations: fiery brown and amber, or brown and green, would seem to be

Woodcock and Yellow.

Woodcock and Mixed.

good combinations in order to imitate a variety of sedge pupae. It is important to note that the darkest colour should always be nearest the eye of the hook to suggest the thorax of a natural pupa.

Woodcock and Harelug

- **Hook**: 14–10
- **Thread**: yellow silk (Pearsall's shade 5)
- **Body**: dark hare's ear fur with a little olive-green seal's fur mixed in; larger guard hairs should be dubbed in under the wing or the fibres picked out with a dubbing needle
- **Tag**: a small tag of flat gold tinsel or Mylar
- **Rib**: fine oval gold tinsel
- **Wings**: inside slips of woodcock primary wing quill feathers
- **Hackle**: no additional hackle is added; the 'hackle' is formed by guard hairs and by picking out the fur
- **Tails**: a few strands of bronze mallard feather

The Woodcock and Hare's Lug Spider and Hare's Lug and Plover (*see* Chapter 7) have been mistakenly taken for original north-country spiders. They were actually hackled patterns I developed some years ago based on the Woodcock and Harelug 'loch' pattern. Ironically, the

Woodcock and Harelug itself did not originate in Scotland. James Ogden of Cheltenham, the inventor of the famous Invicta, was probably the man responsible for this excellent fly. In small sizes the Woodcock and Harelug provides a passable imitation of the pond and lake olives but it is a good sedge pattern too. While its reputation has been principally as a spring fly, it will take trout throughout the season and is a good fly to use when pursuing wild brown trout.

I hope that I have provided the reader with a good selection of traditional loch flies, flies that are still good today and, I would argue, a lot better than some modern patterns dressed with synthetic materials. I am well aware that I have omitted many flies from my list – the Malloch's Favourite, Burleigh and Dabbler series spring readily to mind – but it is not possible to include every pattern and I have been careful to omit patterns that I have not tried myself. The reader may believe that there are better patterns than some of those that I have included. Perhaps in time I will try them and revise this chapter if the opportunity arises. For the time being, rest assured that the flies included in this chapter are interesting to tie, aesthetically pleasing in the fly box and equally attractive to trout.

Woodcock and Harelug.

BIBLIOGRAPHY

Aelianus, Claudius, *De Animalium Natura* (translation by William Radcliffe, *Fishing from Earliest Times* [London, Murray, 1921])

Aldam, W.H., *A Quaint Treatise on Flees and the Art of Artyfichall Flee Making* (London, 1876)

Bainbridge, G.C., *The Fly-Fisher's Guide* (Liverpool, 1816)

Barker, T., *The Art of Angling*, London, 1651 (republished as *Barker's Delight, or the Art of Angling*, 1657)

Berners, Dame Juliana (attributed to), *A Treatyse of Fysshynge with an Angle*, in *The Boke of St. Albans* (Westminster, 1496)

Blacker, W., *The Art of Fly-Making* (London, 1843)

Bowlker, Richard & Charles, *The Art of Angling* (Worcester, 1747)

Bridgett, R.C., *Loch Fishing in Theory and Practice* (Jenkins, 1924)

Bucknall, G., *Fly Fishing Tactics on Stillwater* (Muller, 1966; revised 1974)

Chetham, J., *The Angler's Vade Mecum* (London, 1681)

Clarke, B., *The Pursuit of Stillwater Trout* (London, A & C Black, 1975)

Collyer, D.J., *Fly-Dressing* (Newton Abbot, David & Charles, 1975; *Fly-Dressing II*, David & Charles, 1981)

Cotton, C., *Being Instructions How to Angle for a Trout or Grayling in a Clear Stream*, Part II of *The Compleat Angler*

Courtney Williams, A., *A Dictionary of Trout Flies and of Flies for Sea-Trout and Grayling* (London, A & C Black, 1949; Fifth Edition, 1973)

Cutcliffe, H.C., *Trout Fishing on Rapid Streams* (South Molton, 1863)

Edmonds, H.H. and Lee, N.N., *Brook and River Trouting* (Bradford, 1916)

Francis, F., *A Book on Angling* (London, 1867)

Fogg, W.S.R., *The Art of the Wet Fly* (London, A & C Black, 1979); *Stillwater Dry Fly Fishing* (London, A & C Black, 1985); *A Handbook of North Country Trout Flies* (Congleton, Old Vicarage Publications, 1988)

Gingrich, A., *The Fishing in Print* (Winchester Press, 1974)

Goddard, J., *Trout Fly Recognition* (London, A & C Black, 1966; Third Edition, 1976); *Trout Flies of Stillwater* (London, A & C Black; Fourth Edition, 1979)

Grey, Viscount, *Fly Fishing* (Haddon Hall Library Series, 1899)

Halford, F.M., *Floating Flies and How to Dress*

Them (London, 1886); *Dry-Fly Fishing in Theory and Practice* (London, 1889); *Dry Fly Man's Handbook* (1913)

Harding, E.W., *The Fly-Fisher and the Trout's Point of View* (London, 1931)

Hidy, V.S., *see* Leisenring, J.E

Hills, J.W., *A History of Fly-Fishing for Trout* (Allan, 1921; reprinted by Barry Shurlock, 1973)

Ivens, T.C., *Still Water Fly-Fishing* (London, André Deutsch, 1952; revised and enlarged Third Edition, 1970)

Jackson, J., *The Practical Fly-Fisher* (London and Leeds, 1854)

Kingsley, C., *Chalk Stream Studies* (included in *Miscellanies* [London, 1859] and in *Prose Idylls* [London, 1873])

Kingsmill Moore, T.C., *A Man May Fish*, 1960 (reprinted by Colin Smythe, 1983 and 1985)

Lawrie, W.H., *A Reference Book of English Trout Flies* (London, Pelham, 1967)

Lee, N.N., *see* Edmonds, H.H.

Leisenring, J.E., *The Art of Tying the Wet Fly*, 1941 (reprinted with additions by Vernon S. Hidy as *Tying the Wet Fly & Fishing the Flymph*, Crown, 1971)

MacKintosh, Alexander, *The Driffield Angler* (1806)

Malone, E.J., *Irish Trout and Salmon Flies* (Colin Smythe, 1984)

Moss, D., *Trout From a Boat* (Ludlow, Merlin Unwin, 2007)

Mottram, J.C., *Fly-Fishing: Some New Arts and Mysteries*, 1915 (republished by the Flyfisher's Classic Library, 1984)

Nemes, S., *The Soft-Hackled Fly* (Chatham Press, 1975); *The Soft-Hackled Fly Addict* (Chicago, 1981)

Ogden, J., *On Fly-Tying* (Cheltenham, 1879)

Pennell, H.C., *The Modern Practical Angler* (London, 1870)

Plunket-Greene, H., *Where the Bright Waters Meet*, 1924 (republished by André Deutsch, 1983)

Pritt, T.E., *Yorkshire Trout Flies* (Goodall & Siddick, Leeds, 1885; republished as *North-Country Flies* [London, Low, 1886])

Reid, J., *Clyde Style Flies* (David & Charles, 1971)

Roberts, J., *A Guide to River Trout Flies* (Ramsbury, The Crowood Press, 1989)

Ronalds, A., *The Fly-Fisher's Entomology* (London, 1836)

Skues, G.E.M., *Minor Tactics of the Chalk Stream* (London, A & C Black, 1910); *The Way of a Trout with a Fly* (London, A & C Black, 1921); *Sidelines, Sidelights and Reflections*, 1932 (republished as *The Chalk-Stream Angler* [Barry Shurlock, 1976]); *Nymph Fishing for Chalk Stream Trout* (London, A & C Black, 1939); *Silk, Fur and Feather* (1950)

Stewart, T., *Two Hundred Popular Flies and How to Tie Them* (Benn, 1979) (originally published from monthly *Trout and Salmon* magazine articles in four separate volumes in 1962, 1964, 1969 and 1973)

Stewart, W.C., *The Practical Angler* (Edinburgh, 1857)

Stoddard, T.T., *The Art of Angling as Practised in Scotland* (Edinburgh, 1835)

Swarbrick, J., *Wharfedale Flies* (1807)

Theakston, M., *British Angling Flies* (Ripon, 1853)

Tod, E.M., *Wet Fly-Fishing* (London, 1903)

Turton, J., *The Angler's Manual*, 1836 (Turton's list of flies is reproduced by W.H. Lawrie in *A Reference Book of English Trout Flies* [Pelham, 1967])

Venables, R., *The Experienced Angler* (London, 1662)

Veniard, J., *The Fly-Dresser's Guide* (A & C Black, 1952); *Reservoir and Lake Flies* (A & C Black, 1970)

Voss Bark, C., *A History of Flyfishing* (Merlin Unwin, 1992)

Wakeford, J., *Fly-tying Tools and Materials* (A & C Black, 1991)

Walker, C.F., *Lake Flies and Their Imitation*, 1960 (republished by Andre Deutsch, 1983)

Walton, I. and Cotton, C., *The Compleat Angler* (London, 1676; now published by Oxford University Press)

Webster, D., *The Angler and the Loop Rod* (Edinburgh and London, 1885)

Younger, J., *On River Angling for Salmon and Trout* (Edinburgh, 1840)

INDEX